# 佛教常识答问

# Answers to Common Questions about Buddhism

赵朴初 著
赵 桐 译
柯马凯 审译

Author: Zhao Puchu
Translator: Zhao Tong
English Editor: Michael Crook

外语教学与研究出版社
FOREIGN LANGUAGE TEACHING AND RESEARCH PRESS

(京)新登字 155 号

图书在版编目(CIP)数据

佛教常识答问/赵朴初著;赵桐译. - 北京:外语教学与研究出版社, 2000

ISBN 7 - 5600 - 1834 - 3

Ⅰ.佛… Ⅱ.①赵… ②赵… Ⅲ.佛教 - 基本知识 - 问答 - 英、汉
Ⅳ.B94 - 44

中国版本图书馆 CIP 数据核字(2000)第 15175 号

佛教常识答问
赵朴初 著
赵 桐 译
* * *
责任编辑: 刘相东
出版发行: 外语教学与研究出版社
社 址: 北京市西三环北路 19 号 (100089)
网 址: http: //www.fltrp.com.cn
印 刷: 北京外国语大学印刷厂
开 本: 850×1168 1/32
印 张: 12.5
字 数: 261 千字
版 次: 2001 年 9 月第 1 版 2001 年 9 月第 1 次印刷
书 号: ISBN 7 - 5600 - 1834 - 3/H·1037
定 价: 15.90 元
* * *

生固欣然
死亦無憾
花落還開
水流不斷
我兮何有
誰歟安息
明月清風
不勞尋覓

趙樸初

# 目　　录

序
译者前言
编辑凡例
第一章　佛陀和佛教的创立 …………………… 2
第二章　佛法的基本内容和佛教经籍 ……… 46
第三章　僧伽和佛的弟子 …………………… 114
第四章　佛教在印度的发展、衰灭和复兴 … 164
第五章　佛教在中国的传播、发展和演变 … 218

（一）佛教的传入和经典的翻译 ……… 218
（二）佛教各宗派的兴起 ……………… 252
（三）少数民族地区的佛教 …………… 294
（四）佛教对中国思想文化的影响 …… 302
（五）发扬人间佛教的优越性 ………… 314

附录
巴、英、汉佛教术语对照表 ……………………… 328

# Contents

Author's Preface
Translator's Preface
Editorial Notes

Chapter I. The Buddha and the Origin of Buddhism ………… 3
Chapter II. The Essence of the Buddha Dhamma and the Buddhist Canonical Literature ………… 47
Chapter III. The Sangha and the Buddha's Disciples ……… 115
Chapter IV. The Development, Decline and Resurgence of Buddhism in India ……………… 165
Chapter V. The Spread, Development and Evolution of Buddhism in China ……………………… 219
1. The Introduction of Buddhism into China and the Translation of Buddhist Scriptures ……………… 219
2. The Emergence of Various Buddhist Schools …… 253
3. Buddhism in Minority-inhabited Regions of China ……………………………………… 295
4. The Impact of Buddhism on Chinese Thought and Culture …………………………………… 303
5. Carrying Forward the Advantage of Popular Buddhism …………………………………… 315
Appendix
Buddhist terms in Pāli, English and Chinese ………… 328

# 序

## 赵朴初

这本书是我三十多年前开始写的，因为事务冗忙，时作时辍。原来计划，除现在的五章外，还有三章是有关中国与外国佛教关系史的，因佛教协会已有这方面资料的编辑和著作，所以不重复了。

我写成第一章后，曾以楞严经“如人饮水，冷暖自知”这句话用“饮水”的笔名陆续在《现代佛学》杂志上发表。有一位朋友问我：“你为什么用这样一个小题目？”我说：“我喜欢‘小题大做’，而不愿‘大题小做’，更害怕‘有题空做’。”这本英译的书名很好，很合我的心意。

几年前，一位青年僧人用日文翻译这本书，我应他的要求写序时，曾记下与本书有关的一件事：1957 年我陪一位柬埔寨僧人见毛泽东主席，客人未到之前，我先到了，毛主席便和我漫谈。他问：“佛教有这么一个公式—— 赵朴初，即非赵朴初，是名赵朴初，有没有这个公式呀？”我说：

# Author's Preface

Zhao Puchu

I began to write this book over thirty years ago. Owing to the heavy load of work, I could only write intermittently. In addition to the five chapters as they appear now, I intended to write three more chapters dealing with the history of relations between China and other countries in the Buddhist sphere. Since the Buddhist Association of China has undertaken to compile and write on this topic, there is no need to duplicate their work here.

When I finished writing the first chapter, it was published in installments in the *Journal of Modern Buddhism*. I used the pseudonym, "Yin Shui" (drink water), derived from the text *Śūraṃgama Sūtra* that reads "One perceives whether the water is cold or warm only when one drinks it." A friend of mine asked why I chose such an insignificant title. I replied, "I prefer to make a fuss about trifles rather than underplaying a big issue, not to mention completely ignoring significant subjects." The title of the English version of my book is in conformity with my wish.

A few years ago a young monk translated my book into Japanese. In the preface, which I wrote at his request, I referred to a story connected with the subject of this book. In 1957, I accompanied a Cambodian monk to see Chairman Mao Zedong. Before the guest arrived I had the opportunity to chat with the Chairman. He told me,

"有。"主席再问:"为什么?先肯定,后否定?"我说:"不是先肯定,后否定,而是同时肯定,同时否定。"谈到这里,客人到了,没有能谈下去。后来,我在写这本书的第二章时,想起这一次未谈完的问答,我想,书中谈到缘起性空的思想,可能补充了当时我在毛主席面前所想讲的话。

我曾看到一本毛主席的勤务员李银桥写的书。有一天,毛主席在延安出门散步,毛主席对李银桥说:"我们去看看佛教寺庙,好不好?"李银桥说:"那有什么看头?都是一些迷信。"毛主席说:"片面片面,那是文化。"我因而想起文化大革命结束后,周建人先生写信给我说:文革初期范文澜先生向他说,自己正在补课,读佛书。范老说,佛教在中国将近两千年,对中国文化有那么深厚的关系,不懂佛教,就不能懂得中国文化史。1987年,我到四川一个佛教名胜地方看到被人贴迷信标语的事实,回来写了一份报告,钱学森博士看见了,写信给我说:"宗教是文化。"

"There is a formula in Buddhism: Zhao Puchu is not Zhao Puchu (in the sense of Paramattha), but Zhao Puchu by name. Is this true?" "Yes." I replied. He added, "Why, then, do you affirm it before negating it?" "It is not affirmation before negation," I said, "but simultaneous affirmation and negation." Then the guest arrived and the conversation was interrupted. Later when I worked on Chapter II of this book, I recalled that unfinished talk. I think the idea of the voidness of nature because of Dependent Origination (Paṭiccasamuppāda) in the book might constitute what I would have said to the Chairman at that time.

I have read a book written by Li Yinqiao, one of Chairman Mao's bodyguards. According to this book, when Chairman Mao was taking a walk with Li in Yan'an one day, Mao said to him, "Let's go see a Buddhist temple, shall we?" Li said, "What's the point? It is nothing but a symbol of superstition." "One-sided, one — sided your thinking is. It is culture." This also reminds me of a letter to me from Mr. Zhou Jianren after the end of the Cultural Revolution, in which he told me that in the early period of the turmoil, Mr. Fan Wenlan had sent word to him that he was making up for a missed lesson by reading Buddhist books. Fan said that Buddhism in China has lasted about twenty centuries, it had such a profound influence on Chinese culture that one can hardly understand the cultural history of China without some knowledge of Buddhism. Finally, in 1987, I visited a Buddhist historical site in Sichuan Province and found that anti-superstition slogans were visible everywhere. Therefore, on my return, I wrote a report. Seeing the report Dr. Qian

这三个人，一是伟大的革命家，一是著名的历史学家，一是当代的大科学家，所见相同，都承认佛教是文化，而今天还有不少人的认识水平和当年李银桥的一样。

我最初写这本书的动机只是为了和外国朋友谈话时，翻译人员因缺乏佛教知识而感到困难，想为他们提供一些方便。但这许多年来，得到国内不少人的关怀、鼓励，也得到一些外国朋友的注意。事实说明，这一本小书对于增进人们对佛教的了解，增进国际朋友对中国佛教的了解，不无少许贡献。

我感谢译者为此书所付出的宝贵的心力。我虔诚期待国际朋友对于此书内容给予指教。

Xuesen wrote to me, "Religion is a part of culture".

It is noteworthy that all three of these men, the first, a great revolutionary, the second, a famous historian, and the third, a great contemporary scientist, shared the same view that Buddhism is a part of culture. Yet there are still many people today whose perception remains like that of Li Yinqiao at that time.

At the very beginning, I was impelled to write this book by the desire to help those interpreters who had difficulty in performing their work due to a lack of knowledge in Buddhism. In recent years, however, I have received kindly consideration and encouragement from many people at home as well as friends from abroad. This indicates that this pamphlet has made more than a negligible contribution towards enhancing the public comprehension of Buddhism and helping foreigners understand Chinese Buddhism.

I am indebted to the translator for her arduous endeavors in accomplishing this task. I sincerely look forward to forthcoming comments on the book from friends all over the world.

# 译者前言

《佛教常识答问》一书是赵朴初先生一生对佛学进行研究的总结之作。本书的前三章按照佛、法、僧三宝的顺序精辟地阐释了何为佛、何为法、何为僧。第一章对佛教的创立及创始人作了历史的而不是神话的阐述；第二章深入浅出地阐释了佛法的基本内容，介绍了佛教典籍的形成及其流布；第三章对僧团的建立、僧侣的生活、戒律与仪轨作了生动的描述。本书的后二章不啻是一部印度佛教、中国佛教小史，第四章叙述了佛教在其发源地——印度的发展、衰灭和复兴；第五章是本书内容最详实、最能体现作者本怀的一章，其中深入论述了佛教在中国的传播、发展和演变，分析了佛教与人们日常生活的关系，佛教对于社会的思想与文化发展所起的作用，从而阐发了发扬人间佛教的优越性，使之服务于当今社会文化与生活的主旨。

本书用答问的方式实际上回答了佛教两千五百年来所涉及到的大多数问题，因此，这本书可以说是朴老提出的佛学大纲，对于一般人想全面了解佛教将起到正确导入的作用，对于学者要深入研究佛教与佛学将起到启发思路，找到切入点的作用，对于外国人想了解佛教，尤其是中国佛教的全貌提供了全方位的素材。

# Translator's Preface

*Answers to Common Questions about Buddhism* is the final fruit of a lifetime of study on Buddhism made by Mr. Zhao Puchu. The first three chapters give respectively a succinct exposition of the Buddhist Three Gems, i. e. Buddha, Dhamma (Buddhist doctrine), and *Sangha* (the Buddhist Order). Chapter One gives a historical, rather than mythological, account of the founder and the founding of Buddhism. Chapter Two gives in simple language a profound explanation of Buddhist doctrine, as well as its spread and the compilation of its canonical literature. Chapter Three gives a vivid account of the formation of the Sangha as well as their life and disciplines. The last two chapters are nothing short of a brief history of Indian and Chinese Buddhism. Chapter Four describes the rise and fall and resurgence of Buddhism in its birthplace — India, while Chapter Five is packed with detailed information, and expresses the innermost feelings of the author. By giving a thorough analysis of the spread, the development and evolution of Buddhism in China, and of the relationship between Buddhism and everyday life, the impact of Buddhism on social, intellectual and cultural development, the last chapter contends that we should carry forward the advantages of popular Buddhism, and make it serve contemporary social and cultural life.

In the form of questions and answers, the book addresses and answers practically all the questions raised by Buddhism over the past 2,500 years. The book may be regarded as Zhao Puchu's general survey of Buddhist studies, giving the ordinary public a proper introduction to Buddhism, while giving to the scholars inspiration and points of entry into in-depth study of Buddhism. It also furnishes the foreigners wishing to learn about Buddhism, especially Chinese Buddhism, a comprehensive outline of the field.

本书用活泼的、通俗易懂的、开启心智的方式回答了那些似乎莫测高深的佛学问题，妙语机锋间透露出一位大家的睿智，一位善知识的亲切，一位学者治学的严肃与公允的态度，以及一位真正的佛教徒对佛教正信的立场，因而与一切迷信、假信和伪信划清了界线。

译者于 1996 年受中国佛教文化研究所的委托，开始着手翻译此书。受命之时，万没想到这是如此艰巨的任务，是对译者佛学知识、中文修养，尤其是外语水平的全面挑战。为了不使译者的浅陋有损于原作的光辉，在翻译过程中参阅了大量参考书，务求作到言出有据。对于绝大多数佛教术语，尽量找出它们的巴利语（梵语）原词以及被广泛接受的英文译法，并且，为了方便广大信众、学者掌握佛学英语、巴利语，译者还编辑了《巴、英、汉佛教术语对照表》（附书后）。对于较为复杂的思想、义理，力求在阅读巴利语、英语、汉语原典的基础上理清了思路，领会了作者的意趣之后再遣词运笔。历时三载，数易其稿，方成现在这个样子，此稿虽得到赵朴初先生亲自审阅，并予以嘉许，然自知还有许多不尽人意之处，祈请方家大德、广大善信施慧赐教。

在反复翻译、修改过程中，得到了各方专家的指教。译稿始成，便邀请了不懂汉语、不懂佛教，不懂汉语、但懂佛教，既懂汉语、又懂佛教的多位外国专家予以审读，听取他们的意见，尽量使译文的风格不失去原作的原汁原味。在此，译者要特别向柯马凯先生、魏海伦女士、提瑟·嘎里奥桑姆先生致以最诚挚的谢意，如果译文尚令人满意，全都有赖于他们使之增色。同时，在翻译过程中还参阅了此

The language is vivid yet colloquial, and answers in an enlightening way even those seemingly incomprehensible and abstruse points of Buddhism. Through the apt wording one detects the wisdom of a great philosopher, the sympathy engendered in one with intimate knowledge, the serious and magnanimous approach of a true scholar, and the orthodox stand of the true Buddhist, clearly demarcating it from any superstition or heresy.

This translation was begun in 1996 at the request of the China Institute of Buddhist Culture. At that time, I had no idea what a challenge this work would prove to be of my knowledge of Buddhism, my Chinese skills and my English level. In order that the limitations of the translator do not detract from the splendors of the original work, over the course of translation I consulted a large number of reference books, strove to ensure that translations were made on a sound basis, and for most technical terms, sought out the original Pāli (or Sanskrit) terms, as well as those English forms most sanctioned by usage. For the convenience of the reader wishing to learn English or Pāli Buddhist terms, I compiled a Pāli, English and Chinese glossary (see appendix). When dealing with more complex ideas, I tried through reading works in the original Pāli, English or Chinese to arrive at a clear grasp of the ideas and the intentions of the author before setting pen to paper. The present translation is the culmination of work over three years and many revisions, and while it has been checked by the author, and earned his praise, I am aware that there remain many areas that fall short of total satisfaction. I earnestly beseech the readers indulgence and criticism.

Over the course of translation and its revision, I have benefited from the help of many experts. In order that the translation would not loose its original flavour, from the very first I have consulted a range of foreign experts, including some who know neither Chinese nor Buddhism; some who do not know Chinese but know Buddhism, as well as some who know both Chinese and Buddhism. Here I wish particularly to thank Michael Crook, Helen Wiley, and Tissa Kariyawasam. If the translation brings satisfaction, it is they who have helped it do so. At the same time, through the course of translation, I consulted translations of this work, in other languages as well. For the hard

书的其他几种译文，对于这些译家所付出的艰辛，译者表示由衷的敬意。在翻译过程中，始终得到了赵朴初先生、中国佛教文化研究所的信任、支持与鼓励，使翻译的过程成为我修习的过程，因此真诚地感谢朴老以及佛教文化研究所给了我这个提高与丰富自己的机会。

这本译作是集中了许多人的智慧的成果，译者决不敢专擅其功，这一点也是要特别加以说明的。

赵　桐

1999.12.

work of these translators, I would like to extend my heartfelt respect. And throughout the work, the constant trust, encouragement and support of Mr. Zhao Puchu and the China Institute of Buddhist Culture has made it a learning experience for me. For this, I am sincerely grateful to Mr. Zhao Puchu and the Institute of Buddhist Culture, who gave me this opportunity to better myself.

This translation is the fruit of the labour and wisdom of many people. I make no claim to the credit—this is a point I wish to make clear.

Zhao Tong
Dec. 1999

# 编辑凡例

1. 本书为中、英文对照本，以问题序号相对应。

2. 本书出现的重要佛教术语都给出了对应的巴利文原词。本书的中文版本中原注有一些梵文或巴利文术语，此次出版前，根据赵朴初先生本人的意见，除个别词语外，一律改为巴利文。此项改动是出于佛教巴利语较之佛教梵语应世更早的原因。巴利语原是古印度摩揭陀国一带所使用的大众语，一些专家认为，这一带是佛陀弘法的主要地区，佛陀弘法使用的就是这种语言。在阿育王时期（公元前三世纪）派遣到斯里兰卡弘法的玛亨陀长老把用巴利语记述的三藏带到斯里兰卡，并于公元前一世纪结集为用僧伽罗字母书写的巴利三藏流传下来。这套巴利三藏历两千年而不变，成为当今世界保留得最完整、最系统、最古老的佛教宝典。梵语是古代印度婆罗门经典所使用的语言，或称为雅语，用梵语编定成书的佛教典籍目前已没有完整成套版本留存。

3. 本书译文所使用的缩略语：S.（梵语），P.（巴利语）。

4. 本书附有《巴、英、汉佛教术语对照表》，是按章节和问题序号排列的。

# Editorial Notes

1. This book is laid out as a bilingual book with Chinese original facing its English translation, and it is arranged according to the number of the questions.
2. Most Buddhist terms in this book are given in both the original Pāli and English Translations. Some Buddhist terms in Pāli or Sanskrit were given in Chinese original text, and have been rendered into Pāli in this edition in compliance with Mr. Zhao Puchu's own wishes. The reason for this change is that Buddhist texts appeared earlier in Pāli than in Sanskrit. The Pāli language was popularly used in Magadha State in ancient India where the Buddha gave most of his sermons, and some scholars believe the Buddha taught in Pāli. In the period of Asoka (3 century BC), Ven. Mahinda was dispached to Sri Lanka as a missionary by his father, King Asoka, and he took the oral Pāli Tripitaka there. This was later recorded in Sinhalese script Pāli in the first century BC and handed down to this day. This Pāli Tripitaka has been preserved unaltered during 2000 years and has become the most complete, systematic and oldest Buddhist canonical treasure in the world.
3. The following abbreviations are used in the text: S. (Sanskrit), P. (Pāli).
4. A glossary of Pāli terms is given with both English and Chinese translations in numerical order by chapter and question.

# 第一章
## 佛陀和佛教的创立

1. 问:什么是佛教?

答:佛教,广义地说,它是一种宗教,包括它的经典、仪式、习惯、教团的组织等等;狭义地说,它就是佛所说的言教;如果用佛教固有的术语来说,应当叫做佛法(Buddha Dhamma).

2. 问:"法"是什么意思?

答:"法"字的梵语是达磨(Dharma)。佛教对这个字的解释是:"任持自性、轨生物解。"这就是说,每一事物必然保持它自己特有的性质和相状,有它一定轨则,使人看到便可以了解是何物。例如水,它保持着它的湿性,它有水的一定轨则,使人一见便生起水的了解;反过来说,如果一件东西没有湿性,它的轨则不同于水的轨则,便不能生起水的了解。所以佛教把一切事物都叫做"法"。佛经中常见到的"一切法"、"诸法"字样,就是"一切事物"或"宇宙万有"的意思。照佛教的解释,佛根据自己对一切法如实的了解而宣示出来的言教,它本身也同样具有"任持自性、轨生物解"的作用,所以也叫做法。

3. 问:佛是神吗?

# Chapter I
# THE BUDDHA AND THE ORIGIN OF BUDDHISM

1. Q: What is Buddhism?

A: Buddhism, in a general sense, is a religion with its canonical literature, rites, customs, Sangha Order (congregational organization) etc.; more specifically, it is the Buddha's teachings, and with this specific meaning it should be termed the Buddha Dhamma.

2. Q: What is "Dhamma"?

A: "Dharma" in Sanskrit ("Dhamma" in Pāli) means "retaining one's own nature, such that it can be recognized". That is to say, everything has its own attributes and appearance (S. prakṛti and lakṣaṇa, P. pakati and lakkhaṇa) and maintains its own properties, by which people can perceive it for what it is. For instance, water maintains its property of wetness and acts according to its fixed track, so people recognize it as water when they see it. Conversely, when something is devoid of wetness and obey different rules from water, there then can be no concept of water. Therefore, Buddhism views everything as "dhamma". The terms "all dhammas", "each dhamma" appearing in Buddhist canons indicate "all things" or "universal existence". According to this interpretation, the discourses delivered by the Buddha based on his own empirical comprehension of dhammas are also "Dhamma" since they hold true to the principle of "retaining its own nature, such that it can be recognized."

3. Q: Is the Buddha a deity?

答：不，佛不是神。他是公元前六世纪时代的人，有名有姓，他的名字是悉达多（S. Siddhārtha，P. Siddhattha），他的姓是乔达摩（S. Gautama，P. Gotama）。因为他属于释迦（Sākya）族，人们又称他为释迦牟尼，意思是释迦族的圣人。

4.　问：为什么称他为佛呢？佛的意义是什么？

答："佛"字是"佛陀"的简称，是 Buddha 的音译（如果用今天的汉语音译，应当是"布达"），佛陀的意义是"觉者"或"智者"。"佛陀"是印度早就有了的字，但佛教给它加了三种涵义：(1) 正觉（对一切法的性质相状，无增无减地、如实地觉了）；(2) 等觉或遍觉（不仅自觉，即自己觉悟，而且能平等普遍地觉他，即使别人觉悟）；(3) 圆觉或无上觉（自觉觉他的智慧和功行都已达到最高的、最圆满的境地）。

5.　问：除释迦牟尼外，有没有另外的佛？

答：佛教认为过去有人成佛，未来也会有人成佛，一切人都有得到觉悟的可能性，所以说："一切众生，皆有佛性，有佛性者，皆得成佛。"

6.　问：如来佛是不是释迦牟尼？还是另一人？

A: No, the Buddha is not a deity. He was a man who lived in the sixth century BC. He had his own given and family names, his given name was Siddhattha (S. Siddhārtha) and his family name Gotama (S. Gautama). As he belonged to the Sākya clan, people also called him Sākyamuni, meaning a sage of the Sākyas.

4. Q: Why is Buddha called "Fo" in Chinese? What does it mean?

A: "Fo" is the abbreviation for "Fotuo" which was used to translate the word "Buddha". (The characters used for "Fuotuo" were pronounced "buda" at the time of translation.) Buddha means "an enlightened one" or "an awakened one". The term "Buddha" existed in India from the earliest times, but Buddhism has attributed three additional connotations to the term. They are as follows: (1) enlightenment (Sambodhi, which means thoroughly realizing the properties and appearance of all dhammas as they are); (2) perfect enlightenment (Sammā-sambodhi, which means not only enlightening oneself but also equally and universally enlightening others); (3) supreme or paramount enlightenment (Anuttara sammā-sambodhi, which means the wisdom and achievement have reached the highest and the most perfect sphere in enlightening both oneself and others).

5. Q: Are there any other Buddhas besides Sākyamuni?

A: Buddhism claims that there were people who attained Buddhahood in the past and there will be people to become Buddhas in the future. It is possible for everybody to achieve enlightenment. Therefore, "All living beings have Buddha-nature, everyone with the Buddha-nature may attain Buddhahood."

6. Q: Is the Chinese term "Rulai Fo" identical to Sākyamuni or is he somebody else?

答："如来"这个名词是从梵语 Tathāgata 译出来的。"如"字就是"真如"(tathāta)，即一切法(事物)的真实状况，它又包含"如实"(Yathābhūtam)的意义。佛经对"如来"的解释是："乘真如之道而来"，又说"如实而来"。"如来"是一个通用名词，它是"佛陀"的异名。如释迦牟尼佛，可以称释迦牟尼如来；阿弥陀佛，可以称阿弥陀如来。

7. 问：阿弥陀佛和释迦牟尼佛不是一个人吗？

答：不是。阿弥陀佛是另外一个世界上的佛。阿弥陀佛是梵语 Amitābha 的音译，意义是"无量的光明"。

8. 问："南无佛"是什么意思？为什么读起来是"那摩佛"？

答："南无"是梵语 Namo 的音译，念成"那摩"，是保持原来古代的读音。现代广东、福建一部分地区，仍保持这个古音。它的意义是"敬礼"。今天印度人相见，互道"那摩悉对"，就是说："敬礼了"。

9. 问：释迦牟尼的一生可以简略介绍一下么？

答：可以。释迦牟尼的时代，约当公元前六世纪中叶，正是我国春秋时代，与孔子同时。他是当时迦毗罗国(Kapilavatthu)国王的长子。父亲名净饭(Suddhodana)，母亲名摩耶(Māyā)。摩耶夫人生产前，根据当时习俗，回到母家去，路过蓝毗尼花园(Lumbinī)，在树下休息的时

A: "Rulai" was translated from the Sanskrit word "Tathāgata". "Ru" means "suchness" (tathatā), or "according to the reality" (Yathābhūtaṃ), i. e. the ultimate reality of all dhammas, while "lai" means "come". "Rulai" (Tathāgata) is interpreted in the Buddhist scriptures as "coming by the path of Tathāgata" or "coming according to the reality". Tathāgata is a general term and another name for "Buddha". Thus Gotama Buddha can be called Gotama Tathāgata, and Amita Buddha can be called Amita Tathāgata.

7. Q: Are not Amita Buddha and Gotama Buddha one and the same?

A: No, Amita Buddha or Amitābha is the Buddha of another world. The Chinese term "Amituofo" is the transliteration from Sanskrit of "Amitābha", meaning "boundless light".

8. Q: What is the meaning of "Nanmo Fo"(南无佛)? Why is it pronounced as "Namo Fo"(那摩佛 )?

A: "Nanmo" is the transliteration of Sanskrit "Namo". The Chinesc characters "南无" were used since their pronunciation was similar with "namo" in the ancient time when this term was introduced into China. Such a pronunciation is still preserved now in parts of China's Guangdong and Fujian provinces. "Namo" means salutation or homage. Even today, when Indians meet they say "Namaste" to each other, that is to say "Homage to you".

9. Q: What is known about the life of Sākyamuni?

A: Well, Sākyamuni lived around the sixth century BC, equivalent to the Spring and Autumn Period in China, and was a contemporary of Confucius. He was the eldest son of the King of Kapilavatthu. His father was named Suddhodana; his mother, Māyā. Queen Māyā gave birth to Prince Siddhattha on the way to her parents' home while taking a rest under a tree in Lumbinī Grove, since, according to the custom prevailing in

候，生下了悉达多王子。

10. 问：蓝毗尼花园现在还有遗址留存下来吗？

答：公元七世纪时，我国玄奘法师曾到过蓝毗尼。根据他的记载，他曾经看到在他之前八百多年阿育王（Asoka）在那里建立的石柱，标志着佛陀诞生之处，但当时石柱已被雷击破，柱头倒在地下，已经是衰落的情景了。后来由于没有人能够识得柱上的文字，因此佛陀诞生的地址久已湮没无闻。直到 1897 年才被人发现了阿育王的石柱，考古家认识出上面的文字，这才发掘出蓝毗尼园的遗址，在附近并且发掘出古代的市镇，其中有些可以相信是属于当时的迦毗罗城的。今天尼泊尔政府已经把这个地方作为圣地加以建设和保护。

11. 问：释迦牟尼幼年教养情况是怎样？

答：摩耶夫人产后不久就死了。幼年时代的释迦牟尼是由他的姨母波阇波提夫人（Prajāpati）养育的。他自小从婆罗门学者们学习文学、哲学、算学等等，知识很广博。又从武士们学习武术，是一个骑射击剑的能手。他父亲净饭王因为他天资聪慧，相貌奇伟，对他期望很大，希望他继承王位后，建功立业，成为一个“转轮王”（统一天下的君主）。

India at that time, women should go back to their parents' home for child bearing.

10. Q: Are there any vestiges of Lumbinī Grove remaining today?

A: During the seventh century AD, Tipiṭakācariya Xuan Zang (Hsuan Tsang) of China visited Lumbinī Grove. According to his account, he saw the stone pillar erected there by King Asoka about 800 years before, marking the birthplace of the Buddha. The site at that time, however, was in a state of desolation, the pillar having been struck by lightning and the top having fallen down onto the ground. Subsequently, the birthplace of Buddha sank into oblivion because nobody could read the letters on the pillar. It was not until 1897 when Asoka's pillar was re-discovered and archeologists deciphered the inscriptions that the ravaged ruins of Lumbinī Grove were excavated. Some ancient settlements were also excavated in the vicinity of that site, part of which may have belonged to the old city of Kapilavatthu. Today, the government of Nepal has proclaimed it as Holy Land and undertaken necessary reconstruction and protection.

11. Q: How was Sākyamuni educated in his childhood?

A: Queen Māyā died soon after giving birth. Young Sākyamuni was brought up by his aunt (his mother's sister) Princess Prajāpati. As a child he began to learn literature, philosophy, arithmetic etc. from Brahmin scholars and gained a broad and profound knowledge. He also learned martial arts from warriors and became a master at riding, shooting and fencing. Because of his great intelligence and striking features, his father, King Suddhodana, hoped that he would become a universal ruler (Rāja Cakkhavattin, a King who could unify the whole world) and perform meritorious services after he succeeded to the throne.

12. 问:那么,他后来为什么不继承王位呢?

答:悉达多王子在幼年的时候,就有沉思的习惯,世间许多现象,给他看到,都容易引起他的感触和深思:饥渴困乏、在烈日下耕田的农人,绳索鞭打、口喘汗流拖着犁头耕地的牛,蛇虫鸟兽弱肉强食的情景,衰丑龙钟的老人,辗转呻吟的病人,亲朋哭泣送葬中的死人,这些都促使他思索着一个问题——如何解脱世界的苦痛。他读过的吠陀书(Veda,婆罗门经典)不能解决他的问题。他学到的知识和他未来的王位、权力也都不能解决他的问题。于是他很早就有了出家的念头,后来终于舍弃了王位。

13. 问:他父亲怎么会让他出家呢?

答:净饭王发觉了他儿子的心思后,曾经想过各种办法防止他,特别是企图从生活的享受上羁縻他。悉达多王子十六岁时,净饭王便为他娶了邻国的王女耶输陀罗(Yasodharā)为妃,生了一个儿子叫罗怙罗(Rāhula)。但是这一切都没有能够阻止他,终于在一天夜深人静的时候,他偷偷地出了国城,进入一个森林中,换去王子的衣服,剃去须发,成为一个修道者。关于他出家时的年龄,有两种不同记载,一说是十九岁,一说是二十九岁。

14. 问:出家以后的情形怎样?

答:他父亲曾尽力劝他回去无效,只好在亲族中选派五个人随从他一起,这五个人的名字是:憍陈如(Kaundinya, P. Koṇḍañña),跋堤(Bhadrika, P. Bhaddiya),跋波

12. Q: Why didn't he succeed to the throne later on?

A: Prince Siddhattha in his childhood developed the habit of meditating. Many phenomena he observed touched him strongly and made him think deeply: e. g. the hungry, thirsty and exhausted farmers working under the scorching sun, panting and sweating cattle being flogged as they plough, the struggle among snakes, insects, birds and beasts under the law of the jungle, weak and ugly old people, the moaning and suffering sick, the dead in funeral processions with their families and friends weeping behind. All these presented him with a problem: how to deliver the world from suffering. Neither the Veda he had read nor the knowledge he had acquired, nor his future throne and power could solve this problem. Therefore, he harbored the idea of renouncing the world in his early days, and finally he relinquished his throne.

13. Q: How could his father agree to his renunciation?

A: Having found out what his son had in mind, King Suddhodana tried many ways to detain him, cspecially by surrounding him with worldly pleasures. When Siddhattha was only 16 years old, King Suddhodana arranged for him to marry Princess Yasodharā from a neighboring state. Yasodharā bore him a son named Rāhula. But all this was in vain. He finally slipped out of the capital city in the still of a night. He entered a forest, shed his princely clothes and, shaving his head and beard, became a wandering mendicant. Regarding his age at the time of renunciation, there are two different accounts—one says nineteen, and the other twenty-nine.

14. Q: What about his life after he renounced the world?

A: Having tried in vain to persuade him to return, his father chose five men from his clan to accompany him. They were Kauṇḍinya, Bhadrika, Vāṣpa, Mahānāma, and Asvajit (P. Koṇḍañña, Bhaddiya, Vappa, Mahānāma, Assaji). Prince Siddhattha and his followers successively paid visits to three

(Vāṣpa，P. Vappa)，摩诃男(Mahānāma，P. Mahānāma)，阿说示(Asvajit，P. Assaji)。悉达多王子和他的侍者们先后寻访当时三个有名的学者，从他们学道，但都不能满足他的要求。于是他知道当时哲学思想中没有真正解脱之法，便离开了他们，走到尼连禅河(Nairañjanā，P：Nerañjarā，现在叫做 Lilaian)岸边的树林中，和那里的苦行人(极端刻苦修行的人)在一起。为了寻求解脱，他尝够了艰苦辛酸，坚持不懈，经历六年之久。但是结果徒劳无功，方才悟到苦行是无益的。他于是走到尼连禅河里去沐浴，洗去了六年的积垢，随后受了一个牧女供养的牛奶，恢复了气力。当时随从他的五个人见到他的情景，以为他放弃了信心和努力，便离开了他，前往波罗奈城(Benares)去继续他们的苦行。王子于是一个人走到一棵毕钵罗(Pippala)树下，铺上了吉祥草，向着东方盘腿坐着，发誓说："我今如不证到无上大觉，宁可让此身粉碎，终不起此座。"他便这样在树下思维解脱之道，终于在一个夜里，战胜了最后的烦恼魔障，获得了彻底觉悟而成了佛陀。

15. 问：释迦牟尼成佛处，现有遗迹留存吗？

答：释迦牟尼成佛处，自古称为菩提场或菩提伽耶(Buddhagayā)，那里的毕钵罗树，因为佛坐在树下成道的缘故，得到了菩提树之名。从此，所有毕钵罗树都叫做菩提树。"菩提"就是"觉"的意思。菩提伽耶在今天印度比哈尔省伽耶城(Gayā)的南郊。那棵菩提树在二千数百年中曾两次遭到斫伐，一次遭风拔，但都重生了新芽，现在的

famous scholars and learned from them, but none of them could satisfy his quest. When he realized that no real path of deliverance (or absolution) was to be found in the philosophical thought of that time, he left for a forest on the banks of the Nerañjarā river, now the Lilaian, and lived there with other ascetics. In his search for emancipation, he went through suffering and pain for six years. However, since it proved fruitless, he began to understand that austerities were to no avail. So he went to take a bath in the Nerañjarā River, cleaning off all the dirt of six years. Then, after accepting the milk gruel offered by a herdswoman, his strength returned afresh. When his five followers saw this, they thought he had abandoned his faith and spiritual efforts, so they left him for Benares City (P. Bārāñasī) to continue their ascetic practices. The Prince then went alone to a Pippala tree and made a seat with auspicious grass (kuśa) under the tree. Sitting down with his legs crossed and facing the east he vowed, "Now should I fail to attain supreme enlightenment, I would rather have my body decompose than rise from this seat." In such a manner, he commenced meditating on absolution, and finally one night defeated the moral affliction and Māra's temptations (kilesa and Māra), achieved complete enlightenment, thereby becoming a Buddha.

15. Q: Are there any vestiges remaining of the site where Sākyamuni became Buddha?

A: The site where Sākyamuni attained Buddhahood has been known as the Place of Enlightenment or Buddhagayā ever since. The Pippala tree there, as well as that kind of tree in general later became known as Bodhi tree. Bodhi means enlightenment. Buddhagayā is situated in the southern suburbs of Gayā City in Bihar Pradesh of India today. In the course of more than twenty centuries, the Bodhi tree was twice chopped down and once blown over, but always sprouted again. The present Bodhi tree is a great grandson of the original one. At the plot where

菩提树是原来那棵树的曾孙。树下释迦牟尼坐处有石刻的金刚座。树的东面有一座宏伟庄严的塔寺，名叫大菩提寺，至今约有一千八百多年的历史，附近还有许多佛的遗迹和古代石刻与建筑。1956年印度比哈尔省政府为了这个圣地的建设和管理，设立了一个国际性的咨询委员会。中国佛教协会接受了邀请，指派了两名代表参加该会。

16. 问：释迦牟尼成佛后的事迹，可以简略地谈一谈吗？

答：释迦牟尼成佛的年龄，也有不同的记载，有的说三十岁，有的说三十五岁。此后五十年(或四十五年)中，直到他八十岁逝世前，他没有间断过他的说法工作。他到处游行，向大众宣示他自己证悟的真理。他最初到波罗奈城去找离开了他的五个侍者，为他们说法。佛教把佛陀第一次说法，叫做“初转法轮”。

17. 问：“转法轮”是什么意思？

答：“轮”(Cakka)，是印度古代战争中用的一种武器，它的形状像个轮子。印度古代有一种传说，征服四方的大王叫做转轮王，他出生的时候，空中自然出现此轮，预示他的前途无敌。这里以轮来比喻佛所说的法。佛的法轮出现于世，一切不正确的见解、不善的法都破碎无余，所以把说法叫做转法轮。佛初转法轮处是鹿野苑(Sārnāth)，在

Buddha sat under the tree is a stone-carved diamond pedestal (Vajrāsana). To the east of the tree is a majestic thūpa (S. stūpa) temple known as Mahābodhi Ārāma with a history of over 18 centuries, and nearby are a number of traces of Buddha and ancient carved stones and architecture. In 1956, the government of Bihar Pradesh appointed an international advisory committee to supervise the construction and administration of the Holy Land. The Buddhist Association of China, at its invitation, sent two delegates to that Committee.

16. Q: Would you please give a brief account regarding his life after Sākyamuni attained Buddhahood?

A: There are different versions regarding the age at which Sākyamuni attained enlightenment, some quote it as thirty and some as thirty-five. For fifty (or forty-five) years after that, until the end of his life at the age of 80, he never stopped preaching his doctrine. He traveled widely, preaching to the public the truth he had perceived. At the outset, he went to Benares (P. Bārāṇasī) to look for his five departed followers and preached the truth to them. The first sermon of the Buddha is called "The initial turning of the wheel of Dhamma" (S. Dharmacakra pravartana, P. Dhammacakkappavattana) in Buddhism.

17. Q: What does "Turning the wheel of Dhamma" (Dhammacakkappavattana) mean?

A: Cakka (wheel) was a wheel-like weapon used in wars in ancient India. There was an old legend in India that the rāja (king) that conquered the world would be the Rajacakkavattin, i.e. "The wheel-turning king". At the time of his birth, a wheel appeared in the sky, prophesying that he would be unconquerable in the future. In Buddhism the wheel is used as a metaphor of the Dhamma preached by the Buddha. Once the Buddha's Dhammacakka emerged, all the wrong thinking and evil things

今天波罗奈城(Benares)。经过近代的发掘,鹿野苑发现了不少有价值的文物。有阿育王的石柱,有公元四世纪石刻的佛初转法轮像等等,并且发掘到古代塔寺的遗址。鹿野苑现有佛寺、博物馆和图书馆,都是近几十年来陆续兴建起来的。佛初转法轮处的鹿野苑,和佛诞生处的蓝毗尼园、佛成道处的菩提伽耶、佛逝世处的拘尸那伽(S. Kuśinagara, P. Kusināra),是佛教四大圣迹。值得指出的是:近代学者们对这些圣迹以及其他一些古迹的发掘和修复,主要都是根据我国古代高僧法显、玄奘等的记载。

18. 问:佛初次说法的地方为什么要比其他说法的地方看得重要呢?

答:佛在鹿野苑初转法轮这件事是佛教的一件大事。从那时起,开始建立了佛教;从那时起,开始具足了三宝。

19. 问:"三宝"是什么?

答:佛陀是佛宝。佛所说的法是法宝。佛的出家弟子的团体——僧伽(Sangha)是僧宝。称之为宝,是因为它能够令大众止恶行善、离苦得乐,是极可尊贵的意思。佛初转法轮,憍陈如等五人都归依佛,出家为弟子,于是形成了僧伽。所以说,从那时起开始具足了三宝。

would be smashed and vanish. Hence the preaching of Dhamma is called Dhammacakkappavattana (turning the wheel of Dhamma). The Buddha's initial turning of the wheel of Dhamma took place at Sārnāth (Deer Park) in present day Benares. Through the recent excavations, quite a few valuable relics have been discovered at Sārnāth, including King Asoka's stone pillar, stone-engraved images of the Buddha's first turning of the wheel of Dhamma dating from the fourth century AD etc. Even the ruins of the ancient thūpa temple were unearthed. Buddhist temples, museums and a library now standing there were built over the last few decades. There are four places regarded as the holy places of Buddhism: Sārnāth where the Buddha initially turned the wheel of Dhamma, Lumbinī Grove where the Buddha was born, Buddhagayā where the Buddha attained enlightenment, and Kusināra where the Buddha passed away. It is worthy of note that modern scholars excavated and repaired the holy places and other historical sites mainly on the basis of the records of the eminent ancient Chinese pilgrims like Fa Xian (Fa Hsien), Xuan Zang (Hsuan Tsang) and others.

18. Q: Why is the site of the Buddha's first sermon looked upon as more important than other sermon sites?

A: The Buddha's initial turning of the wheel of Dhamma at Sārnāth was a great event in Buddhism. From that time, Buddhism was established; and after that, the Three Gems (Tiratana) came into existence.

19. Q: What are the Three Gems (Tiratana)?

A: The Three Gems are the gem of Buddha, the enlightened one, the Gem of Dhamma, the teachings given by the Buddha, and the Gem of Sangha, the Order of the Buddha's monastic disciples. These three are called gems (ratana) because they can lead people to stop doing evil and to perform kindness, to free themselves from suffering and to gain happiness. The title of "The Three Gems" also shows the great value placed on them.

20. 问:什么叫做归依?

答:归依的意思是:身心归向它、依靠它。归依三宝的人是佛教徒。“归依”也可以写成“皈依”,“皈”与“归”的读音和意义相同。

21. 问:佛在世的时候,归依的人多吗?

答:是的,佛初转法轮后从鹿野苑到摩揭陀国(Magadha)去的一路上,受到他的教化而归依的人就很多。其中有拜火教的婆罗门姓迦叶的三兄弟,都改变了原来的信仰,率领他们的弟子一千多人归依了佛教。佛到了摩揭陀国首都王舍城(Rājagaha)后,归依的人更多。其中最有名的出家弟子有舍利弗(Sāriputta)、摩诃目犍连(Mahāmoggallāna)、摩诃迦叶(Mahākassapa)等人。后来佛回到故乡去,他的异母弟难陀(Nanda)、堂兄弟阿难陀(Ānanda)、提婆达多(Devadatta)和他儿子罗怙罗等都随他出了家。还有宫廷中一个剃发工奴优波离(Upāli)也出家加入了僧团,后来成为有名的佛教戒律学大师。佛的姨母波阇波提也归依了佛,是第一个出家女弟子。至于不出家而归依三宝的弟子则为数更多。佛的出家弟子,男的叫比丘(bhikkhu),女的叫做比丘尼(bhikkhunī);在家弟子,

When the Buddha initially turned the wheel of Dhamma, Koṇḍañña and others, five of them in all, followed the Buddha, renounced lay life and became the Buddha's disciples, thus forming the Sangha Order. Therefore, the three Gems have been cherished since that time.

20. Q: What is the meaning of "abiding by the Three Gems" ("Ti-saraṇaṃ gacchāmi")?

A: Ti-saraṇaṃ gacchāmi means that one abides by the Three Gems with one's heart and soul. Those who have gone to and relied on the three Gems are Buddhists.

21. Q: Were there many people who came and followed the Buddha during his lifetime?

A: Yes. On the way from Sārnāth to Magadha State after the Buddha's first sermon, many people were converted to follow him and his teachings. Among them were three brothers, Brahmins, by the name of Kassapa. They had been Zoroastrians, but converted and brought along with them more than one thousand of their followers to convert to Buddhism. After the Buddha arrived in Rājagaha, the capital of Magadha, many more people converted, including some who became prominent disciples, like Sāriputta, Mahāmoggallāna and Mahā-kassapa. Afterwards, when Buddha returned to his native land, a number of his relatives: his younger half brother Nanda, his cousins Ānanda and Devadatta, his son Rāhula and others became monastic disciples. Among them there was a barber named Upali who had served the royal family, and later became a famous master of Buddhist disciplines (Vinaya bhānaka). Buddha's aunt Prajāpati also followed to become the first female monastic disciple of the Buddha. Besides, even more devotees converted to the faith without renouncing the home life. Therefore, Buddha's disciples consist of Bhikkhu (monks), Bhikkhunī (nuns), who form the Buddhist monastic Order; and Upāsaka,

男的叫做邬波索迦（upāsaka），女的叫做邬波斯迦（upāsikā），合称为四众弟子。

22. 问：释迦牟尼一生游行教化的区域，是哪些地方？

答：根据记载和发掘的资料，佛自己足迹所到的地方，主要是中印度。他的弟子们分到四方游化，可能更远一些。但是斯里兰卡和缅甸都有佛曾经到过并留下足印的传说。佛居住的地方以摩揭陀国的王舍城和拘萨罗国（Kosala）的舍卫城（Sāvatthī）的时间为最多。在王舍城外有一个竹林，是频毗娑罗王（Bimbisāra）献给佛和僧众居住的，后人称为竹林精舍。在舍卫城有一个林园是当地一个富商须达多（Sudatta）和拘萨罗国王子祇陀（Jeta）共同献给佛的，后人称为祇园精舍。佛常往来两处，所以竹林、祇园并为说法的重地。王舍城南面的灵鹫山（Gijjhakūṭa）也是佛常和弟子们说法的地方。佛逝世前由王舍城北行到毗舍离（Vesālī）城（今印度比哈尔省境内），又由毗舍离向西北行，最后到了拘尸那伽（今印度联合省伽夏城 Kasia），佛是在拘尸那伽逝世的。现在佛逝世处，发掘出佛遗体火化的地方和石刻的佛涅槃像以及其他古迹。印度政府为了纪念佛涅槃二千五百年，曾对这个圣地予以必要的修复和建设。

23. 问：什么叫做“涅槃”？

答：现在暂不详细解答，这里可简单解释为“逝世”。

Upāsikā, who are the male and female lay followers; together they are known as the four groups of disciples.

22. Q: Where did Sākyamuni travel and preach during his life?

A: According to historical records and excavations, Buddha's own footprints mainly covered central India. His disciples, dispersed in all quarters, might have gone further afield. There are also legends in Sri Lanka and Burma about the Buddha visiting and leaving his footprints. During the Buddha's lifetime, he resided for the most part in Rājagaha, in the state of Magadha and Sāvatthī in the state of Kosala. Outside Rājagaha was a bamboo forest, donated to the Buddha and his disciples by King Bimbisāra, which later came to be known as Bamboo Grove Monastery (Veḷuvanārāmaya). In Sāvatthī, there was a garden given to the Buddha jointly by a rich merchant, Sudatta, and Prince Jeta of Kosala. This garden was known later as Jeta Grove Monastery (Jetavanārāmaya or Jetavana Anāthapiṇḍikassa-ārāma). Since the Buddha used to travel between the two places, both became important sites for the propagation of his doctrines. Gijjhakūṭa Hill, situated south of Rājagaha, was another place frequented by the Buddha and his disciples for preaching. Prior to his death, the Buddha went northward from Rājagaha to Vesālī (Bihar Pradesh in modern India). Then he turned northwest, and finally arrived at Kusināra (now Kasia in Uttar Pradesh, India) where he passed away (Parinibbāna). In modern times, excavations have uncovered the site of his cremation, and discovered a stone-carved image of his nibbāna as well as other relics. The Government of India in commemoration of the 2500th anniversary of the Buddha's Nibbāna (S. Nirvāna) has done some essential repair and construction in the holy place.

23. Q: What is "Nibbāna"?

A: This will be fully explained later, it may be simply interpreted as death.

24. 问:佛涅槃前后的情形是怎样?

答:佛在毗舍离城的时候,已经有了重病,在那里度过雨季后,偕弟子们向西北走去,路上受了铁匠纯陀(Cunda)供献的食品,病更加剧。最后走到拘尸那伽一条河边,洗了澡,在一处四方各有两棵娑罗树的中间安置了绳床,枕着右手侧身卧着。后来所有卧佛像(即佛涅槃像)都是这样的姿式。佛告知弟子们将要涅槃,弟子都守候着。夜间有婆罗门学者须跋陀罗(Subhadda)去见佛,阿难陀想挡住他,佛知道了,唤他到床前为他说法,于是须跋陀罗成了佛的最后的弟子。佛在毗舍离临出发前和在途中为弟子们作了多次的教诲,到了那天半夜逝世前又最后嘱咐弟子不要以为失去了导师,应当以法为师,要努力精进,不要放逸。

佛逝世后,遗体举行火化。摩揭陀国人和释迦族等八国将佛的舍利分为八份,各在他们的本土上建塔安奉。其中摩揭陀国安奉在菩提伽耶的一份,到公元前三世纪,被阿育王取出,分成许多份送到各地建塔。1898 年,考古家在尼泊尔南境发掘迦毗罗国故址,发现一舍利塔,塔内藏有石瓶石函等物;有一瓶放在铁和水晶层迭的函内,里面有黄金花,花上安放着佛骨。从函上刻的文字知道这就是释迦族供养的佛的舍利。

24. Q: What were the circumstances before and after the Buddha's Nibbāna?

A: Buddha had been very sick when in Vesālī. After the Rainy Season Retreat (Vassa) in Vesālī he went with his disciples towards the northwest. On the way he took food offered by the blacksmith Cunda and became violently ill. Finally he reached the bank of a river in Kusināra, after taking a bath he lay on his right side with his head resting on his right hand, on a hammock placed among four pairs of sala trees. Subsequently, all the recumbent (Sleeping) Buddha statues or the statues of the Buddha's Nibbāna have been modeled in this posture. Buddha informed his disciples of the approach of his Nibbāba, and all his disciples watched over him. At night, a Brahmin scholar named Subhadda came to see the Buddha. When Ananda tried to stop him the Buddha called Subhadda to his bedside and preached a discourse for him, so Subhadda became the last disciple of Buddha's lifetime. From the time he left Vesālī on the journey, the Buddha preached to his disciples many times and at midnight when he was about to die, he told them for the last time, "You should not think that you no longer have a teacher. Rather you should let the teachings (Dhamma) be your teacher. Be diligent in striving for salvation, never be indolent."

After the Buddha's death, his body was cremated. The remains were divided into eight portions by Magadha, the Sākya, and other states and then enshrined in thūpas constructed in the eight states. By the third century BC a portion of Buddha's Sarīra enshrined in Buddhagayā in Magadha was taken out by King Asoka and was divided into many portions to be stored in thūpas in different places. In 1898, archeologists discovered a Sarīra thūpa on the southern border of Nepal when they excavated an ancient location of Kapilavatthu. Inside the thūpa they found stone vases, urns and other articles. One of the vases was kept in an urn made of layers of iron and Crystal. In the vase there was a golden flower with the Buddha's bones placed on it. The inscription on an urn indicates that this is the Buddha's Sarīra enshrined by the Sākyas.

25. 问:舍利是什么?

答:舍利(Sarīra)就是遗体,但这个名称一般只用于佛和有德行的出家人的遗体。

26. 问:塔是作什么用的?

答:"塔"又称"塔波",是梵语 Stūpa (P. Thūpa)省略的音译,完整的音译是"窣堵波",意义是"高显"或"坟"。塔一般是藏舍利的。也有不藏舍利而作为标志纪念之用的。

27. 问:佛涅槃的年代,有没有不同的计算?

答:关于佛涅槃的年代,东南亚佛教徒一般认为是公元前545年,所以1956年和1957年各国都举行佛涅槃二千五百年盛大纪念。我国关于佛涅槃年代有很多不同的说法,一般公认的年代是公元前486年,与南传佛历相差59年。

28. 问:佛的涅槃日是哪一天?

答:我国一般认为农历二月十五日是佛涅槃日,四月初八日是佛诞生日,十二月初八日是佛成道日。南方各国则以公历五月月圆日(相当于我国农历四月十五日)为佛节日(Vesākhā),认为佛诞生、成道、涅槃都在这一天。

25. Q: What is sarīra?

A: Sarīra means the remains of the dead, but this term is generally confined to the remains of the Buddha and other virtuous priests only.

26. Q: What is the function of a thūpa?

A: Thūpa (S. stūpa), rendered into Chinese as "Ta", "Tabo" or "Sudubo", means "tower" or "tomb". It is usually used for keeping sarīra, though some are built for commemorative purposes.

27. Q: Is there agreement over the year of the Buddha's Parinibbāna?

A: With regard to the year of the Buddha's Parinibbāna, the Buddhists in Southeast Asia generally put it in the year 545 BC, so in 1956 and 1957 many countries ceremoniously observed the 2500th anniversary of the Buddha's Parinibbāna. In China, however, there are different opinions about the year of the Buddha's passing away, the generally acknowledged year being 486 BC, 59 years later than the Theravādin calendar of Southeast Asia.

28. Q: What is the date of the Buddha's Parinibbāna?

A: In China, the 15th of the second month of the lunar calendar is commonly accepted as the Date of the Buddha's Parinibbāna, the 8th of the fourth month as the Buddha's birthday, and the 8th of the twelfth month as the Day of the Buddha's enlightenment. In South and Southeast Asian countries, however, the full moon day of May of the Gregorian calendar (corresponding to the 15th of the fourth month in the Chinese lunar calendar) is the Buddhist Holy Day called

29. 问：听了上面的谈话，对释迦牟尼佛的一生事迹已经有了轮廓的了解。现在想请你谈一谈当时佛教创立的历史背景。

答：这是一个较难的问题，因为第一关于印度古代历史资料缺乏，第二我自己在这方面少研究。但是我仍然愿意将一些我所知道的材料和所想到的线索，提供你参考、研究和判断。

30. 问：很好。我认为，任何宗教和思想都是历史的产物，能够了解一些当时社会的情况，是有助于对佛教的了解的。希望你就几个主要的问题谈一谈，能说明一个大概就行了。

答：先从当时的形势谈起吧。你知道古代印度曾经有一个区域叫做"中国"吗？

31. 问：这倒不知道。那是在印度的什么地区？

答：大约三千五百年到四千年前，雅利安(Ārya)人逐渐由中亚细亚进入印度河流域，征服了那里的土著民族，并且吸收了他们的文明，在那里定居下来，建立了好些国家。因为长期成为雅利安人政治文化的中心(也就是婆罗门文明的中心)，当时那个地区被称为"中国"(Madhya Desa)。至于东方和南方的恒河流域的广大地区，则被称为是化外的"边地"。但是到了释迦牟尼时代，形势有了很大的改变。原来"中国"地方的国家已经开始衰落，而东南

Vesākhā (S. Vaishākya), which is regarded as the Day of Buddha's birth, enlightenment, as well as Parinibbāna.

29. Q: From what you have said we have learned the brief outline of the life of Sākyamuni Buddha. Would you now please give some historical background on the origin of Buddhism?

A: This is rather a difficult question, firstly, because there is a lack of materials on Indian history, secondly, I haven't studied this area very deeply. Yet I would like to share what information I have, as well as clues and leads in my mind for your further reference, research and judgment.

30. Q: Good. I think all religions and ideologies are products of history. It would be helpful to the understanding of Buddhism to learn something about the social circumstances of that time. I hope you can paint a brief sketch of its main points.

A: Let us begin with the situation of that time. Do you know there was a region called the Middle Kingdom (Madhya Deśa) in ancient India?

31. Q: I am afraid I don't. In what part of India was it located?

A: About 3500-4000 years ago, with gradual migration from central Asia into the Indus Valley, the Aryans conquered the original inhabitants and settled there. They assimilated the aboriginal civilization and founded a number of states. For a long time afterward, this area was a political and cultural center of Brahmin civilization and of the Aryan people, thus this region was called the Middle Kingdom (Madhya Deśa). As to the vast areas of the eastern and southern Ganges Valley, these were called uncivilized "frontier" areas. However, by the time of Sākyamuni, a tremendous change had taken place. The states in the original Madhya Deśa began to decline, while those in the

边地的国家则勃然兴起。释迦牟尼居住最久、教化最盛的摩揭陀国就是当时新兴的霸国。这时候，文明的中心已经转移到摩揭陀国的王舍城，拘萨罗国的舍卫城，跋耆国的毗舍离城等新都市，其中王舍城尤为重要。

32. 问：这些新兴国家除了实力强盛之外，在社会、经济、文化方面有没有什么特点？

答：据我初步地研究，有三种情况值得一提：(1) 在种族问题上，矛盾的增多；(2) 在经济问题上，社会生产力的发展；(3) 在思想上，反婆罗门教义的新思想的兴起。这三种情况都反映在“种姓制度”问题上。

33. 问：什么是种姓制度？

答：种姓制度是雅利安人进入印度之后创立的。“种姓”这个词儿是从梵语“Varṇa”（p. Vaṇṇa）翻译过来的，它的原来的字义是“颜色”或“品质”。照他们的说法，肤色白的雅利安人是品质高贵的种族，深色皮肤的达罗毗荼(Dravida)族和其他土著民族是品质低贱的种族。这种制度原来是用以划分雅利安人和非雅利安人的界限的。后来随着工作和职业的分化的发展，本来用以划分雅利安人和非雅利安人的种姓差别，也在雅利安人自己中间起了反映，于是有四姓（四个种姓）的划分。最高的种姓是婆罗门(Brāhmaṇa)，是掌握祭祀文教的僧侣阶级（到后来婆罗门也可以当国王）；其次是刹帝利（Kṣatriya），是掌握军政的国王和武士阶级；其次是吠舍（Vaiśya），是商人、手工业

south-eastern frontier began to prosper. Among them was Magadha, the newly emerging dominant state where Sākyamuni resided for the longest time and taught most extensively. The center of civilization by this time had shifted to the new cities: Rājagaha in Magadha, Sāvatthī in Kosala and Vesālī in Vajji, among them Rājagaha was particularly important.

32. Q: Apart from being powerful and prosperous, were there any particular characteristics in respect to social, economic and cultural spheres in these newly-emerging states?

A: According to my preliminary study, there are three conditions which are worthy of notice: (1) The increasing ethnic conflicts; (2) The development of social productivity in the economy; (3) The emergence of a new anti-Brahmanist trend of thought. All these three were reflected in the caste system.

33. Q: What is the caste system?

A: The caste system was created with the entry of Aryans into India. The word "caste" is used to translate the Sanskrit word "Varṇa" (P. Vaṇṇa). Its original meaning was "color" or "quality". According to their theory, white-skinned Aryans were a superior race; the dark colored Dravidians and other aborigines were inferior races. At first, this system was used to distinguish between Aryan and non-Aryan peoples. Subsequently, with the developing division of trades and occupations, the caste distinction formerly used for separating Aryans from non-Aryans also found reflection among Aryans themselves. Hence the division of four castes: the highest caste was Brāhmaṇa, the class of priests who administered religious rites, and educational and cultural affairs (some later became Kings). The next was Kṣatriya, the class of kings and warriors who administered military and political affairs; the third was Vaiśya, composed of merchants, artisans and peasants engaged in farm work; and the fourth was Śūdra, composed of farm laborers, herdsmen, ser-

者，也有从事农耕的农民阶级；最下的种姓是首陀罗(śūdra)，是农人、牧人、仆役和奴隶。前三者是雅利安人，后者是非雅利安人。各种姓有它的世袭的职业，不许被婚姻混乱，尤其严禁首陀罗和别的种姓混乱。对首陀罗男子和别的种姓女子结合所生的混血种，特别订有法律，给予一种贱名，如首陀罗男子与婆罗门女子的混血种名为旃陀罗(Caṇḍāla)。他们的地位最低贱，不能与一般人接触，被称为"不可触者"。这种人世世代代操着当时认为下贱的职业，如抬死尸、屠宰、当刽子手之类。种姓制度不仅订在法律里面，而且神圣不可动摇地规定在宗教教义和教条中。在婆罗门教势力强盛的"中国"地方，种姓制度最严格。

34. 问：在新兴国家地方也有种姓制度吗？

答：随着雅利安人势力的扩展，这些国家都不能不受到婆罗门文化的影响，当然也都存在着种姓制度，但种姓制度所遇到的困难就比较多得多。第一，在这些国家里，土著人民占的比率大；第二，雅利安与非雅利安种族混合情况比较普遍；第三，为了巩固雅利安人在那些地方的统治，有不少土著部族的首领通过入教仪式被安排在刹帝利种姓之列。在种姓制度下，统治阶层的婆罗门和刹帝利之间一向存在着矛盾，尤其是非雅利安人的刹帝利对婆罗门的优越地位的反抗，更加显著。据研究，摩揭陀国的人多半是吠舍和首陀罗的混血种，婆罗门法典认为他们是半雅利安、半野蛮的下等种族。后来统一印度的摩揭陀国阿育

vants and slaves. The first three castes were Aryan and the last one non-Aryan. Each caste had its own hereditary occupations and were not permitted to inter-marry, and in particular, any mixing between Śūdras and other castes was strictly prohibited. There were special laws governing the offspring of Śūdra males and females of other castes, for instance, the shameful title of Caṇḍāla was given to the child born of a Śūdra male and a Brahmin female. The status of Caṇḍāla was the most degraded and since they were not allowed physical contact with others, they were known as the "untouchables". From generation to generation, such people took the humblest jobs such as corpse-carriers, butchers, executioners and the like. The caste system was not only enacted in laws but also unshakably regulated by religious doctrines and tenets. In Madhya Deśa, the caste system was most strictly enforced under the powerful influence of Brahmanism.

34. Q: Did the caste system exist in the newly emerging countries too?

A: With the extension of Aryan influence, these states could not but be affected by the Brahmanic culture. Although the caste system entered there, it encountered quite a lot of obstacles. Firstly, the original inhabitants were in the majority in these states. Secondly, miscegenation between Aryan and non-Aryan races was relatively common. Thirdly, in order to consolidate the Aryan domination in those areas, quite a few aboriginal chiefs were inducted into the caste of Kṣatriya through embracing rituals. Under the caste system, there were always rivalries between the ruling castes, Brāhmaṇas and Kṣatriyas. This was particularly strong between the non-Aryan Kṣatriyas and the Brāhmaṇas who held the superior position. Research shows that most people of Magadha came from miscegenation of Vaiśyas and Śūdras, therefore, they were regarded as an inferior race — semi-aryan and semi-barbarian — by Brahmanic code. It is said that King Asoka of Magadha who later on

王，据说就是首陀罗的血统。在这种环境中，反对婆罗门种姓制度教义的学说，容易为大众所接受和欢迎，而释迦牟尼倡导的“四姓平等”之说，事实上反映着当时那些新兴国家的人民对种姓制度的不满。

35. 问：释迦是不是雅利安种？

答：关于释迦的种族问题，有不同的说法，有的说是蒙古种，有的说是雅利安种。但是从当时的地理看，迦毗罗国地处僻远，又是小国(有人研究，认为它当时是拘萨罗国的附庸国)，因此它的王族不是雅利安种的可能性较大，而且佛经上不只一次说释迦牟尼的身体是紫金色，这可以为释迦族不属于白色的雅利安种的一个论据。

36. 问：能不能说当时种姓制度问题上的矛盾纯粹是种族的矛盾？

答：不能那么说。据我看，它还反映着当时社会生产力的发展所带来的矛盾。

37. 问：释迦牟尼时代印度的社会是不是奴隶社会？

答：近代在印度河流域的发掘，证明在公元前 3500-2750 年之间，那里的土著民族(可能就是达罗毗荼族)，早已有了惊人的城市文明。他们有城市规划，有下水道，有两三层砖建楼房，有公私浴室。街道上有货摊和店铺，有纺织业和陶业。这个事实推翻了西方学者们一向认定印

unified India had Śūdra blood. In such an environment any theories against the Brahmin ideas of caste system would easily be accepted and welcomed. The doctrine advocated by Sākyamuni saying that "all four castes are equal," mirrored the resentment of people in the newly emerging states towards the caste system.

35. Q: Did the Sākyas belong to the Aryan race?

A: Concerning Sākya's ethnic origin, there are different opinions. Some hold the view that it was of the Mongolian race, and others, Aryan. But as far as the geography of that time is concerned, Kapilavatthu was located in a remote area and was a small state (some believe it was a dependency of Kosala). It is more likely that its royal family was not of the Aryan race. Besides, in Buddhist scriptures there is more than one reference to Sākyamuni having a golden purple body, thus providing further grounds for arguing the Sākyas were not a white Aryan race.

36. Q: Can it be said that caste contradictions at that time were simply a reflection of ethnic contradictions?

A: Not exactly. As I see it, it also reflected the contradictions brought about by the development of social productivity at that time.

37. Q: Was Indian society at the time of Sākyamuni a slave society?

A: Recent excavations in the Indus Valley show that as early as 3500-2750 BC, the aborigines there (probably the Dravidians) already had a remarkable urban civilization. They had city planning, with sewerage, two or three storied brick buildings, and public or private baths. Along the streets, there were stalls and shops. A textile industry as well as a ceramics industry existed. This fact strongly refutes the suggestion of Western scholars that the Indian civilization was brought in by Aryans. As a mat-

度文明是雅利安人带来的说法。事实上是游牧民族的雅利安人接受了土著的高级文明。根据发掘的材料来看,当时土著民族已经进入了奴隶社会,而且可以断定他们有了相当发达的农业。至于雅利安人定居下来很长时期(约一千年)以后,到了种姓制度确立了的时期,那里的社会是否仍然是奴隶社会,值得研究。从婆罗门的法典看来,首陀罗并不是奴隶,只是有一部分人当奴隶,而奴隶只是从事杂役劳动,在生产部门很少参加,显然奴隶不是主要生产者,因此很难断定当时是奴隶社会。

38. 问:据你看当时是什么制度的社会呢?

答:佛经中的资料记载,当时国王每年有一固定的日期,在自己的田地里举行亲耕仪式,人民都在替他耕田。这与婆罗门的法典规定的靠自己劳动为生的首陀罗人要以劳动向国王纳税的条文相合。根据我国古代译师的注释,"刹帝利"的原来字义是"田主"。从这个线索来推断,似乎"种姓"制度开始完备地确立的时期,印度已经进入了封建领主统治的农奴社会。而到了释迦牟尼时代,在新兴的国家里,情形又有所演变。根据佛经的资料,当时的商业很发达,有相当规模的陆运和航运的商队,商人掌握着雄厚的经济力量,例如把一座林园送给佛的大富商须达多,他有力量以黄金布地和拘萨罗的王子比富。手工业也很发达,有细密的分工,自由经营的小工商业在生产上占重要地位。当时有了纳税的自由农民,有佃农。可以设想,在吠舍人和首陀罗人混合种族的新兴国家里,刹帝利

ter of fact, it is the nomadic Aryans who accepted the higher civilization of the original inhabitants. In the light of the excavations, the aboriginal society at that time was a slave society, and it may be concluded that they had already considerably advanced agriculture. As to the period from when the Aryans settled down, up until the caste system was set up (about 1,000 years), it remains to be studied whether it was still a slave society. According to the Brahmanic code, Śūdra did not mean slave, only some of that caste were slaves who engaged in odd jobs, taking very little part in production. It is apparent that slaves were not the main labor power, therefore, it is hard to assert that this was still a slave society.

38. Q: In your opinion, what was the prevailing social system at that time?

A: It is recorded in the Buddhist scriptures that there was a fixed time each year during which the king presided over a ploughing ceremony in the fields, and the people tilled for him. This agrees with the clause of the Brahmin codes, which stipulates that the Śūdras who lived off their own labor should pay taxes to the king through offering their labor. According to the notes made by the ancient Chinese translators, Kṣatriya originally meant "land owner". It may be inferred from this that by the time the caste system began to be well established, India had entered into a society of serfdom ruled by feudal lords. By the time of Sākyamuni, more changes had occurred in the newly emerging states. The Buddhist literature suggests that commerce at that time was flourishing with large-scale trade caravans and mercantile fleets, thus merchants had solid economic strength. For instance, a very rich merchant named Sudatta, who made a gift of a garden to the Buddha, was of such great wealth that he compared riches with the prince of Kosala by paving the whole garden with gold. Handicrafts flourished too, with fine division of labor. Small enterprises of industry and commerce operated freely and played an important role in productive activities. At

可能不是领主，而是新兴地主阶级的代表。印度在公元前一千年间已经有了铁器，到这时期，铁制农业器具更已普遍使用，农业上生产力有了很大的发展。在当时的经济情况下，封建领主的割据，是不利于商业、手工业，特别是农业的发展的。历史证明，统一兴修水利和灌溉系统是促成阿育王统一印度的重要原因。虽然阿育王是佛逝世二百年以后的人，但是佛在世时，人们就有"转轮王统一天下"的理想。佛幼年时，他的父王和国人曾期望他做转轮王。佛虽然舍弃了王位，但是他也推崇转轮王这样的理想人物。"转轮王"思想，实际是反映着当时一般人要求有一个中央集权政府来代替领主割据的愿望，这个要求和愿望必然和种姓制度发生冲突。

39. 问：释迦牟尼和婆罗门、刹帝利的关系怎样？

答：释迦牟尼是公开宣布反对婆罗门教义的，所以一生遭到婆罗门攻击的事很多。但是也有不少婆罗门教徒和学者改变了原来的信仰而归依了他。婆罗门人受了佛教的刺激，就有了《摩奴法典》的出现。这部法典一方面固然是为了维护种姓制度，一方面也可能作了一些修正。在《摩奴法典》里攻击佛教的文句虽不明显，但后出的《述记氏法论》则把攻击佛教的态度明白地表示出来。至于佛和

that time there emerged tax-paying free farmers as well as tenant farmers. It is conceivable that, in the newly emerging states where the majority was of the mixed castes of Vaiśyas and Śūdras, Kṣatriyas might not have been serf-owners, but representatives of a newly emerging landlord class. As early as 1,000 BC ironware had appeared in India, and by this period, iron farm tools were widely used, and agricultural productivity was greatly increased. Under such economic circumstances, partitioning by feudal lords was unfavorable to the development of commerce, handicrafts and of agriculture in particular. History shows that the centralized construction of water conservancy and irrigation works was of importance in King Asoka's unification of India. Even during the Buddha's lifetime, 200 years before Asoka, people had already cherished the ideal of "one world unified by the wheel turning king" (Rāja Cakkavattin). In his childhood, the Buddha's father and compatriots hoped he would become the wheel-turning king. The Buddha, in spite of forsaking his throne, also held the ideal of a wheel-turning King. The idea of the wheel-turning king was indeed a reflection of the people's common aspiration to have a centralized government to replace the state of division by the feudal lords. This desire inevitably came into conflict with the caste system.

39. Q: What was the relationship between Sākyamuni and Brahmins, and between Sākyamuni and Kṣatriyas?

A: Sākyamuni publicly opposed Brahmanic doctrines, so he was subject to numerous attacks by the Brahmins during his lifetime. Nevertheless, a large number of Brahmin scholars and followers shed their original beliefs and turned to the Buddha. The Brahmaṇas, in response to Buddhism, issued the *Manu Code* (Manu-Smṛti), which, while upholding the caste system, made some amendments to it. Although the *Manu Code* didn't overtly attack Buddhism, the subsequent *Manuals of Public and Domestic Rites* (Sarvadarśana Saṃgraha) expressed an explicitly offensive attitude against Buddhism. As to the relationship between

刹帝利的关系，你知道，佛是出身于刹帝利种姓的。当时佛所游化的那些国家的国王们，如摩揭陀国的频毗娑罗王，拘萨罗国的波斯匿王等，都是他的信徒和有力的支持者。后来阿育王更大弘佛法。应当说，新兴国家的刹帝利对佛是极其尊重信仰的。值得注意的是，佛经中提到四姓时，改变了原来以婆罗门为首的次序(即婆罗门、刹帝利、吠舍、首陀罗)，而把婆罗门放在刹帝利之后，这是违反传统习惯的，由此也可以看出他贬抑婆罗门地位的态度。

40. 问:释迦牟尼和平民的关系怎样?

答:释迦牟尼教化的方式是接近平民的。他说法不用婆罗门的雅语，而用当时平民的俗语，就是一个例子。前面说过释迦牟尼曾经接受一个首陀罗人优波离为弟子，佛的兄弟和儿子在僧团内行次在他之下，他们都得向优波离礼拜。对一般人不肯接触的旃陀罗人，佛和弟子们平等接受他们的供养。佛曾经设法和一个不敢见他的旃陀罗人相见，并为他说法。佛对待所有不幸的人都是这样。他的弟子中有乞丐，也有妓女，有一次，佛谢绝了国王的邀请，而到一个不幸的堕落的女人那里去应供。在古代印度社会里，妇女的地位和奴隶差不多。佛接受妇女为出家弟子，让她们参加僧团的事实，被认为是宗教史上一个很大的革命举动。

the Buddha and the Kṣatriyas, as you know, Buddha came from the Kṣatriya caste. The kings of those states where he traveled and preached, such as Bimbisāra of Magadha, Prasenajit of Kosala and others were his faithful followers and strong supporters. At a later time after Buddha, King Asoka more energetically promulgated the Buddha Dhamma. It should be concluded that the Kśatriyas of the newly emerging states had great esteem for and staunch faith in Buddha. It is worth notice that in the Buddhist texts, whenever mention is made of the four castes, Brahman is put after Kṣatriya. That is contrary to the traditional order in which Brahmin came the first. (i. e. Brāhmaṇa, Kṣatriya, Vaiśya and Śūdra) From this break with tradition, one can see the Buddha's depreciation of the Brahmins' position.

40. Q: What was the relationship between Sākyamuni and the common people?

A: Sākyamuni's style of teaching was close to the common people. Instead of the elegant language of the Brahmins, he used vernacular language. As mentioned earlier, Sākyamuni accepted a Śūdra named Upāli to be his disciple to whom the Buddha's brothers and son had to pay homage since their ranks in the Sangha were lower than his. The Buddha and his disciples accepted on equal footing the offerings contributed by the Caṇḍālas, or the untouchables, with whom other people were reluctant to make physical contact. The Buddha contrived to meet a Caṇḍāla and preach to him when he was too shy to come and see him. In the same way the Buddha treated all the unfortunates. Among his disciples were beggars and prostitutes. The Buddha, on one occasion, rejected an invitation from a king and went to take a dāna offered by an unfortunately degenerated woman. In ancient Indian society, the status of women was akin to that of slaves. The fact that the Buddha admitted women into the Sangha Order as his monastic disciples was considered a great revolution in religious history.

41. 问：佛虽然对不幸的人们表示同情，但是他没有教他们向统治者进行反抗，不是吗？

答：诚然，佛没有教他们以怎样的实际行动反抗统治者。佛主要教导人们断除内心的烦恼，以求解脱，同时又说现世止恶行善的因，会获得来世安乐的果，在这方面可以说，佛对现实生活问题，是抱着容忍的态度的。但是，他在思想上推倒了婆罗门的神权，宣布众生平等，说出“诸法无常”的真理，对当时的社会起了进步的作用。

42. 问：当时思想界的情况怎样？

答：和我国春秋战国时代相仿佛，当时印度思想界也正处在一个“百家争鸣”的时期。总的说来，当时思想界有两大潮流，一个是正统的婆罗门教思想的潮流，一个是异端的反婆罗门教思想的潮流，佛教属于后者。

43. 问：婆罗门教的基本思想是什么？

答：婆罗门教是多神教而又带着一神教的色彩，崇拜各种自然的神祇，盛行祭祀祈祷以招福禳灾，而以梵(Brahmā)为创造宇宙万物的主宰。梵从口生出婆罗门，从肩部生出刹帝利，从腹部生出吠舍，从足部生出首陀罗，以此定四姓的贵贱，这就成为种姓制度的根据。人应当服从梵天的意旨，因此应当信奉《吠陀经》，奉事婆罗门，严格遵守种姓制度。后来婆罗门教义有所发展，它把“梵”抽象起

41. Q: Although he had sympathy with the unfortunate and suffering people, isn't it true that the Buddha didn't advise them to revolt against their rulers?

A: True, the Buddha didn't instruct people what action to take against the rulers, and although on the one hand, it maybe said he taught forbearance in real life since he mainly taught people how to eliminate their inner worries and attain deliverance and said to them that desisting from evil and doing wholesome deeds in the present world would bring happiness to future life as effect; on the other hand, his thought played a positive role in society at the time because he repudiated the theory of Brahamin theocracy, proclaimed the equal position of all beings and revealed the truth of impermanence of everything (aniccā).

42. Q: What was the situation in the ideological domain in India at that time?

A: Similar to the Spring and Autumn and Warring States Period in Chinese history, there was also a period of "a hundred schools of thought in contention". Generally speaking, there existed two major ideological trends: one was the school of orthodox Brahmanist thought, and the other, various schools of heretical anti-Brahman thought. Buddhism belonged to the latter.

43. Q: What were the fundamental ideas of Brahmanism?

A: Brahmanism was polytheism with monotheistic lean ings. It worshipped various deities of nature, offered sacrifices and prayers for blessings and warding off calamities, but believed in Brahmā as the superior lord who created the entire universe. Brahmā gave birth to Brahmaṇas from his mouth, Kṣatriyas from his shoulder, Vaiśyas from his abdomen and Śūdras from his feet. Thus, the social standing of the four castes, noble or humble, was decided according to this. And thus people had to abide by the will of Brahmā and keep faith in *Veda*. Ordinary

来做为宇宙的本体，或宇宙生起的最高原理，一方面又从个人观察，认为“我”是个人的主宰和本体，人的身体由“我”而生，人的活动由“我”而起，外界万物也都因“我”而存在，由此推论出“我”与“梵”本来不二，人所应当努力的就是经过修行以达到梵我一致的境地，这样才能免去轮回之苦而得到大自在。

44. 问：当时反婆罗门教的思想有多少派别？

答：根据佛经所说有九十六种之多，最特出的有六个教派，佛经称这些教派的创立者为六师。其中一个就是耆那教(Jaina)的始祖尼乾子(Nigaṇṭha Nātaputta)，其余五人是富兰那迦叶(Purāṇa Kassapa)、末迦梨(Makkhali Gosāla)、阿耆多(Ajita Kesakambala)、婆鸠多(Pakudha Kaccāyana)、散若夷(Sañjaya Belaṭṭhiputta)。除耆那教现还存在、有典籍可考外，其余五人都没有正式记载，现在只能从反驳他们学说的其他教派典籍中看到一鳞一爪。他们有的是否认因果关系的怀疑论者；有的主张纵欲；有的主张苦行；有的认为人由四大(地、水、火、风四个元素)组合而成，死后四大分散，归于断灭，否认来世，是唯物论者。

people had to serve Brahmins, and strictly obey the caste system. With the development of Brahmanist doctrines, on one hand Brahmā was recognized as the noumenon of the universe or the ultimate principle of origin of the universe in the abstract sense, on the other hand, viewed from the individual, Atta (Ātman, Ego) was considered the dominator and noumenon of the individual, the personal body as well as one's actions, thus the phenomena of the external world also arise from Atta. Hence an inference: Brahmā and Atta should not be two but one and the same. So what people had to strive to reach was a state of harmony between Atta and Brahmā through self-cultivation, in this way, they could avoid the suffering of saṃsāra and attain ultimate emancipation.

44. Q: How many anti-Brahmanic schools were there at that time?

A: Buddhist texts mention as many as 96 anti-Brahman schools, six of which were outstanding and whose founders were known in the texts as the Six Teachers. One among the six was Nigaṇṭha Nātaputta, the founding father of Jaina. The other five were Pūraṇa Kassapa, Makkhali Gosāla, Ajita Kesakambala, Pakudha Kaccāyana and Sañjaya Belaṭṭhiputta. Of all these schools only Jaina still exists and has texts one can research, the others have no proper records, but fragments of information can be gleaned from the books of the rival schools which challenged their doctrines. Some of them were sceptics denying the relations of cause and effect; some stood for carnal desires; while others advocated ascetic practices; and still others were materialists who believed that human beings were composed of four Mahābhūta (i. e. the four elements of earth, water, fire and air) which would decompose and vanish after death with no prospect of future life.

45. 问:佛教和各教派的关系怎样?

答:佛教一方面批判婆罗门教义,同时也反对非婆罗门教的各教派。但是佛教和婆罗门教以及各教派的思想都有渊源,佛教接受了他们的某些思想,而根据“缘起”和“业”的理论,予以另一种解释。如“三世因果”(前世造因,今世受果,今世造因,来世受果)、“六道轮回”(随着自己善恶行为,或生天界而为天人,或生人界而为人,或为阿修罗——一种和天人差不多的好战斗的神,或为畜生,或为鬼,或堕地狱。一切众生永远升沉于天、人、阿修罗、地狱、鬼、畜生六道中,犹如车轮没有始终地转着,所以叫做轮回)、“四大和合”(地、水、火、风四元素)等等,并接受了关于天文地理的某些传统说法。

对婆罗门教的神祇,佛教也没有否定他们的存在,只是贬抑他们的地位,当作一种众生看待,认为他们也不免轮回生死之苦,如对于梵天,认为只是天界中的天人,将来也会堕地狱。关于这些,以后还可以谈。

45. Q: What was the relationship between Buddhism and other religious schools or sects?

A: Buddhism not only repudiated Brahmanist creeds but also opposed various non-Brahmanic schools'. However Buddhism, Brahmanism and other religions had some common ideological sources. Although it adopted certain ideas from other schools Buddhism rendered new interpretations according to its own theories of Dependent Origination (Paṭiccasamuppāda) and Kamma. For example, "Cause and effect of three periods of time" (Hetu-phala of tayo addhā) teaches that actions in the past life lead to the present affect, and actions in the present life will produce an effect in future life; and the theory of "Cycles of rebirth in six worlds" which teaches that on the basis of one's own wholesome or unwholesome deeds one might be reborn in heaven as a deity, or on earth as a human being, or become an asura — a bellicose deity-like creature, or an animal, or a ghost, or be born in hell; all sentient beings circulate perpetually up and down, just like a rolling wheel, through the six realms (gatis) of heaven (deva-gati), human world (manussa-gati), asura realm (asuratta), hell (naraka-gati), ghost realm (peta-gati) and animal world (tiracchāna-yonika), in endlessly repeated cycles of rebirth or reincarnation (saṃsāra); and the theory of the blending components of four elements (cattāri mahābhūta) which are earth, water, fire and air. Buddhism also accepted some traditional notions about astronomy and geography.

With regard to gods of Brahmanism, Buddhism did not deny their existence, only degraded their status to that of sentient beings and believed that they also couldn't escape the sufferings of saṃsāra. As for Brahmā, Buddhism deemed it a deity in the deva-gati who might fall into hell. We can return to these questions later.

# 第二章
# 佛法的基本内容和佛教经籍

1. 问:佛法的基本内容是什么?

答:我前面说过释迦牟尼当初出家的目的是为了寻求解脱生老病死等痛苦之道。当时印度许多教派都是有最后解脱的理想的。佛教教义的基本内容简单地说来,就是说世间的苦(苦谛 Dukkha-sacca)和苦的原因(因谛或称集谛 Samudaya-sacca),说苦的消灭(灭谛 Nirodha-sacca)和灭苦的方法(道谛 Magga-sacca)。佛教经籍非常繁多,其实不超出这四圣谛(Cattāri-ariya-saccāni,谛的意义就是真理),而四谛所依据的根本原理则是缘起论(Paṭiccasamuppāda)。佛教的所有教义都是从缘起论这个源泉流出来的。

2. 问:缘起是什么意思?

答:"缘起"即"诸法由因缘而起"。简单地说,就是一切事物或一切现象的生起,都是相待(相对)的互存关系和条件,离开关系和条件,就不能生起任何一个事物或现象。因(Hetu)、缘(Paccaya),一般地解释,就是关系和条件。

# Chapter II
# THE ESSENCE OF THE BUDDHA DHAMMA AND THE BUDDHIST CANONICAL LITERATURE

1. Q: What are the essentials of Buddha Dhamma?

A: As mentioned before, the purpose of Sākyamuni's renouncing the world was to strive for a way of deliverance from the sufferings of birth, old age, illness and death. Many contemporaneous religious schools in India also strove for the ideal of final deliverance. Simply put, the essentials of Buddhist doctrines may be summarized as the Four Noble Truths (Cattāri-ariya-saccāni): the Suffering of all existence (Dukkha-sacca), the Cause of suffering (Samudaya-sacca), the Extinction of suffering (Nirodha-sacca) and the Path leading to the cessation of suffering (Magga-sacca). In fact, all the numerous and voluminous Buddhist texts do not go beyond the Four Noble Truths. However, the fundamental principle on which the Four Noble Truths are based is the Theory of Dependent Origination (Paṭiccasamuppāda). All Buddhist Doctrines flow from this fountainhead – the Theory of Dependent Origination.

2. Q: What is the meaning of Dependent Origination?

A: Dependent Origination means that all dhammas arise through causes or conditions (hetu or paccaya). In brief, all things or phenomena arise out of mutually dependent relations and conditions. Nothing exists without interdependent relationship and conditions. Hetu and paccaya, generally speaking, are cause and condition. The Buddha defined "Dependent Origina-

佛曾给“缘起”下了这样的定义：

若此有则彼有，若此生则彼生；
若此无则彼无，若此灭则彼灭。

这四句就是表示同时的或者异时的互存关系。

3. 问：什么是同时的互存关系？

答：举一个简单例子来说明。如师生关系：有老师则有学生，有学生则有老师，无老师则不成其为学生，无学生则不成其为老师。这是同时的互相依存的关系。

4. 问：什么是异时的互存关系？

答：如种子和芽的关系：因为过去先有了种子，所以今天才能有芽生；也因为今天有芽生，过去的种子才名叫种子，这是异时的互相依存的关系。从另一方面看，种子灭的时候也正是芽生的时候，芽生的时候也正是种子灭的时候，在这里，芽和种子的生与灭现象又是同时的互存关系。总之，无论其为同时或异时，一切现象（法）必然是在某种互相依存的关系中存在的。没有任何一个现象可以说是绝待（绝对）的存在。

5. 问：异时的互存关系是否就是因果关系？

答：照佛教的说法，所谓互存关系，都是因果关系。从

tion" as follows:

When this exists, that exists.
Because this arises, that arises.
When this does not exist, that does not exist.
When this ceases, that ceases too.

These four sentences express the coexistent relationship, both simultaneous and non-simultaneous (sequential).

3. Q: What is a simultaneously interdependent relationship?

A: Let me illustrate this with a plain example, the relationship between teacher and student: If there are teachers, there must be students, and if there are students, there must be teachers; without teachers, there are no students, and without students, there are no teachers. This is a simultaneously interdependent relationship.

4. Q: What is a non-simultaneously interdependent relationship?

A: Take, for example, the relationship between seed and sprout: With the previous existence of seeds, sprouts can come into existence as a consequence; likewise, the coming into existence of the sprouts depends on the previous state known as seeds. This is a non-simultaneously interdependent relationship. From another perspective, the cessation of the state of being seeds coincides with the coming into being of the sprouts. Here the phenomena of the birth of the sprout and the extinction of the seed also form a simultaneously interdependent relationship. In conclusion, all phenomena (dhammas) exist necessarily in certain interdependent relations, whether simultaneous or non-simultaneous. Nothing can be said to exist in the absolute or of itself.

5. Q: Is non-simultaneous interdependent relationship identical to causality?

A: According to Buddhist doctrine, all interdependent relations are causality. In the case of non-simultaneous interdepen-

异时的互存关系来说，种子是因，芽是果，这是异时因果。从同时的互存关系来说，如以老师为主，则老师是因，学生是果；如以学生为主，则学生是因，老师是果，这是同时因果。这当然是简单地举例，其实因果关系是极其错综复杂的。从这一个角度看，这样的因产生这样的果；从另一个角度看，同是这个因会产生另外的果。如某甲，从师生关系看，他是乙的老师；从父子关系看，他是丙的父亲；从夫妻关系看，他是丁的丈夫。以甲为因，则乙丙丁和其余一切都是果，由此而看出一因多果；以其余一切为因，则甲是果，由此而看出多因一果。实际上，没有绝待的因，也就没有绝待的果。世界就是这样由时间上无数的异时连续的因果关系，与空间上无数的互相依存关系组织的无限的网。

6. 问：听说北京西山佛牙舍利塔，砖上和露盘上刻有经文，都是讲缘起的教义的，是吗？

答：是的。那是辽代建的塔。砖上刻着一首缘起偈（偈，是偈陀 Gāthā 的简称，意思就是诗或颂）：

诸法因缘生，缘谢法还灭，
吾师大沙门，常作如是说。

dent relationship, the seed is the cause, and the shoot the effect. This is non-simultaneous causality. In the case of simultaneously interdependent relationship, if the teacher is the subject, then the teacher is the cause and the student the effect; if the student is the subject, then the student is the cause and the teacher the effect; this is simultaneous causality. Of course, these are simple examples, in fact, causality is extremely complicated. From one point of view, a certain cause produces a certain effect, while from another angle, the very same cause may lead to a different effect. For instance, A may be B's teacher in terms of teacher-student relationship; at the same time, he may be C's father in terms of father-son relationship; then he may be D's husband in terms of husband-wife relationship. So if A is taken as the cause, then B, C, D and all others are the effects. From this, we see one cause with a multitude of effects. If all the others are causes, then A is the effect. From this we see a multitude of causes with one effect. In reality, there is no absolute cause, nor absolute effect. The universe is thus a boundless net knitted by uncountable sequential causalities in terms of time, and mutually dependent relations in terms of space.

6. Q: It is said that on the Pagoda (Sarīrika-thūpa) of the Buddha's Tooth Relic in the Western Hills of Beijing, Buddhist texts pertaining to the doctrine of causality were inscribed on the bricks and water-dish crest. Is this true?

A: Yes, that thūpa was first built in Liao Dynasty. On its walls are carved the Gāthā of Dependent Origination (Gāthā means verse or ode) which reads: "All dhammas proceed from causes and conditions (Hetu-paccaya), they will cease with the cessation of their conditions, my teacher, the Great Samaṇa, thus teaches frequently." On its water-dish crest (kalasa) the Sanskrit version of this Gāthā was inscribed:

Ye dharmā hetu-prabhavā
hutuṃ teṣaṃ Tathāgato hy avadat,

露盘上刻的是这首偈的梵文。其实，不只是这座塔，古代佛塔一般都刻着这首偈当作舍利供奉。因为佛说过“见缘起即见法，见法即见佛”。所以这首偈被称为法身舍利偈，这也是说明缘起教义在佛教中的重要地位。缅甸近年拆修一座古塔，砖上也刻着这首偈的巴利文：

Ye dhammā hetu-ppabhavā
tesaṃ hetuṃ Tathāgato āha，
tesañ ca yo nirodho
evaṃ vādī mahāsamaṇo.

7. 问：缘起偈是谁作的？

答：是佛的弟子阿说示(Assaji，最初五比丘之一，意译是“马胜”)说出的。有一天马胜比丘在托钵行乞的时候，遇见了婆罗门大学者舍利弗。舍利弗看见他容貌威仪，不同常人，便问他向谁学道，教义如何。马胜比丘便说出了这首偈，舍利弗听了很欢喜，回去向目犍连说了，两个人便一起归依了佛。这首偈我国有几种译文，偈中“吾师大沙门”，是指释迦牟尼，沙门(Samaṇa)，简单地意译就是出家修道者。当时婆罗门教之外各教派的出家修道者都称为沙门。

8. 问：在当时各教派中，缘起论是不是佛教特有的教义？

teṣaṃ ca yo nirodho
evaṃ vādī mahā-śramaṇaḥ.

In fact, this Gāthā was generally inscribed not only on this pagoda, but on all ancient Buddhist pagodas, as tribute to the Sarīra. Thus this Gāthā is called the Dhammakāya Sarīra Gāthā, since the Buddha had said: "Those who see Dependent Origination, see the Dhamma; those who see the Dhamma, see the Buddha." Hence the importance of the doctrine of Dependent Origination (Paṭiccasamuppāda) in Buddhism. In recent years, when an ancient thūpa was renovated in Burma, the Pāli version of this Gāthā was also found inscribed on bricks:

Ye dhammā hetu-ppabhavā
tesaṃ hetuṃ Tathāgato āha,
tesañ ca yo nirodho
evaṃ vādī mahāsamaṇo.

7. Q: Who was the author of the Gāthā of Dependent Origination?

A: It was uttered by the Buddha's disciple Assaji. (Assaji, meaning "Victory of Horse", was one of the first five Bhikkhus.) One day, when Bhikkhu Assaji was begging with his alms-bowl, he ran into Sāriputta, the great Brahmanic scholar. The latter was arrested by his venerable countenance which was out of the common run, so he inquired of Assaji who was his teacher and what doctrine he was professing. Thereupon, Bhikkhu Assaji uttered this Gāthā. Sāriputta was delighted to hear this and went to tell Moggallāna on his return. Then both of them became followers of the Buddha. There are several Chinese translations of this Gāthā. "My teacher, the great Samaṇa" refers to Sākyamuni. In general, Samaṇa may be simply rendered as ascetics (or mendicant friars) who renounced the home life. At that time, all ascetics regardless of religious sect (except in brahmanism) were called samaṇas.

8. Q: Was the Theory of Dependent Origination (Paṭiccasamup-

答:是的。佛经中说缘起有十一个意义:

(1)无作者义,
(2)有因生义,
(3)离有情义,
(4)依他起义,
(5)无动作义,
(6)性无常义,
(7)刹那灭义,
(8)因果相续无间断义,
(9)种种因果品类别义,
(10)因果更互相符顺义,
(11)因果决定无杂乱义。

这些意义都是不同于其他教派的教义的。

9. 问:可否请你把这十一义简单解释一下?

答:十一义归纳起来,有四个重要的论点:

(一)无造物主,
(二)无我,
(三)无常,
(四)因果相续。

10. 问:无造物主是什么意思?

答:是否定创造宇宙万物的主宰,即十一义中的"无作者义"。因为既承认"诸法因缘生",就不能承认有个独立的造作者。任何一个因都是因生的,任何一个缘都是缘起

pāda) confined to Buddhism exclusive of other religions at that time?

A: Yes. Buddhist scriptures elaborate eleven implications of Dependent Origination. They say that all things come into being

(1) without creator,
(2) from causes,
(3) free from sentient beings,
(4) dependent upon other conditions,
(5) without actor,
(6) with the nature of impermanence,
(7) extinguishing in every instant (khaṇa);
(8) with causes and effects continuously connected without interruption;
(9) with various causes and effects falling into different types;
(10) with cause and effect leading into each other in harmony and in compliance with each other;
(11) with cause and effect functioning in order without confusion.

All these are different from the doctrines of other religions.

9. Q: Would you please explain briefly the eleven implications?

A: The eleven meanings may be summed up into four cardinal points:

(1) There is no god-creator,
(2) There is no ego,
(3) Every thing is impermanent,
(4) Causes and effects proceed continuously.

10. Q: What does "no god-creator" mean ?

A: It means to deny that there is a lord of creation who created the entire universe, this is the first of the eleven doctrines above. If it is accepted that "All dhammas arise from hetu-paccaya", it would be inconsistent to recognize the existence of a

的，因又有因，缘又有缘，从竖的方面推，无始无终，从横的方面推，无边无际。由此而得出结论：没有绝待的一个因。缘起论者，不仅应当否认“从口生出婆罗门”的人格化的造物主，而且也应当否认作为宇宙本源的理性化的存在。从另一方面说，缘起论者固然不承认有一个绝待的第一个因，但同时又反对认为一切出自偶然的观点。他主张任何现象的生起，都不是无因的，而是受必然的因果律支配的，这便是“有因生义”。

11. 问：照你这样说，佛教很像是无神论，但是何以佛教寺庙中又供有很多的神呢？

答：我前面说过，佛教并没有否定婆罗门教的神祇，只是看做是一种众生，后来有些神祇被吸收到佛教中来成为护法神，这是一方面情况。另一方面，也应当承认到后来佛陀被神化了的事实。但是根据佛教教义，佛不是造物主，他虽然有超人的智慧和能力，但不能主宰人的吉凶祸福，佛也是受因果律支配的。

12. 问：什么是“无我”？

答：“离有情义”、“依他起义”和“无动作义”，都是说明无我的道理的。“有情”的巴利语是“萨埵”(Satta)，人和一

separate creator. Every cause (hetu) is generated by other causes, and every condition (paccaya) is generated by other conditions. Each cause has its own preceding cause, each condition has its own conditions. Viewed vertically, there is neither beginning nor end, and viewed horizontally, there is neither boundary nor limit. Thus one comes to the conclusion that there is no absolute cause. Believers of the Theory of Dependent Origination (Paṭiccasamuppāda) should deny not only the personified creator who gave birth to Brahmins from its mouth, but also the existence of any rationally conceived creator of the cosmos. On the other hand, though believers of Paṭiccasamuppāda deny the existence of any absolute initial cause, they also oppose the point of view that everything is fortuitous. They maintain that no phenomenon emerges without cause, it is subject to inevitable laws – the laws of causation. This is what is meant by "Everything arises from causes".

11. Q: From what you are saying, Buddhism seems to be atheist, but why are there so many gods enshrined in Buddhist temples?

A: As I have said earlier, Buddhism does not deny the deities of Brahmanism, but regards them as kinds of sentient beings. Some deities were afterwards brought into Buddhism as guardians of Dhamma. This is on the one hand. On the other hand, we must acknowledge the fact that Buddha was deified later. However, according to Buddhist doctrine, the Buddha is not a creator, nor can he decide weal or woe, joy or suffering of human beings, though he has superhuman wisdom and ability. Buddha is also subject to the law of causality.

12. Q: What is meant by "there is no ego", or "egolessness" (anattā)?

A: "Free from sentient beings", "dependent upon other conditions" and "without actor", all elaborate the theory of Egolessness. "Sentient being" is "Satta" in Pāli, which includes

切有情感的生物都叫做有情。婆罗门教和其他各派主张一切有情都有一个常住的(固定不变地存在的)、起主宰作用的自我(Atta,意义与“灵魂”相当)。缘起论则认为所谓“有情”,无非是种种物质和精神的要素的聚合体。从身体的组织来说,有情是由地、水、火、风、空、识六大(六种元素)所构成的,依借前五大而有身体的机关及其作用——地为骨肉,水为血液,火为暖气,风为呼吸,空为种种的空隙;依借后一大(识)而表现种种的精神活动。再从心理的要素来说,有情的组织分为色(Rūpa)、受(Vedanā)、想(Saññā)、行(Sankhāra)、识(Viññāṇa)五蕴。蕴(Khandha)就是堆,把种种不同的现象分类,每类做为一堆,这就是蕴。简单地解释,“色”就是各种物质,眼、耳、鼻、舌、身五根(根就是人的感觉器官)和色、声、香、味、触五境(境就是感觉对象)等都属于色。受、想、行、识四蕴包括重要的精神要素:受是感觉(感觉苦、乐或不苦不乐等);想是印象(摄取事物的相貌,知道是青、黄、赤、白,是长、短、方、圆,是苦是乐等);行是思维(思维是推动身心活动的力量,所以叫做行);识是了别(对于所认识的对象,予以判断和推理)。佛教根据以上两方面的分析,说明有情不是固定的单一独立体,而是种种要素的聚合体,而任何要素又是刹那刹那依缘而生灭着的,所以找不到一个固定的独立的“有情”在支配着身心,也就是找不到“我”的存在。这便是无我的简单解释。

human beings and all sentient creatures. Brahmanism and other schools maintain that every satta possesses an immortal and determinant Ego or soul (atta). The Theory of Dependent Origination holds that sattas are nothing but the aggregation of various material and spiritual elements. As far as the constitution of body is concerned, satta is composed of the Six Great Elements (cha dhātuyo), namely: earth (pathavī), water (āpo), fire or heat (tejo), air (vāyo), space (ākāsa) and consciousness (viññāna). The first five elements are responsible for the mechanism and functions of the body "—" with earth as bones and flesh, water as blood, heat as warmth, air as breath, space as all sorts of body cavities. With the last element, consciousness, various mental activities become manifest. If we look at psychological constituents, satta are composed of five aggregates (khandhas), viz. corporeality (rūpa), feeling or sensation (vedanā), perception (saññā), mental formations (sankhāra) and consciousness (viññāna). The word "Khandha" means heap or group. All kinds of phenomena are classified into different groups which are named khandhas. In brief, rūpa refers to all parts of corporeality which includes the Five Roots (Pañc' indriyāni) or five physical sense organs of human beings, namely, eye, ear, nose, tongue and body; and the five objective sources of sensation (Pañcāyatana) – Visible objects, sound, odor, taste and tangible objects. The remaining four khandhas – Vedanā, Saññā, Sankhāra and Viññāna constitute important spiritual factors. Vedanā is feeling or sensation (feeling sad, happy, or neither; P. dukkha, sukha, or adukkha-m-asukha). Saññā means perception (to perceive the appearance of things, eg. blue, yellow, red or white; long or short; square or round; suffering or happy). Sankhāra means mental formations (it is so called because it is seen as the driving force of physical and mental activities). Viññāna means the ability of judgment and inference. According to the above analysis, Buddhism holds that satta is not a fixed single (independent) entity, but a composition of various factors which arise and cease with their hetu-paccaya every instant (khaṇa). Hence there is nowhere an independent

13. 问:请允许我插一句。照你所说佛教关于有情的组成要素的说法,它是不是二元论?

答:大体来说,佛教把组成有情的要素分为精神和物质两类,两者结合便是有情的成立。佛教对此有一个专门术语叫做"名色 Nāmarūpa"。名,是精神的要素,即五蕴中受、想、行、识四蕴,也就是六大中的识大;色,就是地、水、火、风、空物质的要素。地水火风空诸要素,都不能单独生起,而必须是互相结合变化的。简单地说,"名色"就是身心合成的存在。从这方面看,有人说它是二元论,有人说它是一种平行论(即心理生理平行),也有人说佛教认为精神物质诸要素都没有独立的单元,所以与二元论和平行论都有所不同。究竟应当怎样看,可以研究,但是它不是唯物论则是明显的。

14. 问:"无动作义"如何解释?

答:"无动作义",就是不承认因果之间有来去。缘起论者承认由因生果,而反对因变成果的说法。譬如以灯传灯,是乙灯的火由甲灯焰生,而不是甲灯的火跑到乙灯去。根据这个道理,佛教虽然也讲六道轮回,但是不承认有个灵魂从这个有情的身体投入另一个有情的胎里去。这个道理是从无我的教义引伸出来的,以后还可以谈。

and permanent "Satta" or Ego, dominating body and mind. This is a simple explanation of Egolessness.

13. Q: Excuse me, another question here. According to your explanation, is the Buddhist notion of the constitution of Satta a form of dualism?

A: On the whole, Buddhism divides the constituents of satta into two categories, spiritual and material. Combination of the two brings about satta, which, in Buddhist terminology, is called "Nāmarūpa" (name and form). Nāma refers to the mental factors, i. e. vedanā, saññā, saṅkhāra and viññāna of the five khandhas, or in other words, the viññāna dhātu (mind) of the six Mahā-bhūta (great elements). Rūpa refers to the material factors consisting of earth, water, fire, wind and space, all of which can not arise independently, but must change and integrate with each other. In brief, nāmarūpa is the combination of body and mind. From this respect, some regard it as dualism, some as parallelism (spiritual-physical parallelism). While some others say nāmarūpa is neither dualism nor parallelism since Buddhism maintains that all spiritual and material elements can not exist as independent units. Thus, how this matter should be viewed remains to be studied. What is evident is that it is by no means materialism.

14. Q: What is the meaning of "no actor"?

A: "no actor" means that there is nothing coming and going between a cause (hetu) and its effect (phala). Believers of the theory of Dependent Origination hold that cause gives rise to effect but deny that cause turns into effect. Taking, for example, the passing of light or fire from one lantern to another, the flame of lantern B is engendered by that of lantern A, it is not that, the flame of A transferred to B. Thus, though Buddhism holds to the doctrine of reincarnation within the six-fold path (saṃsāra), Buddhism denies that there is a soul moving or transferring from one animate being to the seed of another. This idea

15. 问:什么是“无常”?

答:宇宙一切现象,都是此生彼生、此灭彼灭的相待的互存关系,其间没有恒常的存在。所以任何现象,它的性质是无常的,表现为刹那(Khaṇa)刹那生灭的。这就是十一义中“性无常义”和“刹那灭义”。佛经中说:“诸行无常,是生灭法”,就是这个意思。“诸行”,就是指一切事物或一切现象。“行”是迁流变动的意思,一切现象都是迁流变动的,所以叫做“行”。这个字的本身就包含了无常的意义。“生灭”二字,实际上包括着“生、异、灭”三字或“生、住、异、灭”四字。这里每个字表示着一种相状:一个现象的生起叫做“生”;当它存在着作用的时候叫做“住”;虽有作用而同时在变异叫做“异”;现象的消灭叫做“灭”。刹那是极短的时间,佛经中说弹一下指头的时间有六十刹那。刹那生灭,就是一刹那中具足生、住、异、灭。有人问,一个人的寿命一般有几十年,怎么是刹那生灭呢?佛教把人的一生从生到死叫做一期,一期是由刹那刹那相续而有的。对一个人的整体来说,他有一期的生住异灭,即生、老、病、死;但从他的组成各部分来说,则是刹那刹那的生住异灭。佛经说人的身体每十二年全部换过一次。一个物体的生住异灭,一个世界的成住坏空,实际都是刹那生灭相续的存在。照佛教的教义,一切现象没有不是刹那生灭的。佛教把主张“有常恒不变的事物”的见解叫做“常见”,认为是错误的。

is an extension of the principle of Anattā (egolessness) and will be elaborated later.

15. Q: What is "Impermanence" (Anicca)?

A: All phenomena in the universe exist in mutually dependent interrelationships, such that when this arises, that arises; when this ceases, that ceases. There is no permanent existence at all. Therefore, all phenomena are impermanent in nature, arising and ceasing from instant (khaṇa) to instant. This is what is meant by the "nature of impermanence" and "extinction in every Khaṇa" mentioned in the eleven implications of Paṭiccasamppāda, and also meant by the canonical saying: "Impermanent, are all component things; subject are they to birth, and then decay." ("Aniccā vata sankhāra, Uppādavaya dhammino"). "All Sankhāra" denotes all things or phenomena. The word "Sankhāra" means flux and change. Since all phenomena are in fluid and changing, they are named "Sankhāra". The term itself implies the meaning of impermanence. The words "birth" and "decay" actually cover three meanings: origination, destruction and cessation, or four meanings: origination or arising (uppāda or Jāti), maintenance or existence (ṭhitika), destruction or decay (jarā or aññathatta) and cessation (nirodha). Each of the four denotes a characteristic or a state of a phenomenon: the birth of a phenomenon is called origination, the moment when it exists and functions is called maintenance, the moment when it functions but begins to decay is called destruction and the perishing of a phenomeṇon is called cessation. A khaṇa is a very short moment. According to the description in Buddhist texts, the flicking of a finger spans 60 khaṇas. "Extinguishing in every khaṇa" means that origination, maintenance, destruction and cessation are all completed within one khaṇa. Some people ask "why do we speak of 'instantaneously arising and ceasing' when the life-span of a person is usually about a few decades?" The Buddhist answer is that a human being's life from birth to death is a process consisting of a succession of khaṇas. A human

16. 问:请允许我插一句,佛教本身是不是也受"无常"法则的支配?

答:是的。根据佛说,佛法分三个时期:一是正法时期,即佛教兴起时期;二是像法时期,即演变时期,这时期开始有佛像,所以称像法;三是末法时期,即衰坏时期。佛并且曾经说过将来法灭时的情况。"诸行无常",佛教也不例外。

17. 问:什么是"因果相续"?

答:因缘所生的一切法,固然是生灭无常的,而又是相续不断的,如流水一般,前前逝去,后后生起,因因果果,没有间断,这是就竖的方面来说的。从横的方面看,因果的品类有种种无量的差别。种种品类差别的因果关系固然错综复杂,但其间又有井然的法则,一丝不乱。一类的因

life-span, on the whole, also goes through origination, existence, decay and extinction, i. e. birth, old age, sickness and death; but each constituent part consists of continuous arising, existence, destruction and cessation, khaṇa by khaṇa. Buddhist scriptures hold that the human body is completely renewed every 12 years. An entity's arising, existing, decay and ceasing or a world's origination, maintenance, destruction and cessation actually consist of instantaneous originations and cessations. Buddhist theory holds that all phenomena, without exception, originate and cease in every Khaṇa, and that any admission of permanent or unchanging entity, which is called the eternity belief (sassata diṭṭhi), is wrong.

16. Q: If I may ask a quick question: Is Buddhism itself also subject to the law of "impermanence"?

A: Yes. According to the Buddha, Buddha Dhamma covers three successive periods: First, the Period of True Dhamma (Saddhammma), i. e. the period of arising and flourishing of Buddhism; Second, the Period of Image Dhamma (Saddhamma-paṭirūpaka), i.e. the evolution period, in which Buddha's images began to appear; Third, the Period of Termination (Saddhamma-vippalujjati) or the period of decay. Buddha even discussed the circumstance of Dhamma extinguishing in future. "All dhammas are impermanent", Buddhism itself is no exception.

17. Q: What is meant by "cause and effect continuously connected without interruption"?

A: All dhammas are produced by Hetu-paccaya. Though impermanent, constantly arising and ceasing, they are continuously connected without interruption, just like flowing water. The preceding one passing away is followed by the succeeding one, causes producing effects in continuous series without interruption. This is looking at dhammas in a vertical sense in time. Horizontally, there are infinite differences among the varied types of causes and effects. Despite the complicated relation-

产生一类的果，如善因得善果，因与果相符，果与因相顺；一类的因不能生另一类的果，如种瓜只能得瓜，不能得豆。佛教认为因果的法则是决定的，虽三世（过去、现在、未来）诸佛也不能加以改变的。这就是“因果相续无间断义”、“种种因果品类别义”、“因果更互相符顺义”和“因果决定无杂乱义”的简单解释。佛教把主张“现象灭了就不再生起”的见解叫做“断见”，也是反对的。关于因、缘、果的分析，佛教有六因、四缘、五果等说法，这里不一一介绍了。

18. 问：关于上面所说的有关缘起的理论有什么经论可供研究？

答：佛教经论谈缘起道理的地方很多，如上面所说的十一义，出自《分别缘起初胜法门经》（玄奘译），可以一看。又玄奘译的《俱舍论》和鸠摩罗什译的《大智度论》里有关部分，也可以一看。

19. 问：听了你根据“无造物主、无我、无常、因果相续”四

ships between various types of causalities, they are bound by orderly rules without the least confusion. Each category of causes produces effects of the same type. For instance, a good cause leads to a good effect. Causes give rise to concordant effects, and effects correspond to the causes. One type of cause can't give rise to another type of effect, for instance, if one sows melon seeds, one reaps the fruit of melons, and not beans. Buddhism believes that the law of causality is determined and unalterable even by Buddhas of the successive epochs (past, present and future). This is the simple explanation of "causes and effects continuously connected without interruption", "various causes and effects falling into different categories", "cause and effect transferring in harmony and in compliance with each other" and "cause and effect functioning in order without confusion". Again, Buddhism also opposes the view that after its cessation, a phenomenon can not arise again, and terms this "the Annihilation-view" (Uccheda-diṭṭhi). As to a Buddhist analysis of cause, condition and effect, there are theories such as Six Causes, Four Conditions and Five Effects, which I shall not discuss in detail here.

18. Q: Regarding the Theory of Dependent Origination mentioned above, are there any suttas and treatises available for further study?

A: There are many suttas and abhidhamma texts which discuss the Theory of Dependent Origination. For example, the fore-mentioned Eleven Meanings of Paṭiccasamuppāda were quoted from "Fenbie Yuanqi Chusheng Famen Jing" which is worth reading. Also, relevant parts of *Abhidharmakosa-śāstra* (Abhidharma Storehouse Treatise) translated into Chinese by Xuanzang, and the *Mahāprajñāpāramitaśāstra* (Treatise on the Great Perfection of Wisdom) translated into Chinese by Kumārajīva are also instructive.

19. Q: After your explanation of the Eleven Meanings of

个论点来说明缘起十一义之后，对于缘起的理论，大致有所了解。是否可以说这就是佛教对于宇宙万有的解释？

答：四个论点实际只是两个论点——“无常”和“无我”。“无常”就是生灭相续，它不仅包括“刹那生灭”的意义，而且包括“因果相续”的意义。“无我”就是没有主宰，没有一身之内的主宰，也没有宇宙万有的主宰，所以无造物主的意义，实际包含在“无我”里面。“诸行无常、诸法无我”，是佛教对宇宙万有的总的解释，也可以说，是一切法的总法则。所以“无常”和“无我”的教义被称为“法印”。

20. 问：“法印”是什么？

答：印就是印玺。国王的印玺可以证明文件的真实（有通行无阻的作用）。借以比喻佛教的主要教义，也以符合“法印”而证明其为真正佛法（掌握了它，便能对一切法通达无碍），所以称为法印。“诸行无常，诸法无我，涅槃寂静”，并称三法印，或者加上“有漏皆苦”，亦称四法印。

Dependent Origination, based upon the four cardinal points of "no creator, egolessness, impermanence and succession of cause and effect", a basic understanding of the theory of Dependent Origination is achieved. Can this be said to be the Buddhist interpretation of universal existence or the Buddhist cosmology?

A: The four cardinal points are virtually summed up in two points — "Impermanence" and "Egolessness". "Impermanence" means the continuity of arising and ceasing, which includes the notion of "arising and ceasing from instant to instant", as well as "continuity of cause and effect". "Egolessness" means no dominating power either inside oneself or of the universe. So the meaning of "no creator" is virtually included in the concept of "Egolessness". "All phenomena are impermanent, all dhammas are devoid of self" (sabbe sankhārā aniccā, sabbe dhammā anattā) sum up the Buddhist interpretation of universal existence. It can also be called the general law of all dhammas. That is the reason why the doctrines of "Impermanence" and "Egolessness" are referred to as the Seals of Dhamma (Dhamma-lakkhaṇa).

20. Q: What is the meaning of Dhamma-lakkhaṇa?

A: Lakkhaṇa means mark or seal. An imperial seal certifies the authenticity of documents, allowing for passage without hindrance. Here, it is used in analogy for the principal doctrines of Buddhism. If any doctrine is in line with the "Seals of Dhamma", it can be regarded as authentic teaching of the Buddha. (If it has been mastered, all Dhammas will be grasped without obstruction.) That is why they are called the "Seals of Dhamma". If, after "All phenomena are impermanent, all dhammas are devoid of self", we add "Nibbāna is serene", we have what are called the Three Seals of the Dhamma. With the addition of "All defiled (sāsava) dhammas lead to suffering", we have what are designated as the Four Seals of the Dhamma.

21. 问：请解释一下，“有漏皆苦”的意义。

答：“漏”就是烦恼。佛教认为众生不明白一切法缘生缘灭，无常无我的道理，而在无常的法上贪爱追求，在无我的法上执着为“我”，或为“我所有”，这叫做惑，惑使人烦恼，所以又叫做烦恼。烦恼种类极多，贪（贪欲）、嗔（嗔恨）、痴（不知无常无我之理等等叫做痴）是三毒，加上慢（傲慢）、疑（犹疑）、恶见（不正确的见解如常见、断见等）为六根本烦恼。由于烦恼而造种种业（Kamma），业就是行为（身业）、言语（口业）、思想（意业）的活动。烦恼和业引生未来或为天人，或为人，或为地狱、鬼、畜生的身心；于是又起烦恼，又造业，又生身心，这样的生死轮回（Saṃsāra），没有休歇。而生死轮回是苦的。以人生而论，一般地说有八苦：生苦（婴儿在胎出胎时苦）、老苦、病苦、死苦、爱别离苦（与所爱的分离）、怨憎会苦（与所怨憎的聚会）、所求不得苦、五取蕴苦（五取蕴即五蕴，取就是烦恼，人的色受想行识以烦恼为因而生，又能生烦恼，所以叫取蕴。五蕴刹那迁流变坏，为生老病死等苦所集，所以是苦）。总之，佛说世间有无量的苦，苦不是孤立的自己生起来的，也不是造物主给予的，也不是偶然的，而是有因缘的。上面所说因惑而造业，因业而有生死苦，就是佛教对苦的缘起解释。全面分析起来有“十二缘起”。

21. Q: Could you please explain the meaning of "All sāsava dhammas lead to suffering"?

A: Āsava means distress or mental affliction (kilesa). The Buddhist belief is that, because ordinary beings do not understand the truth that all dhammas arise and cease conditionally, with the nature of impermanence and egolessness, they greedily cling to things which are impermanent, and persistently seek for "me" or "mine", in spite of the dhammas of egolessness. This is called illusion which leads to mental affliction (kilesa), so it is also named mental affliction (kilesa). There are many kinds of afflictions, such as lust or greed (rāga), anger or hate (dosa), delusion (moha or avijjā, ignorance of the truth of Impermanence and Egolessness). These three are regarded as the three poisons. Together with arrogance (māna), skepticism or doubt (vicikicchā), and wrong views (micchā-diṭṭhi, such as the belief in permanence or sassata-diṭṭhi, the belief in discontinuity or uccheda-diṭṭhi), they make up the six fundamental afflictions (kilesa). Kilesas give rise to various kammas. Kamma denotes actions of the body (kāya-kamma), speech (Vacī-kamma) and mind (mano-kamma). Kilesa and kamma lead to future rebirth of the body and mind (nāma-rūpa) either as a deity, or a human being, or a being in hell, or a ghost or an animal. There again afflictions arise, kammas are recreated, and body and mind are regenerated. This cycle of life and death (saṃsāra) is endless, and constitutes suffering. In terms of human life, there are, generally held, eight kinds of sufferings (duhkha) – sufferings of birth (the pain suffered in the womb as well as during birth), old age, illness, death, separation from loved ones, association with hated ones, inability to obtain what one desires, and clinging to the five aggregates (Khandhas). (Clinging to the five khandhas is affliction which gives rise to corporeal things, feeling, perception, mental formation and consciousness, the five aggregates in turn give rise to kilesa, and thus are called grasping khandhas. The five khandhas are in the instantly changing fluid which is filled with the sufferings of birth, old age, illness and death. So the five khandhas are suffering.) In sum, as the

22. 问:请简单谈一谈“十二缘起”。

答:佛教的缘起论主要是以人生问题为中心来谈的。对人生问题一般说十缘起或十二缘起。十二缘起是:无明缘、行缘、识缘、名色缘、六入缘、触缘、受缘、爱缘、取缘、有缘、生缘、老死缘。现在简单地解释一下:

(1)老死(Jarā-maraṇa),这是观察人生的起点,老死忧悲苦恼是人生不可避免的。缘何而有老死忧悲苦恼呢?是由于有(2)生(Jāti)。如果没有生,则没有老死,也没有忧悲苦恼。生的条件虽有种种,但是最重要的条件是(3)有(Bhava)。“有”就是存在的意思。简单地说,身口意所造的善业恶业对招引自已的后果潜伏着一种力量叫做“有”。有了业力为缘,必然有后果的生与死。“有”又是缘什么而起的呢?有的缘是(4)取(Upādāna)。取是追求执着的意思,追求色、声、香、味、触五欲,执着可爱事物为我所有,这叫做取。由于以自我为中心追求执着,就能引发身口意三

Buddha says that there is infinite suffering in the world, which is neither self-generated, nor dispensed by some god-creator, nor does it arise by chance. The suffering arises out of causes and conditions. As stated above, kilesas give rise to kammas, kammas give rise to sufferings of birth and death, This is the Buddhist explanation of the Dependent Origination of suffering. For a comprehensive analysis, there are "Twelve Links of Dependent Origination".

22. Q: Please give a brief account of the "Twelve Links of Dependent Origination".

A: The Buddhist theory of Dependent Origination is centered around the problem of human life. There are, generally held, ten or twelve Links of Dependent Origination. The twelve Links are: Ignorance (Avijjā), Mental Formation (Sankhāra), Consciousness (Viññāṇa), Name and Form (or corporeality and mentality, Nāma-rūpa), Six Sense Organs (Saḷāyatana), Contact between sense organs and sense objects (Phassa), Sensations (Vedanā), Desire (Taṇhā), Clinging (Upādāna), Coming into Existence (Bhava), Birth (Jāti), and Old Age and Death (Jarā-maraṇa). Let us explain them briefly:

(1) Old Age and Death: This is the starting point from which to observe an individual's life. Old age, death, worrying, sorrow are inevitable in a person's life. What is the origin of aging, death, sorrow and worrying? It is (2) Birth (Jāti). If a person is not born there are no old age and death, nor sorrow and worrying. Though the conditions for birth are numerous, the most important one is (3) Process of coming into existence (Bhava, meaning existence). In brief, bhava is a kind of latent force created by one's wholesome and unwholesome kammas of body, speech and mind which determines one's future. Given the force of kamma, birth and death are the inevitable outcome. What is the condition for Bhava's arising? It is (4) Grasping or Clinging (Upādāna). Upādāna means craving and clinging, craving for visible objects, for sounds, odors, tastes, and tangible objects, clinging to the possession of lovely things. Such is grasping.

业的活动。取又以(5)爱(Taṇhā)为缘。爱的简单解释就是生命欲,它是生命活动的本源力。有生命欲才有追求执着,有追求执着才有种种身口意的活动而有业力的存在,招引生死之果。所以爱、取、有同是生死的因。说到这里,已经说明了惑、业、苦的因果关系。为了进一步考察生命欲(爱)之所以发生,则必须说明(6)受 Vedanā、(7)触 Phassa、(8)六入 Saḷāyatana 的关系。受是感觉,即对客观境物所起的快感(乐受)、不快感(苦受)或不苦不乐感(舍受)。由于苦乐的感觉,激发和冲动着生命的欲求。感觉来自外界事物刺激的反应,所以依存于触。触是根、境、识三者会合而有的心理活动的开始。如眼(根)对红色(境)时,红色刺激眼根,因而司掌视觉的眼识生起活动。根境识三者会合,才发生红色的触(反应),所以触依存于六入。六入,就是眼、耳、鼻、舌、身、意的六根,是传递色、声、香、味、触、法(法,即前五种事物遗存下来的印象,是意根的对象)六境的机能。

再进一步考察六入依何存在的问题,因而说到(9)名

Because of this self-centered grasping and clinging, activities of body, speech and mind are produced. Grasping arises from (5) Desire (Taṇhā). Taṇhā can be simply explained as the desire for existence or survival. It is the driving force of the activities of life. It is this desire for life that leads to grasping and clinging, which (grasping and clinging) bring about the activities of body, speech and mind, which form the force of kamma that results in birth and death. Therefore, Taṇhā, Upādāna and Bhava together are said to be the causes of birth and death. The above explains the cause and effect relationship between illusion, kamma and suffering. In order to further investigate the origin of the desire for life, it is necessary to explain the relationship between (6) Sensation (Vedanā), (7) Contact (Phassa) and (8) Six Sense Organs (Saḷāyatana). Sensation refers to the feelings associated with the objective existence which can be classified into three groups: pleasant (sukha vedanā), unpleasant (dukkha vedanā) and neither pleasant nor unpleasant (upekkhā vedanā). When pleasant and unpleasant sensations are experienced, the desire for existence is stimulated and given impetus. Sensation is the response to the stimuli of the outside world, thus it depends on contact (phassa) between the sense organs and sense objects. Contact is thus the starting point of the mental coordination of sense organs, sense objects and consciousness. Take, for example, the eye (eye-indriya) contact with the red color (object), when the red color stimulates the eye, the eye-consciousness which is in charge of vision comes into play. With the interaction of organ, object and consciousness, contact with (reaction to) red color occurs. In this way, contact depends upon the six sense organs ( Saḷāyatana ) . The six sense organs are eye , ear , nose, tongue, body and mind, which have the functions of perceiving the six sense objects, namely, visible objects, sound, odor, taste, tangible objects and dhamma (Dhamma here refers to the impression left from the first five elements, or the object of the mental organ).

Furthermore, when investigation is made concerning the origin of the six sense organs, we come to (9) Name and Form

色 Nāma-rūpa。名色的意义前面已经讲过，即身心（色、受、想、行、识五蕴）合成的组织。六根是依存于身心全体组织的东西，有名色所以有六入。名色又以何为缘呢？名色又依存于(10)识 Viññāṇa。识虽是名色中一部分，但是如果把名色当作认识体来看，识乃是它的中心的东西。识对境（认识对象）有总了别作用，使境增加明显，使根增长功能，使受、想、思有所领导。所以名色全体的成立，依存于识，但是识又依存于名色。因为有境对根的刺激，和受、想、思的帮助发生，才有识的现起，识不能离开名色而独立。所以识与名色的关系，是互相依存的关系。

以上所说是十缘起，如果就人们现实的活动的条件来观察，十缘起已经全面了，但如果说明生死何以无穷的原由，则又有行和无明二缘，共十二缘起。

(11)行 Sankhāra，"行"的意义与"有"相同。从现在身口意造作的业来看它潜伏着引生后果的力量叫做"有"，从现在已经成熟的果来看过去所造的业叫做"行"。识与名色，是现在已熟的果，是依存过去的行而生起的。由于过去无始以来"行"的反复，积习成性，隐然有种力量支配着行为，所以生死苦恼现象联绵不断。行又依存于(12)无明 Avijjā。无明是对一切法缘生故生、缘灭故灭、无常、无我

(Nāma-rūpa). The meaning of nāma-rūpa, as mentioned above, is the composition of body and mind (or the five aggregates). The existence of the six sense organs is dependent upon the whole body and mind, or in other words, nāma-rūpa is the basis of the six organs. What condition does nāma-rūpa depend upon? It depends upon (10) Consciousness (Viññāṇa). Consciousness is a part of nāma-rūpa. But when the nāma-rūpa is taken as the object of comprehension, consciousness becomes the kernel of the nāma-rūpa. Consciousness has the functions of recognition and judgment with relation to the objects, which thus make the objects more distinctive, and enhance the abilities of the organs, so that the sensations, perceptions and speculation are governed. Therefore, the unity of body and mind depends upon consciousness, consciousness in turn depends on the body and mind. Consciousness can not stand alone without the functioning nāma-rūpa because its occurrence is based on the stimuli of the objects to the sense organs and the help of sensations, perceptions and speculations. In conclusion, nāma-rūpa and viññāṇa have a relation of mutual dependence.

The foregoing discussion was of the ten links of Dependent Origination. With regard to the present activities of human beings, the ten links of Dependent Origination would be quite comprehensive. However, to explain the endless cycles of birth and death, two more links, Mental formation (Sankhāra) and Ignorance (Avijjā) must be added. Together with the above ten, they constitute the twelve Links of Dependent Origination.

(11) Mental formation (Sankhāra) has the same meaning as (3) Existence (Bhava). When considering the Kamma created by body, speech and mind in the present, it has a potential power to lead to the future fruit that is known as "Bhava" ("coming into existence"). Whereas, when considering the ripe fruit (result) of today, what was formed by past kamma (or actions) is known as "Sankhāra" ("formation"). Consciousness and the name and form are the ripe fruits of today, depending upon the past formations. Owing to the cycles of past "formations" with its beginning unknown, habit becomes second na-

的真实相不认识，特别对自己身心只是因缘所生的道理不能自觉，以为其中有常住的、唯一的、作主宰的我。由于“我”的执着，所以对境而有乐受、苦受、舍受，而起贪嗔痴等烦恼，而造种种善恶业。所以人们的生死痛苦的本源毕竟在于无明。

十二缘起归纳起来仍不外乎上面所说的惑、业、苦的关系。无明、行是过去无始以来的惑和业，招致现在识、名色、六入、触、受的苦果；爱、取、有是现在的惑和业，招致未来的生、老死的苦果。这些都是“有漏皆苦”一句所包括的内容，也就是四谛中苦谛和集谛的内容。

23. 问：现在请解释一下“涅槃寂静”的意义。

答：“涅槃寂静”和“有漏皆苦”相反。涅槃是无漏，是苦果苦因的消灭，也就是十二缘起法的止灭。十二缘起是根据“此有则彼有、此生则彼生”的道理。十二缘起法的止

ture. Just as there is a latent power governing human beings' actions, so the phenomena of birth and death, suffering and worrying occur endlessly. Sankhāra in turn depends on (12) Ignorance (Avijjā). Ignorance refers to being unable to see things as they actually are, or unable to see the reality of impermanent and selfless dhammas which arise when the conditions arise, cease when the conditions cease. An ignorant person especially does not understand the fact that one's own body and mind are merely formed by causes and conditions, while he holds the idea that there is an eternal, unique and dominant self. Because of the affirmation of "self" (atta-abhinivesa), he feels the sensations of pleasant, unpleasant and neutral, and thus has the afflictions of greed, hatred and ignorance, which result in various wholesome and unwholesome kammas. Therefore, the root cause of the sufferings of birth and death of human beings lies in Ignorance (Avijjā).

To sum up, the twelve Links of Dependent Origination are no more than the relationships between illusion, kamma and suffering. Ignorance and mental formations are the result of the illusions and kammas from the endless past, which have incurred the present bitter fruits of consciousness, name and form, six sense organs, contact, and sensation. Desire, grasping and becoming existence are the present illusions and kammas, which will lead to the future bitter fruits of birth, aging and death. All these mentioned above are implied in the words "All āsavas are suffering", which also covers "the Truth of Suffering" (Dukkha-sacca) and "the Truth of the origin of Suffering" (Samudaya-sacca) – two of the four "Noble Truths" (Ariya-sacca).

23. Q: Could you now please explain the meaning of "Nibbāna is serene"?

A: "Nibbāna is serene" is the opposite to "All āsavas are suffering". The term Nibbāna means no flux or no-defilement (anāsava) that is the elimination of the cause and effect of suffering, and the cessation of the twelve Links of Dependent Origination. The basis of the twelve links is the principle of

灭则是根据“此无则彼无、此灭则彼灭”的道理。老死忧悲苦恼，既是由于生缘，消灭生缘则生死忧悲苦恼灭；消灭爱、取、有缘，则生死苦灭。这样推上去直到最后，消灭无明缘则苦果之因“行”灭。无明灭、行灭、识灭，乃至生老死灭，就是涅槃。更明确的来说：凡是属于不清净的污染的缘尽灭，无明转成为不污染的清净智慧，一切法上为清净智慧所照见的实相谛理，这就是涅槃，也叫做“现法涅槃”。涅槃 Nibbāna 的意义是圆寂，就是说：智慧福德圆满成就的，永恒寂静的最安乐的境界。佛教认为这种境界“唯圣者所知”，不能以经验上有、无、来、去等概念来测度，是不可思议的解脱境界。我前面说过可以把涅槃解释为逝世，其实释迦牟尼三十岁的时候，便已经证得涅槃而成佛，不过当时他的肉体还是过去惑、业之果的剩余，所以称为“有余涅槃”。直到他八十岁逝世，方是入“无余涅槃”。

24. 问：如何能达到涅槃的境界呢？

答：上面所说关于涅槃的道理属于灭谛。现在你提的如何达到涅槃的境界的问题属于道谛。道谛以涅槃为目

"When this exists, that exists. Because this comes into being, that comes into being." The cessation of the twelve links follows from the principle "If this does not exist, that does not exist, if this ceases, that ceases." Sufferings of old age, death, worrying, and sorrow are dependent upon the condition of birth (jāti), so the cessation of birth can result in the cessation of the sufferings of old age, death, worrying and sorrow. Likewise, the cessation of desire, grasping and becoming existence results in the cessation of old age and death. And so, ultimately, the cessation of ignorance results in the cessation of mental formations or the cause of all bitter fruits. When the cessation of ignorance, mental formations, consciousness and so on finally results in the cessation of old age and death, then Nibbāna has been attained. To be more explicit, as soon as the complete cessation of impure and defiled causes and conditions has been reached, ignorance will be turned into undefiled and pure wisdom (suddha-ñāna), through which the truth and reality of all dhammas can be seen. This is Nibbāna, which is also called Nibbāna with corporal remainder (Sopadhi-sesa-nibbāna). The meaning of Nibbāna is perfect peace or tranquility, or an eternally happy and joyous state in which wisdom, happiness and virtue are perfectly achieved. Buddhists view such a state as only attainable by holy ones, thus can not be judged by experienced conceptions like existence, non-existence, coming and going etc. It is an inconceivable state of emancipation. As I mentioned above, Nibbāna can be interpreted as passing away. Actually, Sākyamuni attained Nibbāna and became a Buddha at the age of 30, yet his corporal body remained as the residual fruit of his former illusion and kamma. This is Nibbāna with remainder (Sopadhi-sesa-nibbāna). It was not until his death at the age of 80, that he entered Nibbāna without remainder (Nirupadhi-sesa-nibbāna).

24. Q: How can the realm of Nibbāna be reached?

A: The Nibbāna discussed above is the Truth of the Extinction of Suffering (Nirodha-sacca). Your question on how to reach the realm of Nibbāna falls under the category of the Truth

的，以生死根本的烦恼为消灭对象，以戒（Sīla）、定（Samādhi）、慧（Paññā）三学为方法。

(1)戒，是防止身口意三业的过失，有五戒、十戒、具足戒三级。五戒（Pañca Sīla）是不杀、不偷盗、不邪淫、不妄语、不饮酒类。这是出家在家弟子共持的戒。十戒是沙弥（Sāmaṇera）持的戒（出家男子受十戒的叫做沙弥，一般是不满二十岁的人，满二十岁才能受具足戒为比丘）。具足戒是比丘、比丘尼持的戒。当初僧伽成立时，没有约制团体的一定规律。其后随着问题的发生而随时制戒，到佛逝世前，已制定了二百多条。南方国家所传比丘戒二百二十七条，我国西藏二百五十三条，汉地二百五十条，大体相同，仅有某些条款分开和合并的不同，汉地比丘尼戒三百四十八条。

(2)定，是精神上既不昏沉（即不瞌睡），又不纷驰的安和状态。这是印度一般宗教徒所必习的，尤其是佛教徒修持的必要条件。由于定，身心远离爱欲乐触等的粗分别，逐步发得身心轻安，终于能够把心——精神思想集中于任何一境之上，宁静安稳不受扰乱，进而引发一种无漏的智慧。定有世间的四禅和四无色定，有出世间的九次第定、三三昧等。从定而后能引发慧。

of the Path Leading to the Extinction of Suffering (Magga-sacca). Magga-sacca takes Nibbāna as its goal, the elimination of the basic distresses of birth and death as its objective and uses as its method the Threefold Learning (Ti-sikkhā), which consists of morality or moral precepts (Sīla), concentration (Samādhi) and wisdom (Paññā).

(1) Morality aims at preventing faults in the three kammas of body, speech and mind. There are three levels of rules to follow: the five precepts, the ten precepts and the complete precepts for the higher ordained (upasampadā). The five precepts are followed by both lay believers and monastic disciples, that is abstinence from taking life, from stealing, from illicit sexual conduct, from false speech and from intoxicants. The ten precepts are followed by novices (sāmaṇeras) who have just renounced lay life. (Novices are usually under the age of 20 and will get higher ordination to become monks or nuns at the age of 20.) The complete precepts are followed by monks and nuns (bhikkhus and bhikkhunīs). At the beginning of the establishment of the Sangha Order, there were no fixed rules set for the whole Order. Afterwards, precepts were laid whenever problems arose. By the time of the Buddha's Parinibbāna, there were more than 200 rules. The Bhikkhu precepts now number 227 in Theravadin countries, 253 in Tibet and 250 in Han inhabited regions of China. They are mostly the same, with slight differences in grouping of certain items. There are 348 rules for bhikkhunīs in the Han regions.

(2) Meditation or concentration (Samādhi) is a peaceful and tranquil state of mind neither drowsy nor perturbed. It is a necessary practice for general religious practitioners in India, especially for Buddhists in their cultivation. With concentration, the practitioner can distance himself from coarse distinctions of rapture and joy in the body and mind, depart from sense desire (kāma), and gradually develop ease and peace of body and mind, and finally place mind or thought in any chosen state, tranquil, stable and undisturbed. Such meditation can lead to the acquisition of a pure and correct wisdom. Regarding

(3)慧，是分别一切法的自相（特殊性）与共相（一般性），通达四谛的道理而有断除迷惑证悟真理的作用。

戒、定、慧三学包括四念住、四正勤、四神足、五根、五力、七觉支、八正道等修行法门，共称三十七道品。这里不一一介绍，仅简略介绍一下八正道：

(1)正见，就是于一切法上见到无常无我缘起四谛之理而明确认识它，使成为自己的知见；
(2)正思维；
(3)正语；
(4)正业，是使自己的生活行动受正见的指导，使身口意合于法的法则；
(5)正命，是正当的生活方法，反对诈欺仗势骗夺他财以养自己的邪命生活；
(6)正精进，使身口意毫不松懈地努力向正见所指的目的前进；

meditation, there are four stages of trance (cattāri jhānāni) and four higher stages of non-material trance (cattāro arūpa-samādhi) within this world; and there are nine stages of meditation (nava anupubbavihāra samāpattiyo) and three kinds of meditation (tayo samādhī) etc. beyond this world. Through meditation or concentration, wisdom can be acquired.

(3) Wisdom enables one to distinguish the self-nature (sabhāva) of all dhammas from their common characteristics (samañña), to fully understand the theory of the Four Noble Truths, and thus has the function of dispelling illusions (pahīna-kilesa) and attaining truth (adhigama).

The Threefold Learning of morality, concentration and wisdom are emphasized in the practice of the thirty-seven ways to enlightenment (Bodhipakkhiya-dhamma) which are the 4 Foundations of Mindfulness (satipaṭṭhāna), the 4 Right Efforts (padhāna), the 4 Roads to Power (iddhi-pāda), the 5 Spiritual Faculties (indriya), the 5 Mental Powers (bala), the 7 Factors of Enlightenment (bojjhanga) and the 8-fold Path (magga). I won't discuss each in detail here, but I will say something about the 8-fold Path:

(1) Right View (sammā-diṭṭhi) is to see manifest in every dhamma the theories of Impermanence, Egolessness, Dependent Origination and the Four Noble Truths and make them as one's own knowledge;

(2) Right Thought (sammā sankappa);

(3) Right Speech (sammā vācā);

(4) Right Bodily Action(sammā kammanta)means to be guided by the right view in daily life and behavior, so the body, speech and mind are in a conformity with the law of Dhamma;

(5) Right Livelihood (sammā ājiva) means to make one's living in proper ways and oppose the vicious life of supporting oneself by swindling and defrauding others of their properties;

(6) Right Effort (sammā vāyāma) is to strive after the goal shown by the right view without let-up in actions of body, mouth and mind;

(7) Right Mindfulness (sammā sati) is to always keep the

(7)正念，经常忆念着正见，使正见不忘失而经常现前；

(8)正定，在正见指导下修习进入无漏清净的禅定。

25. 问：根据上面所介绍的四谛内容，可不可以说佛教是厌世主义，因为看不出它对世界有任何积极的理想和采取任何积极的手段？

答：从对待有漏的世界来说，可以说是厌世主义，但是佛教当时的创立，反映着对现实生活的不满，它对人间世界也是有一种理想的。例如《增一阿含经》记载，佛陀谈到转轮王统治的社会情况时，他说：那时候世界上土地平整，如镜清明；谷物丰饶，遍地皆生甘美果树；时气和适，四时顺节，人身康乐，少病少恼；富足如意，食不患苦；欲大小便时，地自然开，事已复合；金银珍宝，散在各地，与瓦石同流；人民大小平等，皆同一意，相见欢欣，善言相向；言辞一类，而无差别。从这段话里面，看出一种类似我国古人大同的理想。为实现这种理想社会的各种努力，就是"庄严国土、利乐有情"。这方面的理论在大乘佛教中特别得到发挥，但为当时各种条件所局限，佛教没有提出政治的和社会的措施。

Right View in mind, bring it to mind frequently and never forget it;

(8) Right Concentration (sammā samādhi) is to practice under the guidance of the Right View, to enter the state of pure and undefiled meditation.

25. Q: According to the Four Noble Truths described above, it seems that Buddhism has no positive ideal and takes no positive measures towards the world, can we say Buddhism is a world-weary philosophy?

A: Concerning the attitude of Buddhism towards the tainted world, one can say that Buddhism is world-weary. But still, Buddhism, which originated from dissatisfaction with the temporal life, cherishes a kind of ideal for the human world. It is recorded in the *Ekottarikāgama* that when talking about the social life under the rule of the Wheel Turning King (Rāja cakkavattin), Buddha says that, at that time, the land will be level and bright as a mirror, the crops abundant; trees hanging with sweet and delicious fruits will grow everywhere; the weather will be fine and seasons favorable; the people, healthy and happy without much sickness and worry, will be rich and satisfied, having abundant food to eat; when they go to relieve their bowels, the ground will open automatically and close afterwards; gold, silver and treasures scattering everywhere like tiles and stones; people, old and young, will be on an equal footing and hold the same opinions; they will greet each other cheerfully and in kind words, speaking with the same language without difference. From this passage one can see a kind of ideal similar to that of the Great Harmony dreamed of by the Chinese people in ancient times. Efforts made to realize this ideal society are aimed at "glorifying the country and benefiting the sentient beings." Such an idea was particularly developed by Mahāyāna Buddhism. But due to the limitations of circumstances at the time, there were no political and social measures advanced by Buddhism.

26. 问：什么是大乘佛教？

答：大乘 Mahāyāna 和小乘 Hīnayāna 是佛教的两大宗派。

27. 问：大乘小乘有什么分别？

答：大小乘的分别，主要在于大乘着重利他（利益大众的行为），小乘着重自己解脱。大乘有不同的经典，在教义上有所发挥和发展。这里可以举几个特点：

首先大乘在灭谛上进一步说"无住涅槃"。从理论上说，十二因缘灭，灭的只是不合缘生缘灭真理的无明烦恼，而不是缘生缘灭的法。"涅槃与世间，无有少分别"。所以到了佛的圆满觉悟的境界，就能不住生死，不住涅槃，就能在因缘生灭的世界中，永无休歇地做"庄严国土、利乐有情"的事，而随时随处安住在涅槃的境界。

其次根据缘起的道理，说明一法以一切法为缘而生起，同时又是生起一切法之缘，所以任何人与一切众生都有同体的关系，好像海里面一个小水泡和整个大海水是同体关系一样。所以说，"一切众生是我父母"，又说"视众生如一子"（独子），这样地兴起大慈悲心（慈是同情人之喜乐，悲是同情人之忧苦），"无有疲厌"地"为众生供给使"。大乘佛教特别发扬这种菩萨行的人生观，并且特别鼓励

26. Q: What is Mahāyāna Buddhism?

A: Mahāyāna and Hīnayāna are the two major sects of Buddhism.

27. Q: What are the differences between Mahāyāna and Hīnayāna?

A: The major difference is that Mahāyāna stresses altruism (conduct for benefit of others), whereas Hīnayāna stresses salvation for oneself. Mahāyāna has scriptures different from those of Hīnayāna, and has augmented and developed Buddhist doctrines as well. Here are a few points:

Firstly, in the Truth of extinction of suffering, Mahāyāna further maintains the possibility of " active nibbāna " (apratiṣṭhita-nirvāṇa). According to this theory, with the extinction of the twelve links of origination, it is not the dhammas arising and ceasing based on causes and conditions that cease, but only the ignorance and moral afflictions not in conformity with Dependent Origination that are eliminated. Since "between nibbāna and the temporal world, there is little difference", upon reaching the realm of the Buddha's perfect enlightenment, one can live beyond the cycles of birth and death and never enter extinction, so one can always work ceaselessly for the cause of "glorifying the country and benefiting the sentient beings" in the conditional world, while abiding peacefully in the nibbāna state anywhere at any time.

Secondly, the Theory of Dependent Origination expounds the theory that one dhamma arises with all other dhammas as its conditions, and in reverse, itself is a cause for others. Thus a single person stands in relationship of homogeneity with other beings, just like the homogeneous relationship between one drop of water and the ocean. Hence the saying "All beings are my parents", and "regard all beings as one's only son". This produces a heart of great loving-kindness (mettā) and compassion (karuṇā). Mettā means identifying oneself with all others' joy

“六度”和“四摄”的行为。

28. 问：什么是菩萨？

答：菩萨是菩提萨埵（Bodhisatta）的简称。简单地解释，凡是抱着广大的志愿，要将自己和一切众生一齐从苦恼中救度出来，而得到究竟安乐（自度度他），要将自己和一切众生一齐从愚痴中解脱出来，而得到彻底的觉悟（自觉觉他）——这种人便叫做菩萨。

29. 问：什么叫做六度？

答：“度”的梵语是“波罗蜜多 Pāramitā”，字义是“到彼岸”，就是从烦恼的此岸度到觉悟的彼岸的意思。六度是六个到彼岸的方法。第一是布施（Dāna），有三种：凡以物质利益施与大众的叫做“财施”，包括身外的财物和自身的头目手足和生命；凡保护大众的安全使他们没有怖畏的叫做“无畏施”；凡以真理告知大众的叫做“法施”。第二是持戒（Sīla），戒也有三种，即防止一切恶行，修集一切善行和饶益有情。菩萨最根本的戒是饶益有情戒，就是一切为了利益大众，其余所有戒条都要服从这一条。第三是忍（Khanti），即为利益有情故，忍受毁骂打击，以及饥寒等苦，所谓“难行能行、难忍能忍”，终不放弃救度众生的志愿。第四是精进（Viriya），即不懈息地努力于自度度他、自觉觉他的事业。第五是禅定（Samādhi），第六是般若（Paññā 即

and happiness, and Karuṇā means sympathy with others' grief and sorrow. With such a heart, one should indefatigably serve all beings. Mahāyāna Buddhism especially advocates this "pusa" (Bodhisatta) outlook of life, and particularly encourages the conduct of "Six Perfections" (Pāramitā) and "Four all-embracing virtues" ( cattāri saṃgaha-vatthūni).

28. Q: What is "Pusa" (S. Bodhisattva, P. Bodhisatta)?

A: "Pusa" is short for "putisaduo", the Chinese translation of Bodhisatta. Briefly, any one who cherishes the lofty aspiration to deliver oneself and all beings from misery and sufferings, and attain ultimate happiness (salvation of oneself and of others), and to release oneself and all beings from ignorance into perfect enlightenment (self-enlightenment and enlightenment of others) is called in Chinese "Pusa", i.e. Bodhisatta.

29. Q: What are the Six Perfections (Pāramitā)?

A: The Sanskrit or Pāli word "Pāramitā" literally means "gone to the other shore", that is to cross from this shore of moral affliction to the other shore of enlightenment. Six-Pāramitā are six ways to the other shore. The first Pāramitā is Liberality or Charity (Dāna), which is of three kinds: giving material things to others including worldly possessions, even one's own head, eyes, hands, feet and life, known as material Dāna; another one, giving protection to all beings and to free them from terror, called the free-from-fear givings ( abhaya Dāna); the third, to give all beings the truth, is the Dhamma Dāna. The second Pāramitā is morality or abiding by the precepts (Sīla), this also consists of three categories, (namely,) to avoid evils, to cultivate and accumulate wholesomeness and to benefit sentient beings. The most fundamental sīla for Boddhisattas is to benefit sentient beings, i.e. all being done is for the public interest, while the other precepts are subordinate to it. The third Pāramitā is Patience (Khanti), which means that in service of sentient beings one should be able to endure slander,

智慧），为自觉觉他而修禅定和智慧。

30. 问：什么是四摄？

答：摄（Saṃgaha-vatthu）的意义就是大众团结的条件。第一是布施；第二是爱语（Peyyavajja），慈爱的言语和态度；第三是利行（Atthacariyā），为大众利益服务；第四是同事（Samānattatā），使自己在生活和活动方面同于大众。四摄法是菩萨在众生中进行工作的方法。

31. 问：菩萨为了利行同事，是否应当学习世间各种学问？

答：菩萨为了利益众生，必须广学多闻。佛教要求菩萨行者学习五明（Vidyā 就是"学"）：

(1)声明，即声韵学和语文学；

(2)工巧明，即一切工艺、技术、算学、历数等；

(3)医方明，即医药学；

(4)因明，即逻辑学；

(5)内明，即佛学。

abuse, attack, the sufferings of hunger and cold etc., "Do what is hard to do, bear what is hard to bear", and never give up the vow to save beings. The fourth Pāramitā, Effort or Energy (Viriya), is to make every effort and strive constantly for salvation not only for oneself but for all other beings and enlightenment not only for oneself but for all other beings. The fifth is Meditation or Contemplation (Samādhi). The sixth, Wisdom (Paññā), is to practice meditation and to gain knowledge for the sake of enlightening oneself and other beings.

30. Q: What are the four All-embracing Virtues (cattāri saṃgaha-vatthūni)?

A: Saṃgaha-vatthu are the qualities that ensure public unity. The first is liberality or charity (Dāna). The second, kindly speech (Peyyavajja), is to speak kind words in a kind manner. The third, beneficial conduct (Atthacariyā), means to serve the public welfare. The fourth, equality (Samānattatā), is to live the same life as the ordinary people. These four are the means whereby Bodhisattas carry out their work among human beings.

31. Q: In order to benefit the public welfare and to identify with others, is it necessary for a bodhisatta to study various kinds of worldly knowledge?

A: For the interest of human beings, it is necessary for a bodhisatta to study extensively and to be well informed. Buddhism requires bodhisatta aspirants to learn the Five Vidyā (S. Vidyā or P. vijja, meaning knowledge), these are:

(1) Śabda-vidyā, viz. phonology and philology;
(2) Śilpakarma-vidyā, viz. all technology, techniques, crafts, arithmetic, calendar, etc.;
(3) Cikitsā-vidyā, viz., medical science and pharmacology;
(4) Hetu-vidyā, viz. logic;
(5) Adhyātma-vidyā, viz. Buddhist studies.

五明是学者必须学习之处。“学处广大，悲心恳切”是菩萨的条件。大乘佛教号召难学能学，尽一切学。

32. 问：请再讲一讲大乘佛教的其他特点。

答：其次是根据缘起的道理而说法性空。这就是说，一切法既是因缘和合而起，所以都没有实体；换句话说，一切法都只是因缘和合的现象，在现象上找不到作为主宰的本体。前面所说的“诸法无我”是指人的“我”，现在进一步说法的“我”也没有。前面是破“人我执”，说“人空”；现在是破“法我执”，说“法”空。

33. 问：佛经中有两句话，“色不异空，空不异色”是什么意思？

答：这就是说一切法“缘起性空”。“色”，就是色、受、想、行、识五蕴中的色，是指物质。任何物质现象都是缘起，它有相状，它有功用，但是它的相状和功用里面没有常恒不变的指挥它的主宰，所以说是空。所谓空，不是指的色外空（物体之外的空），也不是指的色后空（物体灭了之后的空），换句话说，并不是离开色而另外有一个空，而是“当体即空”。色是缘起所起，色法上不能有个不变的实性，所以说“色即是空”；唯其没有实性，所以能遇缘即起，

The five vidyās are the realms that must be mastered by scholars. "To be broadly learned, and sincerely compassionate" are the requirements for bodhisattahood. Mahāyāna Buddhism particularly calls for learning whatever is difficult to learn , and all that should be learned.

32. Q: Please tell us more of the features of Mahāyāna Buddhism.

A: Next, I'll talk about the theory of the empty nature (suññatā) of all dhammas, which follows from the notion of Dependent Origination. It holds that all dhammas are simply the cooperation of relative causes and conditions, therefore, there is no substance in them. In other words, all dhammas are nothing but the phenomena of cooperation of causes and conditions, apart from phenomena there is no noumenon as their dominator. When I said previously that "There is no ego within all dhammas", I was speaking of the absence of "self" (atta) of human beings. And now I add the absence of self of all dhammas. The former is to deny self in human beings, and prove "non-substantiality in beings", while the latter is to deny the self in dhammas, and prove "non-substantiality in dhammas".

33. Q: Somewhere in the Buddhist scriptures, it says "Rūpa (matter) is none other than suññatā (emptiness), suññatā is none other than rūpa." What does this mean?

A: It just means that all dhammas are suññatā by nature according to Dependent Origination. "Rūpa", meaning matter or substance, is one of the five aggregates, namely, rūpa, vedanā, saññā, sankhāra and viññāṇa. Every material phenomenon is a product of the combination of causes and conditions, though it has its own form and functions, it has no perpetual and unchangeable entity inside as its dominator. Hence it is empty. This emptiness does not refer to the empty space beyond matter (or the emptiness outside an object), nor does it refer to the emptiness after existence (or the emptiness after the extinction

所以说“空即是色”。这也就是“色不异空，空不异色”的简单解释。

受、想、行、识等精神现象也同样地是缘起性空。“缘起性空”是宇宙万有的真实相状，即所谓“诸法实相”。大乘佛教以实相为法印，称为“一法印”，一切大乘经教，都以实相的道理来印证。如前面所说“无住涅槃”和“菩萨六度四摄”等教义，都是以缘起性空的理论为基础的。

34. 问：关于大乘佛教的特点还有什么可以介绍的吗？

答：上面所说的是大乘佛教各宗派的几个共同的特点。各宗派又有其特点，这里就不谈了。

35. 问：佛经是释迦牟尼亲自写的吗？

答：不是，是佛逝世后，他的弟子记诵出来的。佛逝世的那一年，佛的弟子，以摩诃迦叶为首的五百人集会在王舍城外的七叶窟，将佛一生所说的言教结集起来，以传后世。当时由阿难陀诵出佛所说的经(Sutta)；由优波离诵出

of an object). In other words, emptiness is not apart from matter, but "the object itself is empty." Now since matter arises according to the law of Dependent Origination, it can't possess an unchangeable material existence in each material object, hence "matter is no different from emptiness". And since dhammas have no material existence, so can arise upon the meeting of adequate conditions, "emptiness is no different from matter". This is a simple interpretation of the phrase "Rūpa is none other than suññatā, and vice versa".

Likewise, spiritual phenomena such as vedanā, saññā, sankhāra and viññāna are also emptiness by nature, for they also arise from Dependent Origination. Emptiness, on the basis of Dependent Origination is the true nature (lakkhaṇa) of all that exists in the universe, i. e. the reality of all dhammas. In Mahāyāna Buddhism this reality is regarded as the impress or seal of truth. This doctrine is called the "One Seal of Dhamma". All Mahāyāna doctrines are corroborated with this "One Seal". The aforesaid Buddhist doctrines — "active nibbāna" (appaṇihita-vihāra-nibbāna) and Bodhisattas' "Six Perfections" (Pāramitā) and "Four all-embracing virtues"— are all on the basis of the theory of Emptiness by nature in terms of Dependent Origination.

34. Q: What else can you tell us about Mahāyāna Buddhism?

A: I have mentioned some of the common features of the various sects of Mahāyāna Buddhism. There are still differences between them, since each sect has its own speciality, however, I will not go into the details here.

35. Q: Were the Buddhist texts written by Sākyamuni himself ?

A: No, they were recited and recorded by his disciples after the Buddha's death. In the year of Buddha's Parinibbāna, his five hundred disciples headed by Ven. Mahākassapa held an assembly at Saptaparṇa Cave ( P. Sattapaṇṇa-guhā ) near Rājagaha to compile and edit the Buddha's teachings for posteri-

佛所制的僧团戒律（Vinaya）；由摩诃迦叶当时诵出，后来又补充结集的关于教理的解释和研究的论著（Abhidhamma）。经、律、论为三藏 Tipiṭaka。藏的原语 Piṭaka，是一种可以盛放东西的竹箧。把经、律、论分为三藏，同我国把经、史、子、集分为四库有差不多的意思。这一次结集称为第一结集。照我国通常解释，结集两个字含有编辑的意义。但这个字的梵文 Saṃgīti（巴利语同）却是僧众大会的意思。古代译师用结集二字是含有“会诵”的意思，一方面固然着重在法的结集，同时也包含着人的结集的意思在内。这时还没有用文字记录，只凭口头传诵。

36. 问：第一次结集之外，还有其他结集吗？

答：当时除在七叶窟的五百比丘外，还有未加入摩诃迦叶团体的许多比丘，以跋波（Vappa 最初五比丘之一）为上首，在窟外不远的地方另行结集。所以王舍城结集分窟内窟外二部。所结集的都是小乘三藏。大乘三藏相传是文殊师利（Mañjuśrī）、弥勒（Maitreya）等菩萨和阿难陀等在铁围山结集的。小乘佛教则不承认大乘经典是佛所说。

37. 问：缅甸前几年举行第六次结集，是怎么一回事？

ty. At the assembly Ven. Ānanda recited the Suttas preached by the Buddha, Ven. Upāli recited the Vinaya established by the Buddha, and Ven. Mahākassapa recited, and later supplemented, the Abhidamma which is an exposition and study of the Buddhist creeds. The Sutta, Vinaya and Abhidamma comprise Tipiṭaka. The word Piṭaka originally meant basket for containing things. The compilation of Sutta, Vinaya and Abhidamma into Tipiṭaka is something like the designation of Jing (classics), Shi (history), Zi (academic schools) and Ji (Miscellany) as the "Four Treasures" in China. This Buddhist council was termed the First Saṃgīti. Saṃgīti is generally rendered as "Jieji" in Chinese, while its original meaning in Sanskrit or Pāli is "sangha meeting". The ancient Chinese translators used the word "Jieji" to mean "recital", which implies both the collection of Dhamma, and the assembly of people. The Tipiṭaka was not written down at that time, so it was passed on by oral recital.

36. Q: Were there any more assemblies besides the first one?

A: Yes. At that time, besides the five hundred bhikkhus who gathered at Saptaparṇa Cave (P. Sattapaṇṇa guhā), there were a number of bhikkhus who did not join the Mahākassapa group. Some bhikkhus, headed by Vappa (one of the first five Bhikkhus), assembled at another place not far from the Cave. So the Rājagaha Saṃgīti is composed of two parts, one compiled inside the cave and the other outside the cave, the two compilations together forming the Hīnayāna Tipiṭaka. Tradition holds that the Mahāyāna Tripiṭaka was compiled at Cakkavāḷapabbata by Bodhisattas including Mañjuśrī, Maitreya, as well as Ānanda and others. Hīnayāna Buddhists, however, deny that the Mahāyāna scriptures are authentic Dhamma given by the Buddha.

37. Q: What about the Sixth Buddhist Council (Saṃgīti) held in Burma a few years ago?

答：佛逝世一百十年后，在毗舍离国僧团中有关于戒律上的争论，于是长老（僧龄高的称长老）耶舍（Yasa）召集七百位学德兼优的僧众，依据律藏，断定当时争论问题中有十件事为非法，这是第二次结集。

根据南方佛典记载，佛逝世二百三十五年后，阿育王时代，有很多外道（佛教之外的教派）的人混入佛教徒中，混乱了教义，于是在阿育王支持下，以国师目犍连子帝须（Moggaliputta Tissa）为首的一千比丘在波吒利弗城（Pāṭaliputta，即今天印度比哈尔省省城八纳 Patna）诵出三藏，以清除外道掺杂进去的东西，这是第三次结集。

根据北方佛教记载，佛逝世后四百年左右，在大月氏国迦腻色迦（Kaniṣka）统治西印度时代，以世友菩萨（Vasumitta）为首的五百比丘造论解释三藏，共三十万颂，九百多万言，其中一部就是《大毗婆沙》（Mahāvibhāṣā），是一部重要的论。这是第四次结集。

距今八十多年前，缅甸明顿王邀集众多比丘校勘巴利文三藏，并将三藏全文和校勘记刻在石碑上，现仍保存在曼德勒城。他们称为第五次结集。

1954—1956 年缅甸联邦政府为了纪念释迦牟尼佛涅槃二千五百年，发起第六次结集，邀请缅甸、柬埔寨、锡兰、印度、老挝、尼泊尔、巴基斯坦、泰国等国的比丘二千五百人参加。他们进行了两年工作，根据各国的各种版本和明顿王第五次结集的校勘记，对巴利文三藏进行严密的校勘，印成了最完善版本的巴利文三藏。被称为“第六次结集”。

A: 110 years after Buddha's death, there was a controversy over some of the Buddhist precepts among the monks in Vaiśāli. Thereupon Ven. Yasa Thero (elder priest) summoned 700 learned and virtuous elders and they determined that 10 of the issues involved were violations of the Vinaya. This council was known as the Second Saṃgīti.

According to the records of Southern Buddhist canon, 235 years after Buddha's death, in the Asoka Era, many heretics infiltrated into the Buddhist Order and confused Buddhist doctrines. Thereupon, Ven. Moggaliputta Tissa, with the support of King Asoka, convened a Buddhist council with 1000 participants in Pāṭaliputta (now Patna, Capital of Bihar Pradesh, India) to recite the Tipiṭaka for the purpose of clearing out the heretical adulterations. This was known as the Third Saṃgīti.

According to the Northern Buddhist records, around 400 years after Buddha's death, at the time when King Kaniṣka of Kusana ruled in west India, 500 bhikkhus under Ven. Vasumitta composed commentaries for the Tipiṭaka. These commentaries totaled some three hundred thousand gāthas, more than nine million words. One of these was the *Mahāvibhaṣā*, a very important commentary work (aṭṭhakathā). This generally was known as the Fourth Saṃgīti.

About 80 years ago, King Mindon of Burma invited numerous bhikkhus to collate the Pāli Tipiṭaka and engrave the full texts and an account of the collations on stone tablets which are still kept in Mandalay today. This was called the Fifth Saṃgīti.

From 1954 to 1956 the federal government of Burma, in commemoration of the 2500th anniversary of Sākyamuni's Parinibbāna, sponsored the Sixth Saṃgīti, and invited 2500 bhikkhus from Burma (Myanmar), Cambodia (Kampuchea), Ceylon (Sri Lanka), India, Laos, Nepal, Pakistan and Thailand to participate. They worked for two years and meticulously collated various editions from different countries as well as the collation of Pāli Ṭipiṭaka from King Mindon's Fifth Saṃgīti and finally they produced the most complete edition of Pāli Tipiṭaka in print. This is called the Sixth Saṃgīti.

38. 问:什么是巴利文?

答:巴利(Pāli)是古代印度一种语言,是佛陀时代摩揭陀国一带的大众语。据说佛就是用这种语言说法的,所以弟子们也用这种语言记诵他的经教。巴利语虽然早已不通用了,但是靠了佛经而保存了下来。巴利就是经典的意思。古代印度人民有一种传统习惯,就是把典籍用口口相传的方式背诵下来,而不重视书写。根据《锡兰岛史》记载,公元前一世纪时候,才在锡兰开始传写。到公元五世纪,摩揭陀国三藏法师(通达三藏学者的称号)觉音(Buddhaghosa)到锡兰,重新用锡兰的僧伽罗文字母把巴利文三藏全部记录下来(一说觉音在锡兰时将当时保存很多的用僧伽罗文写的注疏译成巴利文)。原来的巴利文字母已经不存在,现在缅甸、柬埔寨、泰国的巴利文三藏也都是用他们本国字母记录的。最近印度也正在从事用印地文字母记录并印行巴利文三藏的工作。

39. 问:除巴利文之外,还有哪几种文字记录的佛经?

答:还有梵文(Sanskrit)。佛教分南传和北传,传到南方去的用巴利文,是小乘佛教经典;传到北方去的用梵文,多数是大乘佛教经典,也有小乘经典。巴利语是古代俗语,梵文则是古代雅语。

40. 问:中国汉译、藏译佛教经典是从巴利文翻译的,还是从梵文翻译的?

38. Q: What is Pāli?

A: Pāli is a language used in ancient India, to be more specific, it was a popular dialect in Magadha at the time of the Buddha. The Buddha was said to have preached his sermons in this language, so his disciples also used this language to memorize and recite his teachings. Although it is no longer a living language now Pāli has been preserved through the Buddhist scriptures. The word "Pāli" means "classics". The ancient Indians were in the habit of reciting and passing on canonical texts orally instead of in writing. According to *the History of the Island of Ceylon* (Dīpavaṃsa), Buddhist texts began to be written down during the first century BC in Ceylon. By the fifth century AD, Ven. Buddhaghoṣa, Tipiṭakācariya from Magadha, came to Ceylon and made a copy of the whole Pāli Tipiṭaka in Sinhalese script. (According to another account, when Buddhaghoṣa was in Ceylon, he translated a great many Sinhalese commentaries of Tipiṭaka into Pāli.) As the original Pāli alphabet is no longer in existence, the current Pāli Tipiṭaka of Burma, Kampuchea and Thailand are all recorded in the indigenous alphabets. Recently India too has been engaged in the work of recording and publishing the Pāli Tipiṭaka in the Hindi alphabet.

39. Q: Are there Buddhist scriptures recorded in other languages besides Pāli?

A: Yes, there is another system in Sanskrit. Buddhism falls into Southern and Northern traditions. The canons of the Southern tradition were recorded in Pāli, and belong to Hīnayāna Buddhism, while the texts of the Northern tradition were in Sanskrit, mostly being of the Mahāyāna Schools, with a few being Hīnayāna. Pāli was a popular spoken language in ancient India, while Sanskrit a refined one.

40. Q: Were Chinese Buddhist canons and Tibetan ones translated from Pāli or from Sanskrit?

答:汉译佛经,从梵文翻译的居多,也有从巴利文翻译的。藏译佛经则似乎全是从梵文翻译的。

41. 问:现在佛经一般有几种文字?

答:许多国家都用他们自己的文字翻译了佛经。欧洲有俄文、德文、英文、法文、意大利文、芬兰文等,但是都不齐全,其来源不外乎三大系:(1)巴利文,(2)汉文和(3)藏文。梵文经典现在残存的已很少,尼泊尔和我国西藏还有部分古梵文本留存。北传佛教经籍,大部分保存在我国汉文和藏文藏经里。

42. 问:世界佛经是否可以按照语文分为三大系?

答:三大系的划分,是合乎实际情况的。现在佛教界都承认三大系的说法。一般说来,南方国家斯里兰卡、缅甸、柬埔寨、老挝、印度、巴基斯坦、泰国和我国云南省傣、崩龙、布朗等民族的佛教属于巴利语系,是小乘佛教,比较精确的说,应当称为上座部佛教(Theravāda 他们自称的派名)。大小乘过去一直有宗派争执,近来渐有融合的倾向。为了加强各国佛教徒和人民的团结和互相尊重,有许多人主张不再用大小乘的名称,因此称南传佛教为上座部佛教较为合适。我国汉族和朝鲜、日本、越南的佛教属于汉语系。我国藏、蒙、土、羌,裕固等民族以及蒙古、苏联西北利亚地方和印度北部地方的佛教属于藏语系。这两系都属于大乘佛教。

A: The Chinese Buddhist canons were mostly translated from Sanskrit, with a few from Pāli. The Tibetan texts seemed to be all translated from Sanskrit.

41. Q: In how many different languages do the Buddhist texts appear at present?

A: Many countries have been translating Buddhist texts into their own languages. In Europe, there are texts in Russian, German, English, French, Italian, Finnish etc., but none of them is complete. Most of these texts are translated from three source languages: (1) Pāli, (2) Chinese and (3) Tibetan. Besides a small part preserved in Nepal and Tibet, very few of the Sanskrit canons remain. Thus Buddhist scriptures of the Northern tradition are mostly preserved in China in the Chinese and Tibetan Languages.

42. Q: Can the Buddhist canons be classified into three systems according to the languages employed?

A: Yes, the division into three groups conforms to the actual situation. Buddhist circles today all acknowledge the division into three systems. Generally speaking, Buddhism in Southern countries "—" Sri Lanka, Myanmar, Kampuchea, Laos, India, Pakistan and Thailand as well as in the minorities of China's Yunnan Province such as Dai, Benlong and Bulang – falls under the Pāli system, of Hīnayāna Buddhism, or more precisely, Theravāda Buddhism, as they refer to themselves. There used to be sectarian disputes between Mahāyāna and Hīnayāna in the past, but the tendency to blend is increasingly apparent at the present time. Many people advocate that the terms of Hīnayāna and Mahāyāna be dropped with a view to strengthening the unity and mutual respect among the Buddhists and peoples of different countries. Hence it is more appropriate to call Southern Buddhism Theravāda Buddhism. The Buddhism of the Hans in China, as well as of Korea, Japan and Vietnam belongs to the Chinese system. The Buddhism of Tibet, Inner Mongolia, Tujia,

43. 问:汉译三藏有多少卷?

答:有1,692部,共6,241卷,此外中国学者撰述收入藏内的有一千多卷。明代嘉兴版大藏经又收集中国学者撰述5,600卷编为续藏。近代日本也编印续藏,收集的也都是中国撰述的,共1,750部,7,140卷。

44. 问:汉文大藏经有多少版本?

答:我国第一次刻本汉文大藏经是公元971年宋开宝四年刻本。在此以后,历宋、辽、金、元、明、清几个朝代,一千年之间先后有二十余次刻本。1936年在山西赵城县广胜寺发现金代(公元十二世纪)刻本大藏经,因此称为赵城藏。日本帝国主义侵略中国时,企图劫走这部法宝,为八路军抢救,牺牲了八位战士,才保护下来。这部经现藏在北京图书馆。西安开元、卧龙寺藏有宋刻(公元十二世纪)碛砂版藏经,近代有影印本。明代政府刻的南本大藏经(1372年开始在南京刻的)和北本大藏经(1410年开始在北京刻的),还有万历年间刻的方册大藏经(通称嘉兴藏)现在还有留存。清代雍正、乾隆年间(1735-1738)刻的大藏经(通称龙藏),尚有经板留存。

Qiang, and Yugu and other nationalities of China, as well as that of Mongolia, Siberia and northern India belongs to the Tibetan system. The latter two systems belong to Mahāyāna Buddhism.

43. Q: How many volumes, or fasciculi, are there in the Chinese Tipiṭaka?

A: There are 1692 books, totaling 6241 volumes. Besides, over 1000 volumes composed by Chinese scholars are collected in the Chinese Tipiṭaka. In the Ming Dynasty, the Jiaxing edition of the Chinese Tipiṭaka collected some 5600 volumes of Chines scholars' writings to add to the Tipiṭaka as a sequel. In modern times sequels have also been compiled in Japan, which are all drawn from Chinese writings. These total 1750 books, 7140 volumes.

44. Q: How many editions are there of the Chinese Tipiṭaka?

A: The first block-printed edition of the Tipiṭaka in Chinese appeared in 971 AD. or the 4th year of the Kaibao Era of the Song Dynasty. In the following 1000 years, through the dynasties of Song, Liao, Jin, Yuan, Ming and Qing, there were more than 20 block-printed editions published. In 1936, a block-printed edition of the Tipiṭaka from the Jin Dynasty (12th century) was discovered at Guangsheng Temple in Zhaocheng county, Shanxi Province, so it was named Zhaocheng-edition Tipiṭaka. When the Japanese imperialists invaded China, they attempted to rob China of this treasure, but thanks to the Eighth Route Army troops, at the cost of the lives of eight soldiers, it was saved and is now kept in the National Library. In Kaiyuan and Wolong Temples in Xi'an, there is a block-printed Qisha edition from Song Dynasty (12th century), of which a photolithograph has been published in modern times. In addition, there are the Southern-edition (block-printed in Nanjing in 1372) and the Northern-edition (block-printed in Beijing from 1410) as well as the thread-bound edition of Tipiṭaka (common-

我国敦煌石窟所藏晋、魏、隋、唐人的写经，自二十世纪初被发现后，很大部分被盗劫到国外，都是贵重的法宝，北京图书馆还藏有八千多卷。我国还有很多石刻佛经，最重要的是房山县石经山上的石经。那是公元七世纪初我国隋代静琬法师开始刻的，一直继续了千年之久。所刻经板，封存在九个石洞里和埋藏在塔下。1956 年，中国佛教协会在政府支持下，费了两年时间，将那里的经板全部取出拓印了七份，现正在整理和研究中，计刻经一千余部，近三千五百卷；并考证发现辽刻石经是以《契丹藏》为底本，也就是久已失传的《契丹藏》的复刻。房山石经是一部稀有的法宝。

45. 问：藏文大藏经内容请介绍一下。

答：藏文大藏经分两部分：(1)正藏，名"甘珠尔"，"甘"的意思是"言教"，"珠尔"是翻译，就是言教的翻译，包括经和律，因为经和律都是佛的言教；(2)副藏，名"丹珠尔"，"丹"的意思是论著，就是论著的翻译。甘珠尔共 1,108部；丹珠尔共 3,459 部。

ly known as the Jiaxing Edition) block-printed in the Wanli Era, all of which were made by the government of the Ming Dynasty. Printing blocks of the Tipiṭaka made during the Yongzheng and Qianlong Eras of the Qing Dynasty (1735-1738) (commonly known as Dragon Collection) are still in existence.

Hand-written copies of the scriptures made in the Jin, Wei, Sui, and Tang dynasties which are preserved in the Dunhuang Grottoes of China are valuable Buddhist treasures discovered in the early 20th century, but a great portion of them have been stolen (by foreigners) and taken abroad. About 8,000 volumes are now preserved in the National Library. There are also many stone-engraved Buddhist texts in our country, the most important among them are those stored in the caves of Shijingshan (Stone-carved Scriptures Hill) in Fangshan, Beijing. The engraving of these texts was started by Ven. Jing Wan during the seventh century AD. in the Sui Dynasty, and was kept up for about 1,000 years. The blocks are all stored in 9 caves, or buried beneath thūpa. In 1956, the Chinese Buddhist Association with the support of the government, took all of the blocks out and made seven sets of rubbings in two years. These are being catalogued and studied. In total, there are more than 1000 Suttas, nearly 3500 volumes engraved, and the texts carved in the Liao Dynasty are found by textual research to be based upon the Qidan (Khitan) edition which was long lost. The Fangshan stone-carved scriptures are very rare treasures.

45. Q: Could you please tell me about the Tibetan Tipiṭaka?

A: The Tibetan Tipiṭaka consists of two parts: (1) The Proper Collection, called "Bkaḥ-ḥgyur", Bkaḥ means teachings and Ḥgyur means translation. So it is a translation of Buddha's teachings, including the Sutta and Vinaya preached by the Buddha. (2) The Appended Collection, called "Bstan-ḥgyur", Bstan means śāstra or commentary. So it is a translation of śāstras. Bkaḥ-ḥgyur consists of 1108 suttas and Bstan-ḥgyur of 3459 śāstras.

46. 问：藏文大藏经有无刻本？

答：公元十三世纪初年在奈塘刻的大藏，称为奈塘版，是第一次刻本。十五、六世纪明代曾翻刻过两次。十七世纪清康熙、雍正年间在北京翻刻一次，称为北京版，同时西康等地又各翻刻为德格版、卓尼版等。西藏在雍正八年到十年重刻奈塘新版，大体与北京版一致而增订其未尽善之处。约在1921年间十三世达赖喇嘛重刻大藏经，称拉萨版。最近日本印行的西藏大藏经，就是北京版的影印本。

47. 问：巴利文三藏内容是什么？

答：巴利文经藏分五部：

(1)长部(Dīgha-nikāya)，相当于我国长阿含经；

(2)中部(Majjhima-nikāya)，相当于我国中阿含经；

(3)相应部(Saṃyutta-nikāya)，相当于我国杂阿含经；

(4)增支部(Aṅguttara-nikāya)，相当于我国增一阿含经；

(5)小部(Khuddaka-nikāya)，我国缺。

我国小乘经藏只有四阿含(Āgama的字义是集，就是

46. Q: Are there any block-print editions of the Tibetan Tipiṭaka?

A: Yes, there are. Early in the 12th century AD the first block-print of the Tipiṭaka was made in Naitang and is thus known as the Naitang Edition. In 15th and 16th centuries, during the Ming Dynasty, two block print editions were made. In Kangxi and Yongzheng Eras of the Qing Dynasty (17th century), another block-print was made in Beijing, called the Beijing Edition. In the meantime other blocks known as the Dege Edition, Zhuoni Edition, etc. were made in Xikang and elsewhere. In Tibet, a new Naitang Edition was redone between the 8th and 10th year of the Yongzheng Era, about the same as the Beijing Edition, but with certain supplements to overcome its imperfections. Around 1921, the 13th Dalai Lama had another edition of the Tipiṭaka made in Lhasa, known as the Lhasa Edition. Recently, a photo-offset reprint of the Beijing Edition of the Tibetan Tipiṭaka appeared in Japan.

47. Q: What are the contents of the Pāli Tipiṭaka?

A: The Pāli Sutta-piṭaka (the "basket of Buddha's discourses") consists of five parts:

(1) Dīgha-nikāya (Long discourses), corresponding to the Dīghāgama in Chinese Tipiṭaka;

(2) Majjhima-nikāya (Medium-length suttas), corresponding to the Madhyamāgama in the Chinese Tipiṭaka;

(3) Saṃyutta-nikāya (the Discourses organized according to content), corresponding to the Saṃyukktāgama in Chinese;

(4) Aṅguttara-nikāya (the Discourse Collection in Numerical Order), corresponding to the Ekottarikāgama in the Chinese Tripiṭaka;

(5) Khuddaka-nikāya (Minor Anthologies), without complete translation in Chinese.

There are only four Āgamas of Hīnayāna Sutta Piṭaka translated

佛的言教集)。

巴利文律藏分三部:

(1)分别部(Sutta-vibhaṅga),是戒的条文;

(2)犍度(Khandhaka),是僧团中一切生活制度;

(3)附篇(Parivāra),是戒条的解释。

巴利文论藏有七部论;

(1)法聚论,

(2)分别论,

(3)界论,

(4)双论,

(5)发趣论,

(6)人施设论,

(7)论事。

这七部论是关于心理状态,宇宙万有的分析,因果论等重要著作。

48. 问:费了你很多时间。关于佛法基本内容和关于佛教经籍的一些主要情况都承你作了介绍,现在就谈这一些,以后再请教。

答:不见得能够满足你的要求,只能说是提供一些初步材料罢了。

into Chinese (Āgama literally means collection, or collection of Buddha's Discourses).

The Pāli Vinaya-piṭaka (the "Basket of Disciplines") consists of 3 parts:

(1) Sutta vibhaṅga (all of the Precepts);
(2) Khandhaka (procedures for assemblies and rules for daily life in the Sangha);
(3) Parivāra (interpretation of the rules or appendix).

The Pāli Abhidamma-piṭaka (The "Basket of commentaries") consists of 7 parts:

(1) Dhamma-saṅgaṇi (Enumeration of Dhammas or Buddhist Psychological Ethics);
(2) Vibhaṅga (The Book of Analysis);
(3) Dhātu-kathā (Discourse on Elements);
(4) Yamaka (Book of Pairs);
(5) Paṭṭhāna (Book of Causality);
(6) Puggala-paññatti (Description of Human Types);
(7) Kathāvatthu (Points of Controversy).

These 7 Śāstras are important works dealing with the states of mind, analysis of the universal existence, the theory of cause and effect, etc.

48. Q: We have taken up much of your time. You have explained to us the fundamentals of the Buddha's Teachings and the Buddhist canonical works. That is enough for the time being, we'll surely consult you again later.

A: I may not have satisfied your requirements, just provided some basic materials.

## 第三章
## 僧伽和佛的弟子

1. 问:为什么一部分佛教徒要出家?

答:要说明这个问题,先要谈一谈佛教的五乘教法。乘就是车子,能运载行人到远近不同的目的地,借以比喻教法。五戒的教法(戒杀、盗、淫、妄、酒的五条戒)能令修持者得生人间,叫做人乘。十善的教法(不犯十恶即是十善。十恶是指:一、杀;二、盗;三、淫;四、妄语;五、两舌,即挑拨离间;六、恶口,即粗恶伤人的言语;七、绮语,即邪淫言语;八、贪;九、嗔;十、邪见,即否认因果的见解。)能令修持者得生天界,叫做天乘。四谛的教法,能令人断除见惑(我见、常见、断见等错误见解)和思惑(对世间事物而起的贪嗔痴等迷情),证得涅槃,叫做声闻乘。"声"是言教的意思,听闻佛的言教,悟四谛之理而得到解脱的人叫做声闻。在没有佛法的时代,有人独自悟到缘起之理而得到解脱,但他不能把自己悟到的真理说出来,这种人叫做独觉,因此十二因缘法叫做独觉乘。六度的教法,能令修持者行菩萨道,经过无数世的难行苦行,最后达到佛的果位,叫做菩萨乘。

# Chapter III
# THE SANGHA AND THE BUDDHA'S DISCIPLES

1. Q: Why do some Buddhists need to renounce the lay life?

A: Before answering this question, it is necessary to explain the Buddhist doctrine of Pañca-yāna ( Five Vehicles ). Yāna means a vehicle which can carry passengers to their destinations, far or near. It is used here as a metaphor of Buddha's teachings. The doctrine of Pañca-sīla ( Five Precepts: abstaining from taking life from sentient beings, taking things not given, sexual misconduct, false speech, the use of intoxicants ) enables the practitioners to be reborn in the human world, so it is called Manussa-yāna (human-vehicle). The doctrine of Dasa-kusalāni (Ten meritorious acts — avoidance of the ten evils: 1. killing, 2. taking things not given, 3. sexual misconduct, 4. irresponsible speech, 5. speech inciting discord, 6. harsh speech, 7. licentious talk, 8. covetousness, 9. anger and 10. heterodoxy or denial of the hetu-phala doctrine of cause-effect) enables the practitioners to be reborn in heaven, so it is called Devayāna (heavenly vehicle). The doctrine of Four Noble Truths (ariya-sacca, namely, the truth of Suffering, of the Origin of suffering, of the Extinction of suffering, and of the Eight-fold Path leading to the extinction of suffering) enables the people to discard wrong views (diṭṭhānusaya or micchā-diṭṭhi) such as ego-illusion ( atta-diṭṭhi ), eternity-belief ( sassata-diṭṭhi ), annihilation-belief (uccheda-diṭṭhi) etc., and defiled thought ( micchā-sankappa) such as greed (lobha), hatred (dosa), delusion (moha) and so forth, finally, to attain nibbāna(enlightenment). So it is called sāvaka-yāna (voice-hearer vehicle). Voice means the Buddha's

2. 问:五乘教法与出家有何关系?

答:人乘、天乘不要求出家;独觉生在没有佛法之世,虽是山林隐逸而没有出家的仪式;菩萨包括出家的和在家的人,不一定要出家,看住持佛法的因缘和利益众生的因缘可以出家,可以在家。如佛陀时代,文殊师利菩萨和弥勒菩萨都是出家的比丘,维摩诘也是大菩萨,则是居士(在家学佛之士)。只是声闻乘中为了证得现法涅槃,成阿罗汉的目的,要求修行者出家。

3. 问:阿罗汉是什么意思?

答:阿罗汉(Arahat)是修行者得到证悟的果位。到达

teachings. Those who hear the Buddha's teachings, realize the Four Noble Truths and are free from sufferings are called sāvaka. Before the advent of the Buddha-Dhamma, people who independently came to the realization of the Theory of Paṭiccasamupāda (Dependent Origination) and obtained emancipation, but were unable to speak out their self-enlightened truth were called Pacceka-Buddha (Independently Enlightened One). That is why the Dhamma of Dependent Origination is called the vehicle of self-enlightenment (pacceka-yāna). The doctrine of Six Perfections (cha pāramitā) enables the practitioners to act in the way of Bodhisatta, to undergo the countless difficulties and hardships in cycles of birth and death, and to finally attain Buddhahood. So this teaching is called the vehicle of Bodhisatta (Bodhisattayāna).

2. Q: What is the relation between the doctrine of Five Vehicles (Pañcayāna) and renunciation of the world (pabbajjā)?

A: The Human Vehicle and Heavenly Vehicle do not require leaving home. The Pacceka Buddhas (self-enlightened ones), living in the absence of the Buddha Dhamma, led lives of hermits in the mountains and forests, but went through no ceremony of renunciation. As for Budhisattas, some lived at home, and some did not. In their case, it is not necessary to leave home. Whether or not they leave home depend upon the conditions (hetu-paccaya) of their maintaining the Buddha Dhamma and benefiting all living beings. For example, at the time of Sākyamuni Buddha, both Bodhisattas Mañjuśrī and Maitreya (P. Metteyya) were Bhikkhus, whereas Vimalakīrti, though a great Bodhisatta, was a layman (a scholar studying Buddhism at home). So it is only in sāvakayāna those who seek to achieve Nibbāna by becoming Arahats need to leave home and lead a homeless life.

3. Q: What does Arahat mean?

A: Arahat is the status attained by a Buddhist practitioner

这个果位有四个阶段:断除了见惑的叫做须陀洹果,即初果;进而断除思惑,按照其浅深粗细不同而有斯陀含果(二果)和阿那含果(三果);到了阿罗汉的果位(四果),见惑思惑都已断尽,证得涅槃,堪受人天供养。所以阿罗汉的意义之一就是“应供”,这是声闻乘中的终极地位。

4. 问:声闻乘为什么要求出家?

答:根据声闻乘教法,在家修行障碍多,心意难以专纯,只能在理论上断除见惑证得初果,至多断除欲界思惑证得三果,不能证得现法涅槃。出家生活自由无累,容易集注精力从事于无我无欲的修养,所以要证得阿罗汉果,非出家人做不到。

5. 问:出家的制度是佛教创始的吗?

答:出家制度不是佛教创始的。在佛陀的时代,出家修道在印度已成为风气,但是佛陀本人以王子出家的榜样,使出家风气在佛教中得到了鼓励。因此佛教徒中便有出家男女二众和在家男女二众。出家佛教徒一般称为僧人或僧侣。

upon enlightenment. There are four stages to reach this goal: The first stage is to dispel wrong views. That is called Sotāpanna (the fruition of stream winning), i.e. the initial fruition. The second stage, Sakadāgāmi (the second fruition of once return), and the third, Anāgāmi (the third fruition of non-return) are gradually reached by casting off erroneous thought according to their different dimensions and subtleties. When the fourth stage of Arahat is reached, both wrong views and erroneous thought have been completely wiped out and Nibbāna attained. Such an Arahat is worthy of receiving offerings from man and deity alike. So, one of the meanings of Arahat is "deserving offerings". It is the highest status attained by Sāvakas.

4. Q: Why does the voice-hearer vehicle (sāvakayāna) require renunciation?

A: According to the doctrine of voice-hearer vehicle, due to numerous obstacles it is more difficult to cultivate oneself intently and purely at home. Such a practitioner can only achieve the initial fruition of casting off wrong views theoretically, or at most, achieve the third fruition by casting off misleading thoughts of the sensuous world (kāmaloka), and he can never achieve Nibbāna in this life. A homeless life is free and detached, it is easier to concentrate one's mind and energy on self-cultivation to achieve the state of egolessness (anattā) and desirelessness. So it is impossible to attain the status of Arahat without renunciation of the home life.

5. Q: Was the institution of renunciation initiated by Buddhism?

A: No, it was not initiated by Buddhism. By the time of the Buddha, religious mendicancy (paribbājaka) had become common practice in India. But as a prince, Buddha's renunciation set an example to inspire his followers to discard the attachment to home life. Therefore, there are those who renounce home life and become itinerant or monastic disciples, both male and female, as well as lay followers, both male and female among

6. 问:佛教僧侣是不是神职人员?

答:佛教僧侣仅仅是为求得解脱而出家修行的人,不是担任什么神与人之间的神职。他不应当,也不可能代人祈福禳灾,或代神降福免罪。

7. 问:佛教僧侣平时生活应当是怎样的呢?

答:根据佛的制度,一个比丘应当过着清净而俭约的生活,严格遵守不杀、不盗、不淫(包括在俗家的妻子)、不妄语、不两舌、不恶口、不绮语、不饮酒及不非时食(过午不食)、不涂香装饰、不自歌舞也不观听歌舞、不坐卧高广床位、不接受金银象马等财宝,除衣、钵、剃刀、滤水囊、缝衣针等必须用品外不蓄私财,不做买卖,不算命看相,不诈示神奇,不禁闭、掠夺和威吓他人等等及其他戒律。平日昼夜六时中(晨朝、日中、日没为昼三时,初夜、中夜、后夜为夜三时)除一定时间睡眠、托钵、饮食、洒扫、挑水外,其余时间都应当精勤地用在学修方面。

8. 问:学修的内容是什么?

答:教理的研究和禅定的修习,内容不外乎前面说过

Buddhists. The itinerant or monastic Buddhists are generally called Buddhist monks or nuns (Bhikkhus and Bhikkhunīs).

6. Q: Do Buddhist monks and nuns constitute a clergy?

A: Buddhist monks and nuns are merely those who renounce the world to cultivate themselves only for the sake of emancipation. They are not intermediaries between the deity and human beings. As a Buddhist monk, he should not and can not bless, or prevent disaster befalling human beings, nor can he grant blessing or exemption from punishment on behalf of any deity.

7. Q: What style of life should a Buddhist monk (or nun) maintain?

A: According to the Buddha's rules, a Bhikkhu should lead a pure and frugal life, and strictly observe the precepts of abstaining from killing, stealing, sex (including sex with his former wife), irresponsible speech, speech inciting discord, harsh speech, lewd talk, alcoholic drinks, taking untimely food, (i.e., taking food after noon), the use of perfumes and adornments, singing, dancing and watching others sing and dance, sitting or sleeping on high luxurious seats or beds, accepting treasures like gold, silver, elephants, horses, etc. He should not own private property except robes, alms bowl, razor, water-filter, needle, and thread and such necessary articles, nor should he do business, fortune-telling, displaying of magic wonders. He must not confine, plunder or threaten others and must observe some other prescriptions as well. During the six daily periods (three for day, i.e. morning, noon, dusk; and three for night i.e. nightfall, midnight and dawn) he should devote all his time to the zealous pursuit of study and cultivation after allowing time for sleeping, alms begging, eating, drinking, sweeping and cleaning, and carrying water.

8. Q: What are the contents of the study and cultivation?

A: The contents of the study of Dhamma and the practice of

的三十七道品。三十七道品中基本修习的是四念处观(观身不净、观受是苦、观心无常、观法无我),在修四念处观之前,初入道者先学五停心观,即不净观、慈悲观、因缘观、界分别观和数息观。总之,修定修慧的方法很多,这里不一一列举了。

9. 问:佛教僧侣对在家佛徒有什么义务吗?

答:一般说来,在德行上为他们树立模范;教导他们,劝善止恶;为他们讲说佛法;安慰病苦,必要时得参加社会灾难的救济;慈悲柔和,促进众生的福利。

10. 问:照你所说出家风气在佛教中得到鼓励,那么,佛教的理想是不是要求人人都出家呢?

答:根据佛教教义和它的制度来说,出家应当是佛教徒中少数人的事。第一、出家的动机要求真纯——即确是为求解脱,决心舍弃世间贪爱而出家修道。第二、出家后要求对教理及行持都够标准,如果有室家的欲望,应当自动还俗;如果犯杀盗淫妄四根本戒,则应当摈斥在僧伽之

meditation (bhāvanā) are simply the 37 requisites for enlightenment (Bodhipakkhiya-dhamma). The basic practice among the 37 is the "Four Stations of Mindfulness" (cattāro satipaṭṭhānā) i.e. contemplation of the four views: the body is impure, feelings are suffering, mind and mind-objects are impermanent, every dhamma is without self. Prior to the practice of contemplation of the Four Stations of Mindfulness, the beginners should first learn the five systems of meditation, namely, contemplation of impurity (asubhā-bhāvanā), contemplation of mercy (mettā-bhāvanā), contemplation of cause and effect (nidāna-bhāvanā), contemplation of distinction (vibhaṇga-bhāvanā), and contemplation of breath (ānāpāna-sati). In sum, there are many ways to practice concentration and wisdom (samādhi and paññā) which need not be expanded upon here.

9. Q: Are Buddhist monks (or nuns) obligated to serve the lay Buddhists in any way?

A: Generally speaking, the Buddhist monks and nuns serve as models of moral virtue for the laity; advise them to do good and to avoid evil; preach Buddha Dhamma to them; console the sick and the poor and if necessary, participate in the relief work for people in calamities; be merciful and benevolent to promote the welfare of all beings.

10. Q: As you have said, the practice of renunciation was encouraged in Buddhist circles. Is it then the Buddhist ideal to call for everybody to do the same?

A: In terms of Buddhist doctrine and institutions, renunciation should be only for a minority of Buddhists. Firstly, their motives for renunciation and cultivation must be pure and genuine, seeking for deliverance and forsaking worldly craving (tanhā) with determination. Secondly, after renouncing the world, they are required to live up to the standard both in doctrines and in conduct. If they have the desire to get married, they should go back to laity voluntarily. Once they break the

外。第三、出家有许多限制，例如：要得父母允许，要年满二十（求比丘戒、比丘尼戒的），不是肢体不全或精神上有缺陷的，不是逃避刑法、债累的等等。第四、出家受戒要得戒龄满十年的僧侣十人以上介绍、证明和会议通过，舍戒还俗则很容易，只须告知一个人便行。佛教徒本有四众，有出家男女二众，有在家男女二众。出家二众负住持佛法的责任，在家二众负护持佛法的责任，合成为双重的教团，所以佛教并不是要求人人都出家。很多佛教经典，特别是大乘经典如《维摩诘经》、《优婆塞戒经》都是称赞在家学佛的。

11. 问：在家佛教徒修道的条件是怎样？

答：皈依三宝，确信佛法僧三宝为身心归向依靠之处，更不皈依佛教以外的其它宗教与神庙，这是在家佛教徒的必要条件。其次是奉行五戒和持斋。持斋是在每月一定的日子里实行一种克己的生活，即过午不食，不涂香装饰和歌舞观剧，不坐卧高广床座。持斋的日子一般是阴历朔日、初八、十四、望日、二十三、二十九（晦日）。遵守三归、

four fundamental rules (Pārājika) against murder of a human being or abetting a murder, theft, sexual intercourse and exaggeration of one's supernatural power, they should be ostracized from the Sangha Order. Thirdly, there are many restrictions for renunciation. The candidates, for instance, should have their parents' permission, should be over 20 years of age (for ordination of Bhikkhu and Bhikkhunī), should not be deformed or mentally deficient, should not be escaping criminal penalty or debt liabilities, etc. Fourthly, higher ordination (Upasampadā) must be recommended, certified and approved by a council of more than ten elder Bhikkhus (Theras), each with 10 years or more of Upasampadā. On the other hand, it is much easier to return to laity, one need only inform another monk or nun. The Buddhist community is composed of four groups: male and female monastic orders with the responsibility of maintaining the Buddha Dhamma, and male and female laity with the duty of protecting and bolstering the Buddha Dhamma. Together, they form a dual congregation. Therefore, Buddhism does not require everybody to renounce the lay life. Many of the Buddhist scriptures, particularly those of Mahāyāna, such as *Vimalakīrtinirdeśa* and *Upāsaka-sīla-sutta* are eulogies of laymen who undertake Buddhist practice at home.

11. Q: What are the prerequisites for the followers to practise Buddhism?

A: The prerequisites for lay followers are to take refuge in the Three Gems (Tiratana), being firmly convinced that the Three Gems, namely, Buddha, Dhamma and Sangha, are the only resort to turn to and rely on physically and mentally. Nor should they turn to other religions or gods as their refuge. Next, they should observe the Five Precepts(Pañca-sīla) and Eight Precepts of Uposatha. Uposatha means fasting or abstinence on certain days every month, that is, refraining from: eating after midday; using perfume and wearing adornments; singing, danc-

五戒和持斋，对人努力行善，对自己清净身心，这就是佛教在家信徒修持的标准。实际上有不及这个标准的，也有超过这个标准的。佛陀对在家信徒有许多世间法的教导，如对善生童子详细讲了父母子女之间、师弟之间、夫妇之间、朋友之间、主从之间、僧人与居士之间的关系如何善处的问题；对青年跋阇迦谈到方便具足（职业修养的完备），守护具足（节约不浪费财物），善知识具足（交结善友），正命具足（正当的生活）四种安乐法；对当时的国王们讲到如何处理国内政治与睦邻问题。大乘经典则广说在家菩萨应当怎样修六度、四摄等等。

12. 问：事实上出家不是像你前面所说的那样严格吧？

答：事实上在某些时期、某些地区，僧伽中存在着滥收徒众、滥传戒的现象。这种现象，在我国久已引起佛教界的忧虑。从历史的情况来看，佛教最兴盛的时代，并不是僧众最众多的时代；相反的，僧徒太多的时代，往往是佛教

ing and watching entertainment shows; and sitting or sleeping on high comfortable beds. The dates of fasting are generally set on the 1st, the 8th, the 14th, the 15th, the 23rd and the 29th of the lunar calendar. Taking refuge in the Three Gems (Tiratana), observing the Five Precepts (Pañca-sīla), practicing Uposatha, striving to do good for others and keeping one's own body and mind pure — all of these are the demands for self-cultivation for lay Buddhists. In reality, some fall below the above standards and some surpass them. Buddha taught a lot of worldly laws (loka-dhamma) to the lay followers. For instance, he explained in detail to Siṅgālaka (in Siṅgālovāda Sutta) how to properly deal with relations between parents and children, between mentor and disciple, between husband and wife, between friends, between master and servant and between Sangha and laity. He also talked to a young man Dīghajāṇu (or Ujjaya) about the four ways of seeking comfort and balance (Cattāro Dhammā), namely, Uṭṭhānasampadā (perfection of professional training), Ārakkhasampadā (protection of one's own property, frugality without waste), Kalyāṇamittatā (making worthy friends), and Samajīvitā (leading a decent life). He also talked to the kings (rājas) of his time about how to deal with problems of domestic politics and good-neighborly relations. The Mahāyāna codes, on the other hand, discourse generally on how lay Bodhisattas should practise the Six Perfections (cha-pāramitā), Four Embracing Dhamma (Cattāri saṃgaha vatthūni), and so forth.

12. Q: Admission to the Sangha Order actually is not always as strict as you described above, is it?

A: In fact, in certain periods and in certain regions, there has been excessive acceptance of disciples and indiscriminate ordination of Sangha. This has long caused apprehension in the Buddhist circles of China. History shows that the most flourishing periods of Buddhism have not been the times with the largest number of monks. On the contrary, periods with too many monks were usually times of decline of Buddhism. For instance,

衰坏的时代。如唐代初年曾大量淘汰僧众，玄奘法师时代出家很严格，要经过考试，当时玄奘为取得出家资格，还曾经过了困难的手续，但是佛教当时最为灿烂。这不仅我国如此，其他国家也是如此。例如，十五世纪缅甸有一位本来是高僧后来还俗做了国王的达磨悉提，他鉴于当时僧众之滥，曾经通令全国僧众重新受戒加入僧伽。由于他的严格整理，当时缅甸僧侣人数从数十万人减到一万多人，其余不够资格和不愿再度受戒的，均勒令还俗，缅甸佛教因此得到复兴。这件事说明僧伽是不应当盲目发展的。

13. 问：听说有些国家的人民，人人都要出一次家，是吗？

答：缅甸、泰国等都有这个风俗，我国傣族地区过去也是如此。这并不是佛教规定的制度。这些地方一般儿童到七八岁时候，父母便送他们到寺庙出家，在寺庙中识字学经，过僧团生活，过了一定时期可以还俗。出家时期最短的只有几天，有的几个月，有的几年。如果儿童时未出过家的，长大后总要有一个时期出一次家。这种临时出家的人并不受沙弥戒，与发愿长期出家的不同。

in the early Tang Dynasty a large number of monks were dismissed. At the time of Dhammācariya Xuanzang, the conditions for renunciation and ordination were very strict. Candidates were required to pass examinations. Even Xuanzang himself had to undergo difficult procedures to fulfill the qualifications to be a monk. Yet it was precisely at that time, Buddhism came into its most splendid era. The same was true not only in China, but also in other countries. In the 15th century, for instance, there was a high monk named Dhammasiddhi in Burma who later returned to lay society and became a king. In view of the excessive number of monks, he issued an edict ordering that all monks of the country should be reordained. Owing to his rigorous reformation, the number of Buddhist monks in Burma was reduced from a few hundred thousand to ten thousand or so. All the rest, unable or unwilling to meet the requisite qualifications for being reordained, were forced to leave the Sangha. Buddhism in Burma thus came to a renascence. This instance indicates that Sangha should not be developed unrealistically.

13. Q: It is said that in some countries, every one is obliged to experience monastic life once in his lifetime, is that true?

A: True, it is a custom prevailing in Burma, Thailand and some other countries. So it was formerly in the Dai-inhabited region in China. But it is not a regulation laid down by Buddhism. In these regions, children of seven or eight years of age are usually sent by their parents to temples where they learn to read Buddhist scriptures and lead a monastic life. After a certain period, they can return to the lay life. The duration of their stay in the temple varies from only a few days to a few months, or even a few years. One who has not undergone monasticism during childhood is required to do so for some period during adult life. Unlike the volunteers who determine to renounce the lay life for a long time, these temporary practitioners do not receive pabbajjā (junior ordination) as sāmaṇeras (novices).

14. 问:听说日本僧人都有家室,是吗?

答:原来日本僧人都是没有家室的。公元十二世纪时期,净土宗的一派——净土真宗的创始者亲鸾倡导带妻修行,开始娶妻生子。其后几百年中这个制度只限于这一宗派。到明治维新后,僧人结婚的风气便在其它各宗派中流行起来。现在除少数宗派的少数僧人仍然过独身生活外,绝大多数僧人都有家室。他们的子孙世袭僧人的职业。这便形成了以在家佛教徒担任弘传佛教事业的制度。但是这种情况只是属于男僧人,今天日本的尼众还是出家如律持戒的。

15. 问:出家男子为什么称为和尚?和尚是什么意思?

答:"和尚"原来是从梵文 Upādhyāya (P. Upajjhāya) 这个字出来的,这个字到了西域被读成"乌阇",到了汉地又读成"和尚",它的意思就是"师"。和尚本是一个尊称,要有一定资格堪为人师的才能够称和尚,不是任何人都能称的。这个称呼并不限于男子,出家女众有资格的也可以称和尚。但是后来习俗上这个字被用为对一般出家人的称呼,而且一般当作是男众专用的名词,这是和原来的字义不合的。

16. 问:喇嘛是什么意思?

答:喇嘛是藏语,它和"和尚"是一样的意思。这个字

14. Q: Is it true that Japanese monks may marry?

A: Originally, Japanese monks did not have wives and children. In 12th century, Shinran (亲鸾), the founder of Jodo Shinshū (the True Sect of Pure Land) – a branch of the Pure Land Sect, advocated that people could take up Buddhist practice along with their wives. This initiated a way of life among monks of getting married and having children. But for centuries, this custom was confined to this sect alone. After the Meiji Reformation (1868), the custom of marriage became popular among other sects of the day. Today with the exception of a few monks of minor sects, who keep celibacy, the overwhelming majority of monks get married, their Buddhist profession passing on to their offspring. Thus the institution of popularizing the Buddhist cause by lay Buddhists came into existence. However, this state of affairs applies to male priests only, while the nuns in Japan today continue to lead monastic life with abstinence as before.

15. Q: Why are the Buddhist monks termed "Heshang" in China? What does it mean?

A: The word "Heshang" was derived from the Sanskrit Upādhyāya, (P. Upajjhāya), meaning teacher or mentor. The word was pronounced as Pwājjhaw or Khosha in the regions to the West of China. From there to the Han-inhabited area it was changed into Heshang. Originally it was an honorable title only for those who were capable to be masters, and not to anybody else. This title at first had not been confined to Buddhist monks but might equally be applied to qualified Buddhist nuns. Later on, this word came to be used to address any male who is leading a monastic life. It is not in conformity to the original meaning.

16. Q: What is the meaning of "Lama"?

A: "Lama" is a Tibetan word, with the same meaning as "Heshang". This word was misused too since it, in its original

也被滥用了，本来并不是每个出家人都能称为喇嘛的。正确的称呼是：出家的男人受十戒的称沙弥，受具足戒的称比丘；出家的女人受十戒的称沙弥尼，受具足戒的称比丘尼。

17. 问：汉族地区习惯地称出家的男子为“僧”，出家女子为“尼”，这是否是正确的称呼？

答：僧是僧伽的简称，它的字义就是“大众”。僧伽是出家佛教徒的团体，至少要有四个人以上才能组成僧伽。所以一个人不能称僧伽，只能称僧人，正如一个兵士不能称军，只能称军人一样。出家男女二众都在僧伽之内，都能称僧人。把“僧”和“尼”作为男女的区别，是错误的。至于“尼”字是从沙弥尼、比丘尼的字尾而来的，是汉族对出家女众的简称。还有在尼字下加上姑字的，则是习俗的称呼。

18. 问：什么叫做法师？

答：法师(Dhammācariya)本是一种学位的称号，要通达佛法能为人讲说的人才能称法师，不是任何人都可以称的。还有较高的学位，精通经藏的称为经师(Suttācariya)，精通律藏的称为律师(Vinayācariya)，精通论藏的称为论师(Abhidhammācariya)。更高的是三藏法师(Tipiṭakācariya)，是遍通经律论三藏者的学位，如唐代玄奘、义净都受到这个称号。

sense, was not applicable to everyone leading a monastic life. Properly speaking, the title for those who have received ten precepts (pabbajjā) is Sāmaṇera, while for those who have been given the higher ordination (upasampadā) it is Bhikkhu; in the same way, the title for female acceptors of ten precepts is Sāmaṇerī and for the female acceptors of the higher ordination it is Bhikkhunī.

17. Q: In the Han regions, monks are usually called "Seng", and nuns "Ni". Are they correct titles?

A: "Seng" is an abbreviated form of Sangha meaning community. Sangha is a congregation of Buddhist monks and nuns, with at least four members. So an individual can not be entitled Sangha but only a Sangha member, just as a single soldier can not form an army, but only be a military man. Both monks and nuns are included in the Sangha, they are Sangha members. It is a mistake to distinguish between monks and nuns in terms of "Seng" and "Ni". As to the term Ni (nun), it derived from the suffix of Bhikkhunī, being an abbreviation for the Buddhist nuns by the Han people of China. Another common term for them is "Ni-gu".

18. Q: What is a Dhammācariya?

A: Dhammācariya was originally the title of an academic degree, conferred on those with a comprehensive knowledge of Buddha Dhamma and capable of preaching it. It should not be applied to any one else. There are other high degrees: Suttācariya for those who have mastered Suttapiṭaka, Vinayācariya for those with mastery of Vinayapiṭaka, and Abhidhammācariya for those with a thorough knowledge of Abhidhammapiṭaka. Even higher is the Tipiṭakācariya – the title for those with a comprehensive mastery of the knowledge of all the three piṭakas (Tipiṭaka). Xuanzang and Yijing in Tang Dynasty were both awarded the title.

19. 问:什么叫活佛?

答:蒙藏佛教对修行有成就,能够根据自己的意愿而转世的人称为"朱毕古"(藏语)或"呼毕勒罕"(蒙语)。这个字的意义就是"转世者"或"化身"。"活佛"乃是汉族地区的人对他们习俗的称呼,这可能与明朝皇帝封当时西藏地方掌政的噶举派法王为"西天大善自在佛"和清朝皇帝给达赖的封号也沿用了这一头衔多少有些关系,这种封号和称号在佛教教义上都是说不通的,其实蒙藏佛教中并没有"活佛"这个名词。又傣族佛教比丘被称为"佛爷",这也是汉人习俗上错叫出来的,他们自己并没有这种称呼。

20. 问:什么叫做僧王?

答:有些国家如泰国等,全国选出一位僧伽的领袖叫做僧王(Sangha-rāja)。在斯里兰卡则每一僧派选出一位"大导师"(Mahā-nāyaka),每一省或一市选出一位导师(Nāyaka)。僧王或大导师管理全国的僧务,导师管理地方的僧务。

21. 问:为什么出家佛教徒要有僧伽这样的教团?

答:对个人来说,为了在学修上和生活上互相切磋、互相帮助,出家人必须过僧伽的团体生活。对整个佛教来说,要有出家佛教徒组织的教团来担负起"住持佛法"的责

19. Q: What is a Living Buddha?

A: In Mongolian and Tibetan Buddhism, those who achieve exceptional cultivation and are able to reincarnate (get rebirth) according to their own will are called "ḥpbrulsku" (Tibetan) or "Hobilghan" (Mongolian) meaning reincarnater or incarnation. In the Han-inhabited regions, however, they are commonly called living Buddhas. The title probably has something to do with the fact that Emperors of the Ming Dynasty conferred the title of "Western Buddha of Great Goodness and Freedom" on Dhammarāja (religious leader) of the Bkah-brgyud-pa Sect who was the ruler of Tibet at that time, and that the same title was conferred on the Dalais by the Emperors of the Qing Dynasty. In fact such titles do not make sense according to Buddhist doctrine. Besides, there is no such term as Living Buddha in Tibetan and Mongolian Buddhism. Similarly, the Buddhist Bhikkhus of Dai nationality are called by Han people "Foye" (Buddha). This is a misnomer and is not used by the people of Dai nationality themselves.

20. Q: What is Sangha-rāja?

A: In certain countries such as Thailand and others, The Sangha leader elected by the nation is called King of Sangha (Sangha-rāja). In Sri Lanka, a Mahānāyaka is elected from each Buddhist sect, and a Nāyaka from each province or municipality. The Sangha-rājas or Mahā-nāyakas administer national Buddhist affairs, while the Nāyakas administer local Buddhist affairs.

21. Q: Why is it necessary for monastic Buddhists to have congregations of Sangha?

A: For an individual monk or nun, it is necessary to lead a collective life in the Sangha in order to learn from and help each other. Buddhism, as a whole also, needs congregations to undertake the responsibility of "maintaining the Buddha Dhamma". The Sangha has been playing such an important role in the

任。僧伽所以被称为三宝之一，就是因为它在佛教事业中的重要性。

22. 问：僧伽的组织有没有什么原则和制度？

答：有六项原则，就是“六和”：戒和、见和、利和、身和、口和、意和。简单地解释一下：和就是和谐一致的意思，遵守共同的戒律（戒和），见解一致的共同修学（见和），平等受用合法的财物（利和），生活上互相照顾（身和），言语上互相劝善止过（口和），思想上彼此友爱敬重（意和），通过这六项来达到僧伽中的和谐一致。为了实现六和的原则，佛陀曾经为僧伽制定了许多制度。

23. 问：有哪些重要的制度？

答：最重要的是“羯磨”(Kamma)制度。羯磨本是办事的意思，但僧伽中办事的方法是通过会议，所以它的完整的意思就是“会议办事”。比方有什么事情要办，要一定地界内全体僧众集会讨论决定，因事因病不能参加的人必须委托别人代为请假，并表示愿意接受大众的决定。会议开始前，执行主席（羯磨师）询问僧众是否已经齐集，是否有未受戒的人在场，知道僧众已经到齐，外人已经出场后，然后开会。首先报告开会目的，提出议案，大众讨论，做出决定。表决的方式，一般是口头问答，征求同意，同意的不说话，不同意的表示意见，如果大家都不说话，便是通过。有一种事经过这样一次征问，便作决定；有一种较重要的事

Buddhist cause that it is called one of the Three Gems (Tiratana).

22. Q: Are there any principles and systems in the organization of the Sangha?

A: There are six principles known as "the six points of harmony (or unity)", i. e., harmony or unity among disciplines, harmony of views, of interests, in bodily actions, in speech and in mind. To explain briefly, the six points mean: (the Sangha as a whole is) to observe identical commandments, to hold same views when studying side by side, to share equally in the community's goods, to help each other in daily life, to mutually advise to do good and to avoid mistakes, to fraternally love and respect each other in matters of faith. Through these six, the harmony and unity of the whole Sangha can be reached. In order to carry out the above six principles, Buddha devised a number of rules or regulations for the Sangha.

23. Q: What are some important rules?

A: The most important is the Vinaya rules of Kamma. Kamma originally meant action. Since among Sangha, everything is settled through Sangha meetings, so its complete meaning is "action (or settlement of things) through Sangha assembly". For example, if there is something to be done, all the monks in a certain area should gather together to discuss and make a decision. Those who are unable to attend the meeting due to illness or other engagements have to send word through others to ask to be excused and signify willingness to accept the decision of the meeting. Prior to the meeting, presiding chairman (master of Kamma) inquires if all monks have come and if any novice or non-ordained (who are not supposed to attend the meeting) are present. The meeting can not be opened until all the monks are present and outsiders excluded. Then the opening address is made and purpose and proposals of the meeting are tabled for the participants to discuss and decisions are finally made by vot-

要经过两次征问，才作决定；有一种更重要的事（如授戒，或给某人以处分）要经过三次征问，才作决定。最后执行主席说："僧人默然故，是事如是持"（既然大众都没有意见发表，这件事就是这样办了）。另外还有一种表决方式，就是投筹（用颜色的竹筹表示可否，等于投票）。关于这些，佛教典籍中有详细规定。这是世界上最古老的会议法，可以说是佛教的一个重要的创造和贡献。

24. 问：僧伽中有没有定期的会议？

答：每半个月举行一次布萨羯磨（诵戒的集会）。僧众齐集念诵戒本，根据戒律，检查每个人半月中的生活。方式是自己发露（坦白说出过失），别人举过。每年雨季安居期满后，举行集会。这个集会名叫"自恣"，"自"的意思是自己发露，"恣"的意思是恣别人举出自己的罪过，从而忏悔，这仍然是检查生活的集会。至于商办事情是临时召集会议。

25. 问：可不可以说释迦牟尼在僧伽组织中采用了某些原始公社的制度？

答：从它的民主制度和财务分配制度（平均分配、个人不蓄私财）来看，可以这样设想。但是在原始僧伽中，比丘

ing. Voting is generally by oral consent. Those in agreement would remain silent, while those in dissent would speak out their opinions. If all remain silent, the proposal is passed. On some matters, decisions are made by going through the procedure just once. For more important issues, the procedure must be repeated twice for a decision to be made. As to even more important issues (such as ordination or punishment), the procedure must be gone through three times for a decision to be made. Finally the presiding chairman says: "Inasmuch as all monks remain silent, the resolution is passed." Another way of voting is to cast chips (using differently colored bamboo chips to signify for or against, equal to casting ballots). Some Buddhist Canons, with full descriptions of these regulations, are the oldest laws on conference in the world, and are an important creation and contribution of Buddhism.

24. Q: Are there regular meetings of the Sangha?

A: A recitation assembly (Uposatha Kamma) is held every half-month. The monks assemble to recite the text of precepts (Pātimokkha), and to examine, according to Vinaya, everyone's conducts in the past fortnight. The procedure is through confession and exposure by others. At the end of the annual rainy season retreat a ceremony known as Pavārana is held. Pavārana means satisfaction with self-criticism and other's exposure. By this means, each expresses repentance for his own faults. It is, in fact, also a meeting for reviewing the monastic life. As to consultation on other matters, meetings are called whenever necessary.

25. Q: Is it correct to say that Sākyamuni adopted certain institutional aspects of the primitive commune into the Sangha community?

A: It is a tenable position given its democratic system and the system of financial distribution (equally sharing community property without personal possession). During the early days of

是不事生产的。我国汉族僧人有从事农耕的习惯，提倡农禅生活，这是我国僧伽一个优良的特点。

26. 问：羯磨制度，现在还实行吗？

答：布萨和自恣的制度在南方佛教国家中仍然实行，其他宗教性的如传戒羯磨也仍然实行，但是似乎大部分是作为宗教仪式保存着。今天我国也还有寺庙保存着布萨和自恣制度的，至于羯磨的民主精神，由于在长期封建社会中许多封建制度被引用到佛寺中来，特别是由于丛林清规被封建朝廷按照自己的意图加以修改推行，因而久已失去了本来面目。

27. 问：什么叫做丛林清规？

答：丛林就是大寺庙。僧众集合在一处，好像树木丛集成为森林一样，所以叫做丛林。清规就是丛林的僧众日常遵行的规制。这种规制是依据佛所定的戒律结合当时当地的实际情况，包括天时、地理、社会风习、国家法令以及宗派特点等等而定的。中国最古的清规创自四世纪东晋时代的道安，后来各代各派都定有僧制。唐代百丈禅师创立禅宗僧众的清规，久已失传。后来元代皇帝《敕修百丈清规》，那是根据封建统治者的需要而假托百丈之名修出来的东西，与百丈并无关系。后来这个清规经过明洪武、永乐先后下旨推行，于是代替了原来的各种僧制和清规而成为全国僧众遵行的规制。

the Sangha, Bhikkhus were not engaged in production. However, in Han-regions of China monks are used to being engaged in farm work, and advocate a combination of farm work with Buddhist practice. This is an excellent feature of the Chinese Sangha.

26. Q: Is the kamma system still in operation now?

A: Both Uposatha and Pavārana systems are still in practice in the southern Buddhist nations. So are other kammic ceremonies, such as the Ordination Kamma. Yet it seems that, for the most part, they are preserved as religious rites. Today in China, there are also some temples which still maintain the systems of Uposatha and Pavārana. But the democratic spirit of the kamma has long been lost owing to the fact that a number of feudalistic systems were introduced into the monasteries during the long period of feudalism, particularly owing to the fact that the monastery rules (Conglin Qinggui) were revised and enforced by the feudal court in accordance with their needs.

27. Q: What is the meaning of "Conglin Qinggui"?

A: The original meaning of "Conglin" is grove or forest. A thickly populated monastery is just like a forest with plenty of trees, so it is called "conglin", meaning great monastery (Mahāvihāra). "Qinggui" means the rules or regulations daily observed by the monks or nuns in monasteries, which are laid down according to the Vinaya enacted by the Buddha and adapted to prevailing conditions, including climate, geography, social customs, laws and regulations of the state, as well as sectarian characteristics, etc. The earliest monastery rules in China were initiated by Dao'an of the Eastern Jin Dynasty in the fourth century. After that each sect in subsequent dynasties created its own monastery institutions. For example, in the Tang Dynasty a set of codes for monks of the Zen School was created by Master Baizhang. It subsequently was lost. Later on, a "Royal Revised Baizhang Code" was created by an Emperor of the

28. 问:关于僧众的礼节和生活习惯,可否请你谈一谈?

答:戒律中对于这些都有详细的规定,这许多规定南方国家的僧众保持得比较完整。北方佛教僧侣,由于气候、风土等等的差别以及历史的变迁,生活上有了许多改变,这里不能详细列举。请你提出所需要了解的问题,我们可以简单地谈一谈。

29. 问:关于礼节问题,僧众中长幼之间的礼节怎样?

答:僧众的长幼是依受戒的年龄分别的。受比丘戒十年以上的称上座或长老(Thera),二十年以上的称大上座或大长老(Mahā Thera)。戒龄小的应当礼拜戒龄高的。行路时长者先行,幼者后行;坐时长者坐上座,幼者坐下座,或长者不教坐不坐。所以南方国家僧人相见,必须问戒龄。一般比丘见大长老,必须脱鞋,偏袒右肩,然后礼拜。

30. 问:在家佛教徒对僧人的礼节如何?

Yuan Dynasty. This was actually in conformity with the need of feudal rulers, and had nothing to do with Baizhang himself. Subsequently this code was enforced by imperial orders through Hongwu and Yongle eras of the Ming Dynasty, and became a universal system observed by all monks and nuns throughout China, in place of all sorts of original monastic regulations and codes.

28. Q: Would you please give some account of the etiquette and life style of a monastic community?

A: These were stipulated in detail in the Vinaya text. Many stipulations have been preserved intact by Buddhist communities in southern countries, while in northern countries, owing to climatic, conventional and other differences as well as historical transitions, the monastic life has undergone a lot of changes. Details are not easy to list here. If you have specific questions, we can talk about them briefly.

29. Q: What is the etiquette between senior and junior monks?

A: In the monastic community, senior or junior does not refer to older or younger in age, but the number of years since ordination. The title "Thera" (Elder) is conferred on Bhikkhus 10 years after ordination, and "Mahā Thera" 20 years after ordination. Juniors should salute seniors. Seniors precede juniors while walking along. As to sitting, the upper seats are given to the seniors and the lower seats to the juniors, and juniors should not sit unless asked to sit by seniors. So in southern Buddhist countries, the inquiries about ordination time are necessary for monks when they meet each other. Normally when ordinary bhikkhus meet a Mahā Thera, they are required to take off their shoes, and expose their right shoulders, and then make salutation.

30. Q: What is the etiquette of lay Buddhists towards monks and nuns?

A: In southern countries, when a lay Buddhist enters a mon-

答：南方国家，在家佛教徒进入佛寺僧房，首先要脱鞋，见比丘礼拜。比丘教坐时，坐低座或席地坐，不能坐比丘的床位，不能和比丘同桌吃饭。如果比丘到居士家，主人应当以干净的布铺在座椅上，请比丘坐下，然后礼拜。如果自己的儿子当比丘，父母也要礼拜。根据南方佛教习惯，在任何场合，比丘见到居士来访问或入会场，他们从不起立，居士向他们礼拜时，也不回礼，有时仅说一句："愿你吉祥。"向他们送供品时，也是如此。小比丘和沙弥礼拜大比丘时，大比丘也不答礼。在我国比丘受居士或小比丘、沙弥礼拜时，可合掌答礼，座位高下除正式宗教仪式外不甚严格。

31. 问：请你谈一谈关于饮食问题，如过午不食问题，吃素吃荤问题。

答：按照佛制，比丘午后不吃食物。原因有两个：1、比丘的饭食是由居士供养，每天只托一次钵，日中时吃一顿，可以减少居士的负担；2、过午不食，有助于修定。这个制度，今天南方国家仍普遍实行。最严格的只喝白水，连牛奶、茶、椰子水都不喝。但一般的僧人午后可以喝茶、汽水、果汁，也可以吃糖。我国汉族禅宗僧人从古有自己耕种的习惯，由于劳动的缘故，晚上非吃东西不行。所以在多数寺庙中开了过午不食的戒，但是被视为"药食"，持过午不食戒的僧人为数也仍不少。

astery or a monk's room he should take off his shoes before worshipping bhikkhus. At the bhikkhu's request to sit down, he should take a lower seat or sit on the ground, and he must not sit on the bhikkhu's bed. He should not eat together with bhikkhus at the same table. If a bhikkhu comes to a layman's home, the host should place a piece of clean cloth over the chair, and invite the former to sit down before salutation. Even if a son becomes a bhikkhu, his own parents should likewise salute him. According to the Southern Buddhist customs, whatever the occasion, when a lay Buddhist comes to visit or enters the meeting hall, the bhikkhus never stand up, nor do they return the greetings, or sometimes merely say "good luck". When offerings are given to them, they do the same. Likewise, senior bhikkhus do not return the greetings from junior bhikkhus and sāmaṇeras. In China, bhikkhus may return the greetings from lay Buddhists or junior bhikkhus and sāmaṇeras by bringing their palms together in courtesy, and ranking of seats is not strictly observed, except during formal religious ceremonies.

31. Q: Would you please say something about dietary habits, such as abstaining from taking food after midday, vegetarianism and so on?

A: There are two reasons for monastic Buddhists not to eat after midday according to Buddhist regulations, they are: 1. Abstaining from taking food afternoon reduces the burden on the laity since they provide the food; 2. It is conducive to practicing contemplation (bhāvanā). In Southern countries, this institution is still in common practice today. The strictest adherents only drink water, without taking milk, tea, coconut juice or anything else, while others may drink tea, soda water or fruit juice, as well as take candies after midday. In China, the Han monks of Zen sect have been used to doing farm work since ancient times, and due to their physical work, they have to eat something in the evening. So in most monasteries, this regulation is relaxed, but supper is regarded as part of a "medicinal diet". Even so, many monks continue to observe the rule of

32. 问:戒条是可以开的吗?

答:比丘戒中除了不杀不盗不淫不妄四根本戒外,其余戒条平时应当"遮护",在一定的情况下可以"开"(菩萨戒,一切服从"饶益有情戒",在家菩萨为饶益有情故,四根本戒也可以开)。"开"与"遮"是戒律上的术语。如以过午不食为例,平时应当遮,但遇有某种疾病,必须午后进食的人则可以开。我国僧人因劳动的缘故必须开过午不食的戒。禅宗寺庙把吃晚饭叫做房餐,本来是给参加劳动者在房里吃的,而不是在斋堂中大家吃的,但是后来不劳动的人也吃起晚饭来了。

33. 问:南方国家的僧人吃"荤",是否也是开戒?

答:南方国家僧人的饭食,或是到别人家托钵乞食,或是由附近人家轮流送饭,所以他们有什么吃什么,不论素食或肉食。比丘戒律中并没有不许吃肉的规定。我国大乘经典中有反对食肉的条文,我国汉族僧人是信奉大乘佛教的,他们受比丘戒外,并且受菩萨戒,所以汉族僧人乃至很多居士都不吃肉。从历史来看,汉族佛教吃素的风习,是由梁武帝的提倡而普遍起来的。蒙藏族僧人虽然也信奉大乘,但是他们的地方蔬菜极少,不食肉不能生活,所以

abstention from eating after midday.

32. Q: Can the rules (sīla) ever be broken?

A: Among the precepts in Pātimokkha, apart from the four fundamentals of no killing, no stealing, no sexual conduct and no lying on spiritual attainment, all the rest should be maintained in general, but can be relaxed under certain circumstances. According to the Boddhisatta Rules, all must serve the needs of benefiting sentient beings (Sattvārtha-kriyā sīla). Thus for lay-Boddhisattas, even the Four Fundamentals may be relaxed as required for benefiting sentient beings. "Maintain" and "relax" are the terminology used in Vinaya text. For instance, abstention from eating after midday must be observed in normal times, yet in case of illness, it can be broken if the afflicted need to take food after midday. The Chinese monks have to relax the precept of not eating after midday because they take part in farm work. In the temples of Zen Sect, supper is called "chamber meal", since it was originally provided to the laborers in their rooms instead of in the dining hall. However, in later times, those who did not take part in labor also began to have supper.

33. Q: The monks of southern countries eat meat. Do they break the Vinaya rules?

A: The food of monks in southern countries is obtained by begging from door to door with alms bowls or provided by nearby families in turn, so they eat whatever is offered to them, regardless whether it is vegetarian. In the Bhikkhu's Vinaya, there is no rule prohibiting meat-eating. While in Chinese Mahāyāna scriptures there are clauses against meat-eating. The Chinese Han monastics, keeping faith in Mahāyāna Buddhism, accept not only Bhikkhu's precepts but also Boddhisatta sīlas, so Han monks, nuns and even many lay followers abstain from eating meat. Historically, the custom of vegetarianism among the Han Buddhists became popular with the advocacy of Emperor Wu of Liang (North and South Dynasty). As for the Mongolian

一般都吃肉。但他们和南方国家佛教徒一样,对汉族佛教吃素的习惯,都是很赞叹的。至于“吃荤”的“荤”字,是专指大蒜、葱这些气味浓烈、富于刺激的东西,是大小乘戒律所同遮禁,南北佛教徒所共同遵守的。我们把“吃荤”和“吃肉”混同起来说,那是错误的。

34. 问:听说南方国家居士们供饭,必须将盘碗送到比丘手上,不这样,比丘就不能吃,是吗?

答:是的。因为比丘要守“不与不取戒”(即不偷盗戒),不仅是饭菜,供养任何东西都是这样,不交到他们手上,他们便不能取。

35. 问:听说还有比丘手不捉持银钱的,是吗?

答:是的。比丘戒中本有这一条,这是为了防止蓄私财,起贪念。现在还有人遵行。南方比丘旅行时须带俗人随从替他管银钱的事。但是为了种种不便,这个戒条在南方国家中现在也不太严格了。

36. 问:请谈一谈僧人的衣服问题。

答:根据佛教的制度,比丘衣服有大中小三件:一是用

and Tibetan Buddhists, though they follow Mahāyāna Buddhism, they can't live without eating meat since there is a great shortage of vegetables in their regions. Nevertheless, all the Buddhists in southern countries as well as in Mongolia and Tibet highly praise the habit of vegetarianism of Han Buddhists. As to the Chinese word "hun", it refers to things with strong and pungent smells like garlic and onion. They are proscribed by both Mahāyāna and Theravāda Vinayas, which is observed by both Southern and Northern Buddhists in common. It is a mistake to confuse the term "hun" with simply eating meat.

34. Q: It is said that in southern countries, when the dāyakas (lay-Buddhists) offer food to the monks they have to put the bowls into the hand of the latter, otherwise the monks can't take it. Is it true?

A: Yes. Because the monks should observe the rule of "abstaining from taking what is not given" (i.e. the rule against stealing). Not only in the case of alms-giving, whatever is offered by laity must be put into the hands of monks, or they can't take it.

35. Q: It is also said that some monks never touch or hold money with their hands. Is that true?

A: Yes. There is indeed such a clause among the precepts for monks, which is to prevent them from keeping private property and giving rise to greed. Today it is still observed by some monks. In southern countries when such monks travel, they are accompanied by a lay follower who can handle money for them. Owing to certain inconveniences, however, this rule is not very strictly observed today even in the southern countries.

36. Q: Could you please say something about the clothing of monks?

A: According to the Buddhist rules, monks should possess three robes: a large, a medium and a small. The small one,

五条布缝成的小衣，我国俗称为五衣，是打扫劳作时穿的；一是七条布缝成的中衣，我国俗称七衣，是平时穿的；一是九条乃至二十五条布缝成的大衣，我国俗称祖衣，是礼服，出门或见尊长时穿的。三衣总称为袈裟(Kasāya)。袈裟本是一种颜色的名称，因为佛制僧人必须穿染衣，避用青黄赤白黑五正色，而用一种杂色，即袈裟色。我国旧译袈裟色是赤色，南方佛教典籍则说是一种橙黄色，可能是一种赤黄混合色。根据我国佛典记载，佛教在印度分了部派后，各部派衣色便有了区别，有的是赤色，有的是黄色，有的是青黑木兰色。但据六世纪印度来华高僧真谛法师说，各部派衣色实际都是赤色，所谓青黑木兰，仅是些微的差别。现在缅甸、斯里兰卡、泰国、柬埔寨、老挝、印度、尼泊尔诸国的僧服都是黄色，仅有深浅的不同。我国汉族僧人的袈裟，祖衣是赤色，五衣七衣一般都是黄色。蒙藏僧人的袈裟，大衣是黄色，平时所披的中衣近赤色。北方气候寒冷，僧众三衣不够，所以我国僧众在袈裟里面另穿一种常服，这种常服是就古代俗人的服装略加改变的。常服的颜色，明代皇帝曾作过规定，修禅僧人常服为茶褐色，讲经僧人蓝色，律宗僧人黑色。清代以后，没有什么官方规定，但律宗寺院自清初见月律师重兴后，一般僧人常服均为黄色。缅甸佛教徒特别忌穿黑衣，因为在缅甸古代曾有一种邪教僧人穿黑衣，多行非法之事，后来严行禁绝。蒙藏教徒也忌穿黑色衣服。

made of five strips of cloth, known as Five-strip robe in China, is for doing manual and cleaning work. The medium one, made of seven pieces of cloth, commonly called seven-strip robe in China, is the normal form of dress. The large one, usually made of nine to twenty five strips of cloth, commonly called "ancestral robe" in China, is the ceremonial dress for traveling or visiting elders. The three suits are collectively called *jiasha* (kasāya). Kasāya originally was the name of a tincture used to die robes, because the Buddhist monks had to dress in dyed robes of mixed color, or Kasāya color, to avoid five pure colors of indigo, yellow, red, white and black. The kasāya color, which was said to be reddish in ancient Chinese translations, and saffron in the southern Buddhist canons, is presumably a mixed color of red and yellow. The Chinese Buddhist scriptures record that, with the division of Buddhist sects in India, the colors of robes of different sects varied from each other, some being red, some yellow, and some indigo. However, according to the Buddhist master, Ven. Paramattha, who came to China in the sixth century from India, the robe colors of different sects were basically red with minute differences. Today in Burma, Sri Lanka, Thailand, Kampuchea, Laos, India and Nepal the robes of monks are all yellow in color, with slightly different shades. As to the robes worn by the Han monastics in China, the ceremonial robe is red, the five-strip and seven strip robes are generally yellow. Of the Mongolian and Tibetan ones, the large robe is yellow and the medium, worn at ordinary times, is close to red. Because of the cold climate in the north, the three robes are not warm enough, so monks in China wear an additional suit underneath the kasāya called common garb, which is simply ancient Chinese layman's clothing with a slight variation. The color of common garb was stipulated by an Emperor of the Ming Dynasty, that is, for monks who were practicing meditation, it should be teabrown ; for the Dhamma - preaching monks , it should be blue, and for the monks of Vinaya Sect, it should be black. After the Qing Dynasty, there were no official regulations.

37. 问：请谈一谈关于僧人剃发的问题。

答：根据佛制，剃发、染衣、受戒是取得僧人资格的必要条件。剃发染衣的用意是为了舍弃美好装饰，实行朴素无华的生活。一般出家人也不留胡须，但我国有一部分僧人留须，他们认为出家时应剃须，此后可以留。南方国家的僧人则一律不留须。至于受戒并不需要在头顶上烧戒疤。除汉族外，其他民族僧人都没有烧戒疤的规矩。这可能与《梵网经菩萨戒本》燃身供养之说有关。唐朝已有炼顶（以艾燃顶）的习俗，这个习俗形成普遍的制度，据说是在元代。当时异族统治者想借以识别真假，防止抗拒法令的人民逃到僧众里面去。这话尚待查考。

38. 问：关于僧人生活习惯的问题，已经知道了一些了。现在想请你谈一谈佛陀时代僧伽中一些主要的人物。请问释迦牟尼的弟子中最著名的有哪些人？

答：有十大弟子：舍利弗（Sāriputta），目犍连（Moggal-

Yet, with the restoration of the temples of Vinaya School in early Qing Dynasty by Vinaya master, Ven. Jianyue, the common garb of the rank and file monks of this sect were yellow. Burmese monks particularly avoid wearing black since a group of heretic monastics in ancient Burma who dressed in black committed many crimes, were later strictly banned. Mongolian and Tibetan monks also avoid black clothes.

37. Q: What about the practice of tonsure for Buddhist monks?

A: According to Buddhist regulations, a shaved head, dyed garments, and ordination are the prerequisites for gaining the monkhood. The purpose of the tonsure and dyeing of garments is to signify giving up beautification and leading a frugal and austere life. The monks generally do not wear beards, excepting some monks in China who shave their beards upon ordination, but believe that beards can be kept afterwards. No monks in southern countries grow beards. Regarding burning dot-scars on the top of head at the time of ordination, the monastics of other nationalities do not have such regulations, it is only the Han monks who do. This tradition may be related with *Brahmajāla Sutta—Bodhisatta Sīla* which mentions burning one's own body (or parts of body) in dedication to the Buddha. In the Tang Dynasty there was already a custom of scarring the top of the head with moxa cone. This was said to have become common practice during the Yuan Dynasty, when the alien rulers tried to distinguish the false monastics from the genuine ones in an attempt to prevent the law-breaking people from fleeing into the Sangha. This explanation remains to be verified.

38. Q: Now that you have told us about the monastic lifestyle, could you please tell us about some of the chief figures in the Sangha at the time of Buddha? Who were the most distinguished disciples of Sākyamuni?

A: There were ten distinguished disciples: Sāriputta, Moggallāna, Mahākassapa, Subhūti, Purāṇa, Mahā kaccāna, Anu-

lāna)、摩诃迦叶(Mahākassapa)、须菩提(Subhūti)、富楼那(Purāṇa)、摩诃迦旃延(Mahākaccāna)、阿那律(Anuruddha)、优波离(Upāli)、罗怙罗(Rāhula)和阿难陀(Ānanda)。这十大弟子各有特长,其中如舍利弗被称为智慧第一,目犍连神通第一,优波离持戒第一,阿难陀多闻第一。舍利弗、目犍连二人最为佛所器重,是僧众的上首,他们都在佛涅槃前逝世。佛涅槃后,代佛统率大众的是摩诃迦叶,其后是阿难陀。

39. 问:一般佛寺中,立在释迦牟尼像两旁有两位比丘像,他们是谁?

答:有一老一少的像,老的摩诃迦叶,少的是阿难陀。也有两比丘像是年龄相若的,则是舍利弗和目犍连。这种像只是我国汉族佛寺中有的,南方国家的佛寺一般只供释迦牟尼佛像,供弟子像的很少。

40. 问:佛的弟子中有什么遗迹留存吗?

答:1851年英国人孔宁汉(当时的印度考古局长)在印度孟买东北五百四十九英里一个名叫山奇(Sanchi)的地方,对那里的几座古塔进行发掘。在一座塔里面,掘得两个大石函,函盖上分别刻着舍利弗和目犍连的名字,里面藏着他们两位的灵骨。这两份灵骨被英国人劫走,存置在伦敦维多利亚爱尔保博物馆。印度独立后,才向英国交涉取回,现仍供在山奇。山奇这个地方过去不甚知名,但是近代发现很丰富的佛教文物。公元前三世纪阿育王所造

ruddha, Upāli, Rāhula and Ānanda. Each of them had a special distinction. For example, Sāriputta was known as the chief in wisdom; Moggallāna, the chief in psychic power (abhiññā); Upāli, the first in observing vinaya rules, and Ānanda, the chief of learning (bahu-ssuta). Sāriputta and Moggallāna, the two foremost disciples in the Sangha, were most highly regarded by the Buddha. They died before the Buddha's passing away. After Buddha's Parinibbāna, it was Mahākassapa who acted as the leader of the Sangha, and then Ānanda.

39. Q: There generally are two images standing at each side of the Buddha's statue in the Buddhist monasteries. Who are they?

A: If the images are one old and one young, the old is Mahākassapa, and the young Ānanda. If they look about the same age, one is Sāriputta and the other Moggallāna. However, these images exist only in Han Buddhist temples, while in temples of southern tradition, Buddha's image is enshrined alone, unaccompanied by disciples.

40. Q: Are there any relics of the Buddha's disciples remaining today?

A: Sir Alexander Cunningham, an Englishman, (Director of the Indian Archeological Bureau) excavated several ancient thūpas in 1851 at a locality named Sanchi, 549 miles northeast from Bombay, India. In one of the thūpas, they found two large stone caskets with the names of Sāriputta and Moggallāna engraved respectively on the covers and their divine skeletons inside. The skeletons were stolen by the British and preserved in the Victoria and Albert Museum in London. After the independence of India, through negotiations with Britain, they were returned and once again enshrined at Sanchi. In Sanchi, not a well-known place then, a wealth of Buddhist relics have been

的大塔仍然完整的存在，据说是他所造的八万四千塔中唯一留存的一座。塔的四面各有雕刻的石门，极为精美。由于许多宝贵的古迹，特别是由于两位大阿罗汉舍利的发现，山奇现在已经成为印度重要的佛教圣地之一。

41. 问：汉族佛寺中常见到十八罗汉像，那是什么人？

答：应当是十六罗汉（罗汉即阿罗汉的简称，又称十六尊者）。据经典说，有十六位佛的弟子受了佛的付嘱，不入涅槃。公元二世纪时师子国（今斯里兰卡）庆友尊者作的《法住记》中，更记载了十六阿罗汉的名字和他们所住的地区。这部书由玄奘法师译出之后，十六罗汉便普遍受到我国佛教徒的尊敬。到五代时，绘图雕刻日益普遍起来。后来画家画成了十八罗汉。推测画家原意可能是把《法住记》的作者庆友和译者玄奘也画在一起。但后人标出罗汉名字时，误将庆友列为第十七位住世罗汉，又重复了第一位阿罗汉的名字成为第十八位。虽然宋代已经有人指出了错误，但因为绘画题赞的人有的是名书画家和文学家，如贯休、苏东坡、赵松雪等人，所以十八罗汉便很容易地在我国流传开来。

discovered in modern times. A big thūpa built under King Asoka's edict in the third century BC still exists today in good condition, and is said to be the only one surviving among the 84,000 thūpas Asoka built. On the four sides of the thūpa are exquisitely engraved stone gates. Owing to the discovery of numerous valuable relics, particularly of the sarīras of the two great arahats, Sanchi has become one of the most important Buddhist holy sites in India today.

41. Q: In the Han Buddhist temples, usually the images of eighteen Arahats can be seen. Who are they?

A: In fact, there should be sixteen arahats, or sixteen āyasmas (Arahat is transliterated into Chinese as Aluohan, or simply Luohan). According to the Buddhist canons, under the Buddha's instructions, sixteen of his disciples would not enter into Nibbāna. In *Nandimittāvadāna* written by Āyasma Nandimitta of Siharatta (now Sri Lanka) in the 2nd century AD, the names of the sixteen arahats and localities of their residences were recorded. After the book was translated into Chinese by Dhammācāriya Xuan Zang, the sixteen Arahats were held in universal esteem by the Chinese Buddhists. By the time of Five Dynasties, with the growing popularity of paintings and sculptures, representation of sixteen arahats was gradually superseded by representations of eighteen arahats. Presumably the painters intended to add Nandimitta and Xuan Zang, the writer and the translator of *Nandimittāvadāna* into the list. However, when later generations put the names of Arahats on the paintings, Nandimitta was mistakenly listed as the seventeenth resident Luohan, and the name of the first Arahat was repeated as the eighteenth. Though this mistake was already found out in the Song Dynasty, the formulation of Eighteen Luohans became widespread in China, probably because of the many inscriptions and paintings made by famous calligraphers and painters as well as men of letters such as Guan Xiu, Su Dongpo, Zhao Songxue and others.

42. 问:我国许多佛寺中有五百罗汉像,他们是什么人?

答:印度古代惯用“五百”、“八万四千”等来形容众多的意思,和我国古人用“三”或“九”来表示多数很相像。五百比丘、五百弟子、五百阿罗汉,在佛教经典中固然是常见的,但并不意味着是固定的数字。可是随着十六罗汉的崇奉,五百罗汉像也便在五代时期见于绘画和雕塑,不久便有许多寺庙建立了五百罗汉堂。后人又附会地列举五百罗汉的名字,其实都是没有根据的。至于近代某些寺院中塑造的五百罗汉像,许多形象都是出自匠人的臆造,或者采自神话小说,以至流于怪诞,失去了佛的出家弟子应有的合乎戒律的威仪。

43. 问:佛教寺庙中有许多菩萨像,他们是什么人?

答:汉族寺庙中供的菩萨像,主要的是文殊师利(Mañjuśrī)、普贤(Samantabhadra)、观世音(Avalokiteśvara)、地藏(Kṣitigarbha)。

44. 问:你前面不是说过,任何志愿自度度他、自觉觉他的人都可称为菩萨,为什么这些菩萨被当做神一般地崇拜呢?

答:志愿自度度他、自觉觉他,叫做发大心,又叫做发菩提心。初发大心的人固然也可以称为菩萨,但没有得到实证以前仍然是在凡夫的地位。发了大心,依照戒定慧三

42. Q: In many Chinese Buddhist temples, there are images of 500 Luohans. Who are they?

A: In ancient India, the figures " 500", "84,000", etc. were often used to indicate multitudes, just as the ancient Chinese were in the habit of using 3 or 9 to denote large numbers. 500 bhikkhus, 500 disciples and 500 arahats frequently appeared in the Buddhist canons. Frequent as they were, they do not mean definite figures. Along with the veneration to the Sixteen Arahats, however, the images of 500 Luohans, too, began to appear in paintings and sculptures during the period of the Five Dynasties, and before long Halls of 500 Luohans were built in a number of temples. Subsequently, the 500 Luohans were given names without any basis. With regard to the statues of 500 Luohans appearing in many temples in recent times, many of them were created out of craftsmen's imagination, or adapted from fairy tales, so they appeared grotesque, and inconsistent with the dignified posture requested by Vinaya which should be duly upheld by the Buddha's disciples.

43. Q: In Buddhist temples, there are many images of Bodhisattas. Who are they?

A: In Han Buddhist temples, the Bodhisatta images enshrined are mainly Mañjuśrī, Samantabhadra, Avalokiteśvara (or Guanyin), and Kṣitigarbha.

44. Q: You have said before, any one who aspires to deliver himself and others and to awaken himself and others can be called Bodhisatta. Why then are the four worshipped like deities?

A: The ideal of releasing not only oneself but also others and of awakening not only oneself but also others is known as the lofty aspiration, or "bodhicitta". All men who begin to be imbued with bodhicitta may be called Bodhisattas, but they

学修习，实行六度四摄，经过无数生死，最后才能成就佛果，其间有三贤十地五十二位等阶梯。文殊师利等是居于菩萨的极地的，是等觉位菩萨。大乘经典特别称道文殊师利的大智、普贤的大行、观世音的大悲、地藏的大愿，所以这四大菩萨特别受到教徒的崇敬。我国五台山被认为是文殊师利的道场，峨嵋山是普贤的道场，普陀山是观世音的道场，九华山是地藏的道场，称为四大名山。由此可以看出四大菩萨在我国佛教徒心目中的重要地位。

45. 问：四大名山国际上也知名吗？

答：五台山是文殊师利道场，这是见于大乘经典的，所以古代有不少从印度和西域来的高僧来朝拜。尼泊尔并且有这么一个古老的传说：加德满都（尼泊尔首都所在地）山谷地区，原来是一个大湖，文殊师利由中国五台山到那里去，劈开了一座山岭，将湖水排去，让随他同去的人们安居下来，这才建立了尼泊尔国。所以尼泊尔人民对文殊师利和五台山特别有亲切的感情。至于普陀山之成为观世

remain as worldly men until they acquired certain attainments. This involves many steps from making the great vow to gaining Buddhahood, there are the Three Virtuous States, the Ten Excellent Positions or stages (dasa-bhūmi) and the Fifty-two Stages. From the day of arising of bodhicitta, one should practice the Three Studies (Tisikkhā) of discipline (sīla), concentration (samādhi), and wisdom (paññā), carry out the Six Perfections (pāramitā) and the Four Fundamental Virtues (cattāri sangaha-vatthūni), and go through countless cycles of birth and death until finally achieving Buddhahood. Mañjuśrī and the others have reached the highest state of being Bodhisatta, or Sammā-sambodhi Bodhisatta. The Mahāyāna scriptures particularly eulogize the great wisdom of Mañjuśrī, the great conduct of Samantabhadra, the infinite compassion and pity of Avalokiteśvara and the great vow of Kṣitigarbha. Therefore, the four Great Bodhisattas command particular veneration of Buddhists. In China, Wutai Mountains is regarded as the sermon place of Mañjuśrī, Emei Mountains as that of Samantabhadra, Putuo Mountains as that of Avalokiteśvara and Jiuhua mountains as that of Kṣitigarbha. They are known collectively as the Four Famous holy Mountains, an indication of the significant positions of the four Bodhisattas in the hearts of Chinese Buddhists.

45.Q: Are the Four Holy Mountains also well-known in the world?

A: Wutai Mountains as the preaching place of Mañjuśrī was recorded in Mahāyāna Buddhist scriptures, so in ancient times, it was worshipped by quite a few eminent monks from India and Central Asia. There was even an old legend in Nepal saying that the Kathmandu Valley (where the capital of Nepal is located) used to be a large lake. It was Mañjuśrī, after he arrived there from Wutai Mount, China, who cleaved apart a mountain, drained off the lake water, and settled down with his followers, thus founding the State of Nepal. That is why the Nepalese people hold Mañjuśrī and Wutai Mountains in particular affection. As to how Putuo Mountains became the preaching place of

音道场、九华山之成为地藏道场，则和日本、朝鲜佛教僧人有关系。

46. 问：汉族寺庙的前殿一般供着一个笑面和尚像，他是谁？

答：是弥勒菩萨。佛教预言，将来释迦牟尼佛的教法灭尽了之后，经过很久远时期，弥勒菩萨将在这个世界上成佛说法。由于这个原因，弥勒菩萨也受到普遍的崇敬。中国历史上常有假托弥勒降生以号召农民起义的事，如元代弥勒教之类。至于笑面和尚像，并不是弥勒像，而是五代一个和尚名叫“契此”的像，这个和尚经常背着一个布袋，人称为“布袋和尚”，相传是弥勒化身，所以后人塑他的像作为弥勒来供奉。有人认为，汉族寺庙供奉布袋和尚像，可能受了弥勒教的影响，因为弥勒教的产生地就是布袋和尚的家乡，浙江奉化，所以有理由推断布袋和尚的形象是因弥勒教而普遍流行开来的。

Avalokiteśvara and how Jiuhua Mountains became that of Kṣitigarbha, these are said to be related with the Buddhist monks from Japan and Korea.

46. Q: In the front hall of the Han Buddhist temples, there is usually enshrined a statue of a monk with a smiling face. Who is he?

A: He is Maitreya Bodhisatta. According to Buddhist prediction, long after the extinction of the teachings of Sākyamuni Buddha in the far future, Maitreya Bodhisatta would become Buddha and preach in the world. For this reason, he has been held in universal esteem as well. In Chinese history, there were instances in which peasants were called to rebel under the pretext that Maitreya was born, for example, the Maitreya Cult of the Yuan Dynasty and the like. As to the statue of the smiling monk, however, it is not the true image of Maitreya, but the image of a monk named Qici of the Five Dynasties period. He usually carried a bag made of a piece of cloth on his shoulder, so he was known as the Cloth-bag Monk. He was said to be an embodiment of Maitreya. That is why later people chose his form to be enshrined as Maitreya. Some believe that this tradition may have developed under the influence of the Maitreya Cult which originated in Fenghua, Zhejiang Province, since this area was the home town of the Cloth-bag Monk. So it is logical to infer that the image of the Cloth-bag Monk spread under the influence of the Maitreya Cult.

# 第四章
## 佛教在印度的发展、衰灭和复兴

1. 问:请简略地介绍一下佛教在印度的历史概况。

答:佛陀逝世后一千六百余年中,印度佛教在组织上和思想上经过分化、发展和衰坏的过程,最后消灭于公元十二世纪时代。

2. 问:印度今天不是还有佛教吗?

答:印度今天的佛教是公元十九世纪后期才由斯里兰卡重新传入的。在此之前七百年中,印度没有佛教。

3. 问:印度佛教在它的一千六百多年历史中有哪些重要的阶段?

答:从学说的思想发展来看,可以把印度佛教分为五个时期:第一,佛逝世后约一百年之间为原始佛教时期;第二,在这之后约四百年之间为部派分裂时期;第三,此后约四百年为大乘中观学派兴盛时期;第四,此后又约四百年为大乘瑜伽学派兴盛时期,这一时期的后期,密宗颇为流行;第五,最后约三百年为密宗盛行时期。

## Chapter IV

# THE DEVELOPMENT, DECLINE AND RESURGENCE OF BUDDHISM IN INDIA

1. Q: Please give me a general introduction to the history of Buddhism in India.

A: During the 1600-odd years after the Buddha's passing away, Buddhism in India underwent a process of schism, development and decline in organization and thinking. Finally it vanished from India in the 12th century AD.

2. Q: Buddhism still exists in India today, doesn't it?

A: Yes, it does. But the Buddhism of India today was retransmitted from Sri Lanka in the late 19th century. About 700 years before this, Buddhism disappeared from India.

3. Q: What were the important stages in the 1600-odd-year history of Indian Buddhism?

A: In the development of its doctrines, Indian Buddhism can be divided into 5 periods: first, the primitive period of Buddhism – the first 100 years or so after Buddha's Parinibbāna; second, the period of Nikāyas' Schism – about 400 years following the first; third, for about 4 centuries after that – the period when the Mādhyamika School of Mahāyāna flourished; fourth, for another 4 centuries after that – the period when the Mahāyāna Yogācāra School flourished (in the later part of this period, the Tantric School became popular); fifth, for the final 3 centuries roughly – the period of the prevalence of the Tantric School.

4. 问:所谓原始佛教时期的情况是怎样?

答:在这一时期中,佛弟子们在教团生活上一般维持着佛在世时一向的设施和惯例,在学修上奉行着四谛、八正道的根本教义,没有什么重大的争论。这一时期,用佛教的话说,是“和合一味”的时期。但是所谓和合一味,仅能说是大体上的一致,不是没有见解上和主张上的歧异。即以这一时期开始时的第一结集为例,在结集中就曾有关于“小小戒”(微细的戒律)是什么和要不要废除的不同意见。另一方面,由于时间和地点的条件,多数僧众没有能够参加结集,分散在各地的大弟子们也有未能参加的,他们不会没有认为需要补充或修正的意见。如富楼那(十大弟子之一)除在事后承认结集的佛法外,又声明:“我从佛得闻之法,亦当受持”。他和摩诃迦叶讨论戒律时,对“内宿”(僧人住处留藏食物)等八条戒条,他认为那是佛制定之后又开了的,迦叶则认为是开了之后又重制定的,终于各行其是。

典籍中又有跋波(最初五比丘之一)在窟外另行结集的记载。这些事实说明当时的统一之中存在着差异。佛在世时,于不同的时机,对不同的人,说不同的教法。弟子们或因佛说法的时机不同而有听受的不同,或因各人的根性、专长和学修方法的不同而有了解和悟入的不同,这也是可以想见其然的。

4. Q: What was the primitive period of Buddhism like?

A: In this period, Buddha's disciples generally maintained the facilities and conventions of Sangha life as they were in Buddha's lifetime, and practised the fundamental creeds of the Four Noble Truths and the Eight-fold Path on self-cultivation with little dissension. Thus this period was, in Buddhist terms, the period of harmonious unity. But the so called "harmonious unity" was merely a general consensus which did not mean there were no differences in thought and opinions. Take the First Buddhist Council for example, which was held at the beginning of this period, in which there were disagreements over what the "lesser and minor precepts" (khuddānukhuddaka sikkhāpada) were and whether or not they should be abolished. As a matter of fact, most Bhikkhus were unable to take part in the Saṃgīti, and even some of the chief disciples scattered everywhere were unable to attend because of time and distance, and they were sure to have had proposals for additions or revisions to the Dhamma which resulted from the Council. For example, Pūrna (P. Puṇṇa, one of the ten eminent Disciples) declared, "The Dhamma I had heard from Buddha in person must be upheld too", though he had agreed with the Vinaya and the Dhamma recited at the Saṃgīti. When he discussed the disciplines with Mahā-kassapa, they differed on eight rules, for example, the precept against "keeping food in a monastic bedroom", he thought that the rules were enacted by the Buddha first and then were loosened; while the latter thought that the rules were reinstituted after being broken. Eventually each of them followed his own way.

In the Buddhist archives, there were also records about Vappa (one of the first five bhikkhus) holding another Saṃgīti outside the Cave. These facts show the discrepancy in the unity at that time. The Buddha, during his lifetime, preached different teachings to different people at different times. It is conceivable that his disciples might have had different understanding due to their different occasions of listening and had different comprehension owing to the differences of their nature, special-

在第一结集之后，长老们分别率领僧众在各方弘化，师弟相承，渐渐各自形成传承的系统。他们传授的教法和戒律互有异同。各个传承系统很自然地按照地域划分其势力范围，日久之后，不能不受到各地环境的影响而具有各自的特色。在学说思想方面，有的态度偏于自由进取，对佛所说的教法，但取大意，对戒律的受持，也有所通融；有的偏于固执保守，拘泥教条，不敢出入；有的介乎二者之间。这种情形，发展下去，势必引起后来部派的分裂。

5. 问：部派分裂时期的情况怎样？

答：佛教教团最初分裂为上座部和大众部两大派，这是佛陀逝世后约一百或一百余年的事。当时直接引起分裂的原因是由于僧众们在戒律问题上的争执。据说有一位西方波利族比丘名叫耶舍的，游化到东方的毗舍离城，看见跋祇族比丘们劝令在家信徒布施金钱作僧众购买所需之用。耶舍认为比丘乞受金银不合戒律，于是提出异议，遭受到跋祇僧众的摈斥。耶舍便往西方各地邀请上座比丘们到毗舍离集会，结果判决跋祇比丘们为非法（根据上座记载，除乞受金银外，尚有其他九事非法）。这便是第二结集，因为集合的有七百人，所以又称“七百结集”。跋祇比丘们大多数不承认这个判决，他们另外召集了一万比丘举行结集。这便造成了教团的分裂。

ties and methods of self-cultivation.

After the First Council, the Mahātheras (senior monks) led their followers to do missionary work separately in different areas. With the disciples succeeding their own masters, each group eventually formed its own lineage of succession. The Dhamma and Vinaya passed on by each group, thus, had differences as well as similarities. Each tradition naturally gained its own sphere of influence according to geographical divisions, and its own distinctive features relevant to the local circumstances in the course of time. In the area of theory and doctrines, some tended to be liberal and progressive, adopting the general ideas of the Buddha's teachings and being elastic in observance of disciplines; while some were obstinate and conservative, strictly abiding by dogmas without even slight deviation; and some were between the two. Such a situation was going on and inevitably led to Nikāyas' schism.

5. Q: What was the situation in the period of Nikāyas' Schism?

A: The Buddhist community was initially divided into two major sects: Theravāda and Mahā-saṃghika. This happened about 100 or more years after the Buddha's death. The direct cause of the schism was the controversy over the issue of sīla among monks. It was said that there was a bhikkhu from Bārāṇasī (Kasi) named Yasa, who traveled to Vesālī in the east and saw the Vajjian monks inducing the laity to donate money to the Sangha so that they could buy their necessities. Considering the acceptance of gold and silver a violation of the rules in the Vinaya, Yasa raised an objection, but as a result he was excommunicated by the Vajjians. Thereupon, he went to various places in the west and appealed to orthodox bhikkhus to assemble at Vesālī. As a result, the verdict of the assembly declared the conduct of Vajjian monks to be unlawful. (According to Theravāda records, apart from receiving alms of gold and silver, they committed another nine offenses.) This was the Second Saṃgīti or the Council of the Seven Hundred, since there were 700 participants in the assembly. Most of the Vajjian bhikkhus

6. 问:为什么这种判断是非的集会也称为结集呢?

答:两个集会都进行了经律的结集。七百比丘的结集,费时八个月之久。万人结集的时间虽未见记载,想也不会很短。可见两派要求解决的不只是关于乞受金银这一问题,而是要求通过经律的再一次编定来贯彻自己一派的主张。拿两派的戒律两相比较,大众部的僧祇律较简略而多通融,上座部的十诵律则繁密而严格;僧祇律对微细戒条多有舍弃,对于开戒(包括乞受金银在内)多有方便,十诵律则与此相反。显然,第二结集是第一结集之后百年间教团内部矛盾发展的必然结果。七百结集的参与者多数是上座长老,所以这一派被称为上座部(Theravāda)。今天南方国家的佛教徒自称为上座部,因为他们出自上座部的传承。跋祇族比丘举行万人大会,这一派人数众多,所以称为大众部(Mahāsaṃghika)。

7. 问:两派的矛盾是否仅是戒律问题?

答:最初主要是戒律问题上的争论,但是两派为学的精神不同是其主导原因。上座部严格持守戒律,致力于修

refused to obey the decision and held another Saṃgīti which was attended by ten thousand monks. This contributed to the schism in the Buddhist Order.

6. Q: Why was this sort of assembly which passed judgment also called saṃgīti?

A: Because both assemblies engaged in the recital of Sutta (Piṭaka) and Vinaya (Pāli). The Saṃgīti of 700 lasted for about eight months, the duration of the "Saṃgīti of 10,000" was presumably not very short, though there are no records. It can be seen that the parties sought not only to resolve the issue of acceptance of gold and silver, but sought to validate their ideas by revising the Sutta and Vinaya. Comparative study of the two vinayas of these two sects shows that the Mahāsaṃghika-vinaya was simpler and more accommodating, whereas the Sabbatthivāda-vinaya was more comprehensive and strict; the Mahāsaṃghika-vinaya cut out some of the minor precepts and loosened some rules (including alms begging for gold and silver), whereas the Sabbatthivāda-vinaya took a diametrically opposite position. Obviously, the second Saṃgīti was the inevitable outcome of the development of the contradictions inside the Buddhist Community in the 100 years after the First Saṃgīti. As most of the participants of the Saṃgīti of 700 were orthodox Theras, the sect formed by them was named Theravāda. Today, Buddhists in southern countries call themselves Theravādins for they inherited their teachings from this tradition. Since the Vajjian Bhikkhus held the assembly of 10,000, the sect of this majority was known as Mahāsaṃghika.

7. Q: Was the dispute between the two sects confined to the matter of discipline?

A: At first, the dispute was confined to discipline, but its chief cause was the different approach to the cultivation and study between the two sects. The Theravādins strictly observed and maintained the Vinaya precepts, engaging themselves in

习禅定，注重自己内心的修持。大众部则广学多闻，致力于弘传教法，注重接引群众。这两种不同的精神，不仅引起了戒律问题的争论，而且促使后来佛教在教理上、学说上在各个时期不同的发展。

8. 问：在第二结集之后，还有没有部派分裂的事？

答：最初分立的上座、大众二部称为根本二部。后来由于佛教流传地区日广，各地的传承既有不同，而各地风土人情的不同又必然要求说法和制度的改变，因之学派渐渐繁多起来。从第二结集到佛陀逝世后约四百年之间，上座、大众的根本二部又先后分裂为十八部或二十部。关于诸部派分裂的次第、年代乃至名称有不同的传说。由上座部直接分出的最大的一部是说一切有部（Sabbatthivāda），此外较重要的是跋祇子部（Vajjiputtaka 或称犊子部）和化地部（Mahiṃsāsaka）。据大众部传说，上座部最初分出分别说部（Vibhajjavāda），它采取大众部的一些学说，成为独立的部派，与上座、大众成鼎足之势。但根据上座部的说法，分别说部乃是上座部的异名。大众部早期分出的三部是一说部（Ekavyohārika）、说出世部（Lokottaravāda）和鸡胤部（Gokulika 或称牛王部）。大众部后期分出的制多山部（Cetiyavāda）是最大的一个部派。

9. 问：各部派的学说有很大的不同吗？

study and practice bhāvanā, and paying much attention to their own spiritual cultivation, while the Mahāsaṃghikas sought for large-scale learning, and engaging in propagating the Buddha Dhamma and guiding the masses. These two different orientations not only led to the dispute over the commandments but also impelled subsequent variant developments in Buddhist doctrines and philosophy at different times.

8. Q: Were there any other schisms after the Second Saṃgīti?

A: The first split resulted in Theravāda and Mahāsaṃghika, these were known as the two basic sects. Later on, as Buddhism spread far and wide in the course of time, there were different traditions in different localities, thus changes in propagation and institutions inevitably occurred to meet the needs of the local conditionss and customs. This gradually resulted in the emergence of various schools of Buddhism. From the Second Saṃgīti to about four centuries after the Buddha's passing away, the two basic sects of Theravāda and Mahāsaṃghika were successively divided into 18 or 20 subgroups. There are different traditions regarding the sequence, time, and names of each schism. The largest branch directly spilt from Theravāda was Sabbatthivāda (S. Sarvāstivāda), the other rather important subgroups were Vajjiputtaka and Mahiṃsāsaka. According to Mahāsaṃghika tradition, the Vibhajjavāda was the first to split from Theravāda. It adopted some Mahāsaṃghika ideas and became an independent sect, standing apart from both Theravāda and Mahāsaṃghika. However, according to Theravāda tradition, the Vibhajjavāda was a variation of Theravāda. The three sects which broke away from the Mahāsaṃghika in early times were Ekavyohārika, Lokottaravāda and Gokulika. Afterwards, the Cetiyavāda was the largest sect that split away from Mahāsaṃghika.

9. Q: Were there significant differences in the doctrines of various sects?

答：上座、大众根本两部在教义上有较大的差别，至于支末部派，一般地说，与根本部差别不大。上座部学说可以拿说一切有部为代表，因为说一切有部是上座部中最早的和最大的一个部派，它传下来丰富的论藏典籍。大众部没有什么论著留传下来，只是从某些史籍记载中看到它的一些论点。

10. 问：可否把上座部和大众部的学说简略地介绍一下？

答：可以举几个问题来谈。

第一、对于事物（法）的认识问题。在未谈之前，先要介绍两个术语：(1)有为法，一切依借因缘而有造作生灭的事物都叫做有为法；(2)无为法，不依借因缘，本来不生灭的事物是无为法，如涅槃、虚空（万物都在虚空中生灭，而虚空的无碍性则不依借因缘而本自存在）等，都是属于无为法。说一切有部和大众部都认为无为法是实在的。至于对有为法的看法，大众部认为一切有为法依借因缘而生灭，过去的已经灭了，没有实体，未来的没有生起，也没有实体，仅仅现在一刹那中有体和用（作用）。说一切有部认为一切有为法，如果本来没有，即使具备了条件，也不能生起，如龟不能生毛，兔不能生角，所以任何一法，它的体都是永恒存在的，只是作用没有生起的名为未来，作用已经生起的名为过去，作用正在生起名为现在。因此这个部派的主张是三世（过去、未来、现在）实有与法体恒有。法体虽有，但是它的作用的生起要依借于诸法的集合以及前后的关系（因缘），决没有单独能起作用的。既然各各法的自

A: There were considerable differences between the doctrines of Theravāda and Mahāsaṃghika. As to the subgroups, they generally had only minor differences from their basic sect. The doctrine of Theravāda could be represented by Sarvāstivāda's as it was the earliest and largest sect among Theravādins, and bequeathed a wealth of canons of Abhidhamma Piṭaka. Of the Mahāsaṃghika, on the other hand, few works were preserved, only some of its doctrines being known through certain historical accounts.

10. Q: Would you please explain some of the doctrines of Theravāda and Mahāsaṃghika?

A: I cite a number of issues for discussion.

First, pertaining to the interpretation of dhammā (all things). Before dealing with the issue, two terms should be defined. (1) Conditioned Dhamma (Saṅkhata Dhamma): Anything which comes into being, or ceases from being, by causes and conditions (hetu-paccaya) is called Conditioned Dhamma. (2) Unconditioned Dhamma (Asaṅkhata Dhamma): Items that do not depend on other causes and conditions for their existence, which exist in and of themselves without arising and cessation are Unconditioned Dhammas, such as Nibbāna and Space (Ākāsa). (Every thing arises and ceases within space, while space itself exists bearing the nature of infinity, free from hetu-paccaya.) Both Sarvāstivāda and Mahāsaṃghika held that Unconditioned Dhammas exist. As to the Conditioned Dhammas, Mahāsaṃghika believed that the Conditioned Dhammas arise and cease depending on causes and conditions, the past has no real existence since it has ceased, nor has the future, as it is yet to be born, only the present dhammas existing in an instant (Khaṇa) have real existence and function. Sarvāstivāda believed that all Conditioned Dhammas, if they have not arisen and existed, can not arise at all even given necessary conditions, just as the tortoise can not grow hair and the rabbit can not grow horns. Therefore, the ultimate essence of every Dhamma con-

体没有作用，所以没有常一主宰的我。这一种说法是我空法有论，而大众部说法接近于我法两空论。

第二，对于佛陀的认识问题。大众部认为生灭于人间的释迦牟尼佛是化身而不是实身，佛陀的实身是积累极长时期的修行而成的；佛陀的色身、寿命和威力都是无边际的，佛陀永远化度众生无有疲厌；佛所说的一切语言都是随机说法，佛以一音说一切法。说一切有部不承认释迦牟尼是化身佛之说，认为佛所说的语言并不全部都是经教，佛并不是以一音说一切法。

第三、对于声闻和菩萨的认识问题。大众部强调菩萨广度众生的慈悲愿力，轻声闻而贵菩萨。说一切有部虽承认声闻、缘觉、菩萨能修行的根性和所修行的道路有差别，但认为佛与二乘（声闻与缘觉）所得的解脱是没有差异的。

stantly exists, only the manifestations vary: those functions which have not yet manifested are called the future, those functions which have already manifested are the past, those which are functioning are the present. So this sect holds that the essence of the dhammas exists at all times (past, present and future), the dhammas of the three times really exist. Although the essence of dhamma is there, the arising of its function depends on the aggregation of various dhammas as well as their causal relations (hetu-paccaya), and it is by no means able to function independently. Inasmuch as the self-essence of dhammas can not function by itself, there is no "ego" (atta) as a permanent dominator. This is the theory of non-substantiality of ego and substantiality of dhamma, while the Mahāsaṃghikas held a theory close to non-substantiality of both ego and dhamma.

Secondly, pertaining to the conception of the Buddha, the Mahāsaṃghika held the view that what was born, lived and died in the human world was Sākyamuni Buddha's phenomenal body (Nimmāna-kāya) rather than his noumenal body (Saṃbhoga-kāya), the Buddha's noumenal body came into being with the accumulation of merits over a very prolonged period; that the Buddha's body (rūpa-kāya), length of life and power were boundless, the Buddha tirelessly teaches and rescues all beings, all of his words are teachings in a modified form, the Buddha's every utterance is a sermon covering all dhammas. The Sarvāstivāda on the other hand, denied the thesis that Sākyamuni was the temporal body of the eternal Buddha, asserting that not all words of the Buddha were teachings and that the Buddha didn't preach all dhammas with every utterance.

Thirdly, in their conceptions of the Sāvaka and the Bodhisatta, the Mahāsaṃghika stressed the Bodhisatta's power of metta-karuṇā to enlighten sentient beings, and attached less importance to the Sāvakas. The Sarvāstivāda did not believe there was any difference between the liberation attained through the Buddha, and that attained through Sāvakas and the Pacceka-buddhas, though they admitted the differences in the capability and

此外，在其他一些问题的认识上和修行实践的方法上都有不同之处，这里不列举了。

11. 问：在部派分裂时期中还有什么其他重大的事件发生吗？

答：佛教史上一件关系极为重大的事发生在这个时期，那便是阿育王大弘佛法。在阿育王之前佛教的传播只局限于中印度恒河流域一带，由于阿育王的努力，佛教不仅传遍五印度（东、西、南、北、中印度），而且传到亚洲、北非、希腊许多国家，一跃而成为世界性的宗教。

12. 问：阿育王是怎样的一个人物？

答：阿育王（Asoka，或译为阿输迦王，或意译为无忧王）是公元前三世纪摩揭陀国的国王。他的祖父是印度古代著名的民族英雄旃陀罗笈多（有人根据他的名字而考证他是有旃陀罗种姓的血统的，阿育王也曾被称为旃陀罗阿输迦）。旃陀罗笈多是公元前四世纪摩揭陀国人，被国王放逐流徙在西北印度。当时亚历山大侵入印度，占领五河一带，威胁恒河平原。旃陀罗笈多举起义旗，聚合西北民众赶走了希腊驻军，然后回到摩揭陀国，推翻了难陀王朝，成为摩揭陀国孔雀王朝第一代君主。他统一中、西、北印度，使摩揭陀国成为强大的帝国。公元前 273 年，雄才大略的阿育王继承他父亲宾头沙罗登了王位。他发扬光大了先人志业，在历史上第一次实现了全印度的统一。他征

path of cultivation among them.

Besides the above, there were differences in their perceptions of certain problems and on the method of cultivation, which I shall not enumerate here.

11. Q: Did any other important events take place during the period of schisms in Buddhism?

A: One of the most important events in the history of Buddhism took place in this period, namely, King Asoka's promulgation of Buddha Dhamma. Prior to King Asoka, the spread of Buddhism had been confined to the Ganges Valley in Central India. Owing to King Asoka's efforts, Buddhism became a world-wide religion, spreading over not only the five parts of India (Eastern, Western, Southern, Northern and Central India) but also extending to many countries in Asia, North Africa and Greece.

12. Q: What kind of man was King Asoka?

A: Asoka ( meaning Sorrow-free) was the King of Magadha in the 3rd century BC. His grandfather, Chandragupta, was a famous national hero in ancient India (on the basis of his name, some suggest that he was of the Chandra Caste. King Asoka was also known as Chandrasoka). Chandragupta, who lived in Magadha in the 3rd century BC, was exiled to Northwest India. At that time, Alexander the Great invaded India, occupied the region of the Five Rivers (Punjab), and threatened the Ganges plain. Chandragupta rose in opposition, rallying the northwestern people to drive the Greek invaders out. Returning to Magadha he overthrew the Nanda Dynasty to become the first Monarch of the Maurya Dynasty of Magadha. During his reign he unified Central, West and North India, and made Magadha a mighty empire. In 273 BC., the talented and bold strategist Asoka succeeded his father Bindusāra to the throne. He carried forward his ancestors' aspirations and feats, and accomplished the unification of the whole of India for the first time in Indian

服南印度羯陵伽国的时候，看到了战争的惨状，大动悔悟之心，从此放弃了由武力征服的办法，而归依了佛教。他一方面实行转轮王理想的政治，兴办巨大的水利灌溉工程，修筑从摩揭陀国到伊朗的国际大道，发展国内经济和国际贸易；一方面大力传播佛教。他设置一种司掌宗教工作和慈善事业的官职，名叫"正法大官"，派遣他们和传教师们到各地宣传佛教，他的儿子摩晒陀(Mahinda)、女儿僧伽密陀(Saṃghamittā)，(两人都出了家为比丘、比丘尼)也先后被派往师子国(斯里兰卡)。当时东至缅甸，南到斯里兰卡，西到叙利亚、埃及、希腊等地，都有佛教的传播。

13. 问：我国旧时传说，秦始皇时代曾有印度僧人室利房等十八人来华传教，有没有这件事？

答：这件事不见我国的正史纪载，但是秦始皇和阿育王是同时代的人，当时阿育王派遣一批传教师来到中国也是可能的事。阿育王的祖父时代一部文献中曾提到中国丝织品(梵文里有关丝的字，如 Cīnapaṭṭa 即成捆的丝，Cīnasukka 即丝织衣服等，都有 Cīna"支那"这个字作组成部分)，可见秦始皇之前，中国与印度已经有了往来。

14. 问：阿育王弘扬佛教的原因是什么？

history. Yet, when he witnessed the tragic scenes of the war in his conquest of the Kāliṅga Kingdom he repented greatly and decided to undertake no further military campaigns, becoming a staunch follower of Buddhism. On the one hand, he carried out the political ideal of rāja-cakkavatti (universal king), set up huge irrigation projects, built the international road from Magadha to Iran, and developed the domestic economy and international trade. On the other hand, he vigorously disseminated Buddhism. He established a high official post, entitled "Saddhamma Minister", to be in charge of religious affairs and charity. He dispatched these officials together with missionaries to propagate Buddhism in various places. Both his son Mahinda and daughter Saṅghamittā (Buddhist bhikkhu and bhikkhunī respectively) were sent in turn to the State of Lion (now Sri Lanka). In his lifetime Buddhism expanded as far as Burma in the east, Sri Lanka in the south, and Syria, Egypt and Greece in the west.

13. Q: An ancient Chinese tradition holds that at the time of the First Emperor of Qin, known as Qinshihuang, 18 Indian monks, headed by Shilifang, came to China on a mission. Is that true?

A: It is not recorded in the official Chinese history, but it is possible that King Asoka dispatched a group of missionaries to China, as Emperor Qinshihuang and King Asoka were contemporaries. At the time of Asoka's grandfather, a document had already mentioned Chinese silk products (in Sanskrit, words relating to silk, such as Cīnapaṭṭa, meaning bundle of silk, and Cīnasukka, meaning silk clothes, bear the root "cīna" as their component). Thus it can be seen that even before Emperor Qinshihuang there had been intercourse between China and India.

14. Q: What was the reason for King Asoka's promulgation of Buddhism?

答：摩揭陀原来是释迦牟尼教化的根据地。佛教最初就得到摩揭陀国及其邻国国王们的支持，阿育王的祖父笈多王也是一位佛教的护持者。这个事实反映着当时印度的刹帝利（国王）和婆罗门（僧侣）的冲突，而且，据我看，也反映着当时恒河流域的新兴国家中新兴地主们和商主们对领主割据势力的冲突。历史事实证明，孔雀王朝的国王们本身就是善于经营的大商主。婆罗门神权和种姓制度所支持的领主割据势力严重阻碍着农业上灌溉系统的兴建和商业上国内外贸易的畅通，因此，反对神权及种姓制度、主张众生平等的佛教受到当时民众的拥护，尤其是受到新兴地主阶级和商人们的欢迎。另一方面，佛教慈悲安忍的教义，在摩揭陀帝国统治者看来，对国内统一事业的巩固和国际友好关系的发展，是有利无害的。当阿育王从亚历山大穷兵黩武的后果中，从他自己征伐时遭到顽强抵抗的经验中，认识到必须改变武力政策而采用怀柔政策的时候，他便选择了“法轮”作为他的政治武器。

15. 问：阿育王弘扬佛教在学术文化上起了一些什么影响？

答：当时佛教的传播对亚洲各国以及东方和希腊、叙利亚、埃及等国家的文化交流，起了深远巨大的作用。阿育王生前巡礼各地佛迹时铭刻了许多石柱，他又在各地崖壁上刻了许多法诰（根据佛法而颁布的各种教诰），这些遗

A: Magadha was the base area where Sākyamuni proclaimed Buddhist teachings. From the outset, Buddhism was supported by the kings of Magadha and its neighboring countries, Asoka's grand-father Chandragupta was one of them. This was a reflection of the conflict between the Kśatriyas (P. Khattiya) (kings) and Brāhmaṇas (priests) in India at that time. In my opinion, it also reflected the confrontation of the newly emerging landlords and merchants with the rule of the local lords in the new-born nations of the Ganges Valley at the time. History suggests that the kings of the Maurya Dynasty were themselves great merchants skilled in the conduct of business. The rule of the hereditary local lords supported by the Brahmin theocracy and the caste system seriously hindered the construction of the irrigation system in agricultural areas and the smooth running of domestic and foreign trade. Therefore, Buddhism which stood against theocracy and the caste system and stood for the equality of all sentient beings was supported by the masses of people, and especially favorably received by the newly-emerging landlords and merchants. On the other hand, the rulers of the Magadha Empire viewed the Buddhist tenets of compassion and forbearance as helpful, not harmful, to the consolidation of unity at home and the development of friendly relations with other nations. When he saw the consequences of Alexander's militarism and the stubborn resistance he experienced during his conquests, King Asoka learned that he had to change his military campaign into a more moderate one, so he decided on the Wheel of Dhamma (Dhammacakka) as his political weapon.

15. Q: What was the impact on learning and culture of King Asoka's propagation of Buddhism ?

A: The spread of Buddhism at that time played a far-reaching role in the cultural exchange among Asian countries and between the Orient and Greece, Syria, Egypt etc. In the course of his pilgrimages to the Buddhist holy places, King Asoka had engraved many stone pillars and inscribed on mountain cliffs many decrees of Dhamma (decreeing policies and teachings

物至今还有留存和陆续发现的，对古代历史提供了极为重要的资料。

16. 问：阿育王传布佛教之举对当时部派的兴起有没有影响？

答：阿育王时代，佛教大约已经分为四个部派。各部派分往各地传教后，受到了各地不同环境的影响，在形式上和学说上有了不同的发展，这便促成了更多部派的产生。

17. 问：关于阿育王时代举行的第三次结集的情况可否再谈一些？

答：关于第三次结集的经过，我在前面谈到佛教经籍时，已经讲过了。根据南方佛教记载，阿育王大弘佛教之事，就在结集之后。最近在八纳（阿育王故都）发掘出阿育王建筑的一座宏大寺院的遗址，里面有一百根石柱的大讲堂，并有许多僧房和水池。有人说这可能就是第三结集的处所。但是关于第三结集的事，北方所传典籍中没有记载。

18. 问：阿育王之后又有什么大事发生？

答：阿育王大弘佛法后，三百年中，佛教在中亚各国获得坚固的根据地，更向东发展而传来中国，流布地域日见推广。但是在印度境内，佛教却遭遇了厄运。阿育王逝世后不到五十年，孔雀王朝为巽伽王朝所代替。受到婆罗门国师的助力而篡得王位的富奢蜜多罗王崇拜婆罗门而严

according to the Buddha Dhamma). Many remain even today and more are discovered from time to time, providing very important information about ancient history.

16. Q: Did King Asoka's promulgation of Buddhism have an effect on the emergence of the Buddhist sects?

A: At the time of Asoka, Buddhism was probably already divided into four sects. Since each of the sects sent missions to various places and were, therefore, influenced by different circumstances, variations in forms and in doctrines appeared in each of them. Such a variety in turn gave rise to further growth of sects.

17. Q: Would you please say more about the Third Council (Saṃgīti) held at the time of King Asoka?

A: As to the proceedings of the Third Saṃgīti, I have already mentioned it while talking about the Buddhist Canons. According to the Southern Buddhist accounts, King Asoka's spread of Buddhism took place immediately after that saṃgīti. Recently, the ruins of a magnificent monastery built by King Asoka have been excavated at Pāṭaliputta (King Asoka's capital, Patna of today). Inside the monastery was an auditorium (pāsāda) with 100 stone pillars as well as many monastic chambers and pools. Some believe that this was the very site where the 3rd Saṃgīti was held. However, there was nothing recorded about the 3rd Saṃgīti in the northern Buddhist classics.

18. Q: What great events took place after King Asoka's time?

A: For more than 300 years after King Asoka's propagation of Buddha Dhamma, Buddhism took a firm hold in all nations in Central Asia and extended eastward to China, spreading in increasingly wider areas. However, within India itself, Buddhism met adversity. In less than half a century after King Asoka's death, the Maurya Dynasty was replaced by the Śuṅga

厉地排斥佛教，毁坏塔寺，杀戮僧众，使印度佛教一时陷于黑暗的时代。幸而巽伽王朝的统治权力仅限于中印度，他的排佛运动没有波及到南印度与西北印度。当时佛教徒多避难于西北，也有逃到南方的，因而促进了北方佛教的兴盛和南方佛教的发展。当时统治北印度的是大夏国弥兰陀王（希腊族），弥兰陀受了那先比丘的教化归依了佛教。至今传存着他和那先比丘关于佛教的问答，汉文译本称《那先比丘经》，巴利文本称为《弥兰陀问经》。大家都知道的犍陀罗佛教美术，就是从这时候开始逐渐兴起的。

19. 问：当时南方佛教的情况怎样？

答：关于当时南方佛教情况，缺乏资料。可以知道的是：由于阿育王派到南印度去传教的是大众部僧众，所以大众部学说在南方盛行而为兴起于南方的达罗维荼民族所接受。达罗维荼人建立的案达罗国在公元前 28 年灭了中印度的康发王朝（巽伽王朝的后一朝代）而并有其土地。此后，中印度的佛教似乎稍稍有了起色。与案达罗人入主中印度同时，大月支人灭了西北印度的大夏王朝而创立贵霜王朝，印度历史自此进入南北朝时代，直到公元四世纪笈多王朝时才再统一。在此时期中，南朝佛教情况很难知道其详，北朝佛教则在公元二世纪迦腻色迦王（Kaniśka）时期最为兴盛。

Dynasty. King Puṣyamitra, who usurped the throne with the aid of a Brahmin Imperial preceptor, upheld Brahmanism and rigorously suppressed Buddhism by destroying stūpas, vihāras, and slaughtering Buddhist monks and finally plunged Indian Buddhism into a dark age. Fortunately, the reign of the Śuṅga Dynasty was confined to Central India only, so its anti-Buddhist movement didn't spread to South and Northwest India. At that time, most of the Buddhists took refuge in the Northwest, and some to the South, thus they could promote the flourishing of Buddhism in the North as well as its development in the South. The ruler of that time in North India was King Milinda (a Greek) of Bactria, who was converted to Buddhism by Bhikkhu Nāgasena. The dialogues on Buddhism between Milinda and Nāgasena have been preserved to this day, the Chinese translation being entitled *Nāgasena Bhikkhu Sutta* and its Pāli version *Milinda Pañhā*. The well-known Buddhist art of Gandhāra also began at that time and gradually flourished.

19. Q: What was Southern Buddhism like at that time?

A: References to Southern Buddhism at that time are scarce. What we have learned is that the mission sent to South India by King Asoka was of Mahāsaṃghika, so the doctrines of Mahāsaṃghika prevailed in the South and were accepted by the local Dravidians, who were emerging there. In 28 BC, the Andhra (P. Andhaka) Kingdom founded by the Dravidians overthrew the Kaṇva dynasty (the successor of the Śuṅga Dynasty) in central India, and occupied its territory. Consequently, Buddhism picked up slightly in Central India. At the same time that the Andhakas gained dominance in Central India, the Kuṣanas overthrew the Bactria Dynasty in Northwest India, and founded the Kṣāṇa Dynasty. After that the history of India entered into a period of Northern and Southern dynasties until its reunification by the Gupta Dynasty in the 4th century AD. Scarcely any details are known about Buddhism in the South in that period. On the other hand, Buddhism in the North reached

20. 问:迦腻色迦是怎样的人物?

答:关于迦腻色迦的事迹很少有纪载,但是在护持佛教方面,他有阿育王第二之称。据说他从前也像阿育王初期那样多所杀伐,后来得到胁比丘(Pārśva)的教化,归依佛教。从遗迹看来,迦腻色迦时代建造的塔寺和佛像很多,而且在艺术上有很大发展。如在佛塔的形式方面,改变了印度向来的复钵式,而创建了五层楼阁式的佛塔;在造像艺术方面,参酌希腊、印度两地不同形式而自成风格,使犍陀罗佛教美术发展到高峰。迦腻色迦王又由中印度罗致当时佛教大文学家马鸣(Assaghosa)到迦湿弥罗(Kasmīra),使佛教文学获得辉煌的发达。从这些事实中可以想见佛教在这时代兴盛的情况。迦腻色迦王对佛教贡献最大的就是在他发起和护持下举行了一次重要的结集。相传他曾向一些人询问教理,所得到的解答各有不同。他感到学说纷纭,莫衷一是,于是依从胁比丘的指导,招集世友(Vasumitta)以下的硕学比丘五百人在迦湿弥罗纂辑三藏,并加以编述注释,共三十万颂,九百多万言,历时十二年方始完成。其中一部分就是《大毗婆沙论》,是属于说一切有部的一部重要的巨著,我国有新旧两种译本。

21. 问:这时期,除了有部得到提倡弘扬之外,其他部派的情况怎样?

its peak in the 2nd century AD under the reign of King Kaniṣka.

20. Q: Who was King Kaniṣka?

A: Historical records about King Kaniṣka are few, but he was known as "the Second King Asoka" for his patronage and upholding of Buddhism. It was said that his early life followed the same lines as that of King Asoka, with widespread bloodshed, and that later he was converted to Buddhism by the Bhikkhu Pārśva. Architectural ruins show that, in Kaniṣka's era, many stūpas, vihāras and sculptures of the Buddha were built and magnificent progress made in the arts. For example, the form of the stūpa evolved from the traditional Indian domed style (like an inverted alms-bowl) to the 5-storied terraced tower, while in sculpture the Greek and Indian styles were blended to form a new distinct style that brought the Gandhāra Buddhist arts to a climax. King Kaniṣka also invited the great Buddhist writer Assaghosa from Central India to Kasmīra, which helped bring about a brilliant development of Buddhist literature. The flourishing of Buddhism at the time is evidenced by a number of facts. One of King Kaniṣka's greatest contributions to Buddhism was the convocation and support of an important council. It was said that he inquired of a number of people about the Dhamma and received different answers. Considering the varied opinions and being unable to come to a conclusion, he followed Bhikkhu Pārśva's advice to summon 500 learned bhikkhus headed by Vasumitta to Kasmīra to compile and edit the Tipiṭaka with commentaries, which resulted in 300,000 stanzas totaling more than 9,000,000 words, and took 12 years to complete. Among these works was the *Mahāvibhāṣā-śāstra*, an important work of Sarvāstivāda which has two versions, new and old, in Chinese translation.

21. Q: What about the development of other Buddhist sects in this period besides the Sarvāstivāda?

A: At that time, in the Kasmīra area, the Sarvāstivāda Sect

答：当时迦湿弥罗地区，有部最为兴盛，但其他各部派也都很发达。与大众部有关而和有部对立的大乘思想这时流行于印度各地，在思想界中有着广泛的影响。迦腻色迦王所尊事的马鸣就是一个具有大乘思想的人。这时期可以说是大乘学说经过长期酝酿而趋于成熟的时期，但是大乘佛教的大兴，还有待于稍后一个时期的龙树大师。

22. 问：龙树是怎样一个人？

答：龙树（Nāgārjuna）是公元二、三世纪间的南印度人，原来是一个婆罗门学者，后来归依佛教，出家受戒，在雪山从一位老比丘受到大乘经典，由此智慧无碍。当时许多哲学家们都被他的雄辩所折服。他感到所读到的佛经虽然深妙，但是道理还有未尽发挥的，随后又从别处得到许多大乘经典，他便造了许多论著以阐明发挥经义。他的学说迅速地流布印度各地，从此大乘佛教便大为兴盛起来。

23. 问：龙树学说的主要内容是什么？

答：龙树主张的是“诸法实相论”。前面说过，在对于事物的认识问题上，有部认为一切法的自体是永恒存在的，只是它的作用的生起，要依借于因缘。龙树则与此相反，认为一切有为法只是因缘和合所生的现象，没有常住不变、单独存在的自体。譬如众木聚生而为林，林只是个假名，除众木外，别无自体（无自体也叫做“无自性”）。所以龙树说：“因缘所生法，我说即是空，亦为是假名，亦是中

was the most flourishing one, while other sects also developed considerably. The Mahāyāna doctrine, which was related to the Mahāsaṃghika and opposed to the Sarvāstivāda, prevailed in various parts of India and had extensive influence in intellectual circles. Assaghosa, who was held in esteem by King Kaniṣka, was imbued with Mahāyāna ideas. This period may be called the era in which the Mahāyāna doctrines came into maturity after a protracted incubation. However, the high point of Mahāyāna Buddhism was not reached before the appearance of the great master Nāgārjuna, who came shortly afterwards.

22. Q: Who was Nāgārjuna?

A: Nāgārjuna, a South Indian who lived in the 2nd-3rd centuries AD, was at first a Brahmanic scholar and later converted to Buddhism and became a monk. He received the Mahāyāna sūtras from an old bhikkhu in the Himālaya Mountains, after which his wisdom was boundless. His eloquence persuaded many philosophers at the time. He thought that although the Buddhist scriptures he had read were profound, they left much to be expounded. So he got more Mahāyāna texts to read and wrote quite a number of theoretical treatises to elaborate upon the meanings of the scriptures. His philosophy quickly spread over all parts of India, thus the flourishing era of Mahāyāna Buddhism came into being.

23. Q: What are the main elements of Nāgārjuna's philosophy?

A: What Nāgārjuna argued for was "the ultimate reality of all dhammas". As mentioned before, with regard to the cognition of the existence of all things, the Sarvāstivādins believed that the self-nature (sabhāva) of all dhammas exists eternally, with their functions arising dependent upon causes and conditions (hetupaccaya). Nāgārjuna held the contrary view that all conditioned dhammas are nothing but phenomena originating out of the concordance of causes and conditions, without perpetual, unchangeable and independent self-essence. For instance, a

道义。未曾有一法，不从因缘生，是故一切法，无不是空者。”“空”乃是一切法的真实相状。

24. 问：这是不是一种否定一切的怀疑论？

答：为了便于判断，需要再作些说明：(1)一切法空的理论是建立在一切法互相依存的因果律的基础之上的，所以它不是否认因果律的。(2)这里所说的空，不是空无之空，它是绝待的，不能认为是有，也不能认为是无，不能认为是生，不能认为是灭，一切经验上有无、生灭、来去等等概念都说不上，不是我们的觉知分别所能得其实际，所谓非有非无，非生非灭，一切皆空，所以说是“空不可得”。(3)对于事物的认识，龙树说有二谛，这是就一件事物的两面来说的：从现象来说为世俗谛（相待的世间真理），从本质来说为第一义谛（绝待的真理）。从世俗谛来看，宇宙万有，无量差别，种种相状，种种功用，种种生灭、来去、同异、是非、得失等现象和因果关系，历历分明而有；从第一义谛来看，虽有万象差别，而当体空不可得。空与有在因缘所生法上是统一的，因此世俗谛与第一义谛是二而不二的，这便是“不坏假名，而说实相”的道理，这也便是龙树的“中道义”。

forest, being composed of many trees, has no identity of itself apart from the many trees, "forest" is only a term without self-substance or self-nature. Therefore, Nāgārjuna said: "All dhammas arising out of hetupaccaya, I regard as Suñña (emptiness), or a false name, or the meaning of the Middle Path (P. Majjhima-paṭipadā, S. Madhyamā-pratipad). There is no dhamma which does not arise from hetupaccaya, so all dhammas are nothing but Suñña." "Suññatā" is the ultimate reality of all dhammas.

24. Q: Is this theory a kind of skepticism negating everything?

A: In order to make a judgment, further explanations are needed: (1) The theory that all dhammas are suñña is based on the interdependent causality of all dhammas. Therefore it does not refute the law of causation. (2) The above-mentioned emptiness (suñña) is not in the sense of nothingness. It is considered, in the ultimate sense, as neither existent nor non-existent, neither arising nor ceasing. All empirical conceptions such as existence and non-existence, arising and ceasing, coming and going etc. are irrelevant, since to see the reality is beyond the power of our sensation and differentiation. It is said to be neither existing nor empty, neither arising nor ceasing, and all dhammas are suñña (emptiness), therefore "suñña means unobtainable". (3) In regard to the understanding of worldly things, Nāgārjuna propounded the double Truth, or Two Levels of Truth, referring to the two aspects of everything: the phenomenon is referred to as "conventional truth" (relative truth) and the noumenon (essence) is referred to as the first truth (absolute truth). In terms of the Conventional Truth (Sammuti-sacca), there exist countless phenomena in the universe, which present the multitude of differences, the variety of appearances, all kinds of functions, all manifestations arising and ceasing, coming and going, identity and diversity, right and wrong, gain and loss etc., all kinds of phenomena and causality can be distinguished, hence exist. However, in terms of the First Truth (Paramattha-sacca), despite the multitude of manifestations,

25. 问:龙树之后,大乘有什么发展?

答:龙树之弟子提婆是龙树的得力的继承者和弘扬者。提婆也有许多著作,着重于破斥外道(佛教对非佛教的宗教和哲学,均称为外道),因此遭到杀害,但是大乘学说更为发达,同时,有部、经量部和其他部派始终与大乘相抗行,也都很发达。大乘佛教和部派在互相争论辩难中,都在思想上有所发展。到了公元四、五世纪的笈多王朝,大乘佛教产生了一个新的学派——瑜伽系(Yogācāra)与原来龙树的学派——中观系(Mādhyamika)并称为印度大乘佛教的二大思潮。

26. 问:请简略介绍一些笈多王朝的情况。

答:笈多王朝在印度史上是与孔雀王朝媲美的一个王朝。它是公元320年左右在中印度兴建起来的,月护王是这个王朝的创始者。第二代海护王统一了五印度,国势大盛。第三代月护二世王更向西方扩展,并发展了海外贸易交通,远及埃及诸地。随着政治与经济的兴隆,当时印度的文化学术也呈现着灿烂的光彩。笈多时代的佛像雕刻

the entity itself is empty and unobtainable. Existence and non-existence (bhava and suñña) are united in terms of dhammas which arise out of causes and conditions (hetupaccaya), so the Conventional Truth and the First Truth are "different, yet not different". This is the theory of "yielding the ultimate reality (paramattha) without breaking with the empirical concepts (paññatti)", and is Nāgārjuna's meaning of the Middle Path.

25. Q: What development was made in Mahāyāna Buddhism after Nāgārjuna?

A: Nāgārjuna's disciple Deva was a competent successor and propagator of this theory, who also wrote many books, chiefly refuting heresies (Buddhism termed all non-Buddhist religions and philosophies heresies). For this he was murdered. Yet, the Mahāyāna doctrine flourished all the more. In the meantime Sarvāstivāda, Sautrāntika and the other sects, which were all along in opposition to Mahāyāna also made headway. Mahāyāna Buddhism and the other sects, due to their debates and mutual challenges, all developed their own doctrines. By the Gupta Dynasty in the 4th-5th centuries AD, another new Mahāyāna school — Yogācāra came into being. Together with the original school — Mādhyamika, they made up the two main trends of Indian Mahāyāna Buddhist thought.

26. Q: Could you please give a brief overview of the Gupta Dynasty?

A: The Gupta Dynasty was founded by Candra Gupta in central India around 320 AD., and can be compared to the glorious Maurya Dynasty in Indian History. His son, King Samudra Gupta, the second monarch in the lineage, unified five Indian states, making the country a very strong power. The third ruler of the Gupta Dynasty, Candra Gupta II, further expanded westward, and developed overseas trade and communications as far as Egypt and elsewhere. Along with the flourishing of politics and economy, culture and scholarship in India also displayed

被认为是印度历代雕刻中很完美的作品。其它艺术、文学方面都有很高的成就。我国法显法师五世纪初西游印度时,正是月护二世王在位时期,他的《佛国记》中曾记载他当时见闻的盛况。至于宗教哲学方面,当时婆罗门教神学有很大发展,其他学派如数论、胜论等颇为兴盛;佛教在这时期也有了重要的建树,出了不少大学者,其中无着(Asanga)和世亲(Vasubandhu)两兄弟是最为特出的人物,他们就是瑜伽系的创立者。

27. 问:无着和世亲是怎样的人物?

答:无着是北印度人,原来是有部的僧人。传说,他因为对有部教理感到不满足,乃上升兜率天(弥勒菩萨所居住的天上),向弥勒菩萨请问大乘空义(一说弥勒下降为他说法),于是大得悟解。他传出了弥勒的五大部论,并且写了许多著作,以阐明大乘教义。有人考证,无着所师事的弥勒,大概是一位属于瑜伽师(有部中专修禅定的人,称瑜伽师,即禅师)的大乘学者,而不是兜率天的弥勒。世亲是无着之弟,原来也是有部的学者,后来听从无着的劝导,改学大乘,大弘无着的学说。世亲著作极多,被称为千部论师。

dazzling brilliance. The sculptures of Buddha images of this period are regarded as the consummation of Indian sculpture. Remarkable achievements were also made in the spheres of arts and literature. It was during the reign of Candra Gupta II that the Chinese monk, Ven. Fa Xian, visited India in the early 5th century. In his work *Records of the Buddhist Countries*, he gave an account of the grand spectacles he saw and heard in person. Meanwhile, in respect of religious philosophy, Brahmanic theology showed a great development, and other schools like Sāṃkhya, Vaiśeṣika (P. Visesika), etc. thrived too. Buddhism in this time also made important advances with the emergence of many great scholars, the two brothers Asanga and Vasubandhu who created Yogācāra system being the most eminent among them.

27. Q: Who were Asanga and Vasubandhu?

A: Asanga, born in North India, was originally a Sarvāstivādin monk. According to a legend, being dissatisfied with Sarvāstivādin doctrine, he ascended to the Tusita Heaven, (where Bodhisattva Maitreya resided,) to consult Maitreya about the Suññatā theory of Mahāyāna and gained a thorough comprehension of it. (Another story says that Maitreya descended from Heaven to preach Dhamma to him.) He then brought out Maitreya's Five Śāstras, and wrote many works to expound the Mahāyāna thought. Some scholars hold that the Maitreya who instructed Asanga was probably a Mahāyāna scholar from the Yogācāriyas (those Sarvāstivādins who engaged in jhāna were known as "Yogācāriyas" or "Jhāyins") rather than the Maitreya of the Tusita Heaven. Vasubandhu, a younger brother of Asanga, was also a Sarvāstivādin scholar at first and later converted to Mahāyāna under Asanga's influence. He advocated Asanga's doctrine enthusiastically and was honored with the title of Thousand-volume Ābhidhammika due to his great many works.

28. 问:瑜伽系学说的主要内容是什么?

答:瑜伽系的学说,内容极为繁博,包括方面甚广,现在只就宇宙观问题简略地介绍一些。在这个问题上,瑜伽系继承诸法实相论而加以补充和发展。它认为实相应该有两方面,既不是有自性,又不是一切都无所有,这样的认识才是离开有与无的执着,才是中道。瑜伽系说诸法自性有三种:一切法都是依众缘而起,这便是"依他起性";依他起的万物由于凡夫的种种虚妄思量分别(周遍计度),而有种种虚构的体相在心上现出来,其实这种种体相完全是没有的,这便是"遍计所执性";在依他起上离开虚妄分别,便证到圆满成就的真实,或叫做"真如",或叫做"实相",这便是"圆成实性"。这三性可以用一个比喻来说明,遍计所执好像是夜间行路看见一条绳而误认为蛇,其实蛇没有而似有;依他起好比是绳,绳的体由因缘所生,只是假有;圆成实比如绳体的麻,则是真有。从三性的里面来观察,又有三无性:第一,遍计所执的相是没有的,这便是相无性;第二,凡夫认为自然而有的事物,只是因缘所生而已,这便是生无性;第三,诸法的实相,是空不可得,这便是胜义无性。

28. Q: What are the main points of Yogācāra doctrine?

A: Yogācāra doctrines have a very comprehensive content, encompassing a wide range of spheres. Here I shall only say a little about its cosmology. On this question, Yogācāra School built up and developed the Theory of the Reality of All Dhammas. It holds the view that the reality of dhammas has two sides: on the one hand, self-nature (sabhāva) cannot be said to exist, yet on the other hand, all is not nothingness. Only with such a conception can one realise a detachment from existence and non-existence, and arrive at the Middle Path. Yogācāra maintains that the nature of all dhammas falls into three levels ("Trisvabhāva"): that all dhammas arise from causes and conditions is the Paratantra-svabhāva (the nature of being dependent in origin); that ordinary beings attribute to the dhammas produced by cause and conditions all kinds of illusory imaginations and judgments (false imaginations in their minds which do not correspond to reality), is the Parikalpita-svabhāva (the nature of regarding the seeming as real); that the completely true nature, or tathatā (the absolute reality) can be attained by eliminating the illusory inventions is the Parinișpanna-svabhāva (the absolutely true nature). The above three can be illustrated with a metaphor: Parikalpita is like one walking at night and mistaking a rope by the road for a snake, there seems to be a snake but actually there is not. Paratantra is like the rope with its substance arising from cause and conditions, which is only the hypothetical existence. The perfectly true reality resembles the jute, the substance of the rope, which is real in an ultimate sense. Further observation through the three natures shows that there are another three natures presenting non-existence (Trividhā-niḥsvabhāvatā): 1. The parikalpita inventions are not real, this is the nature of non-existence in form (lakṣaṇa-niḥsvabhāvatā); 2. The worldly things that ordinary beings take to exist are just produced by causes and conditions, this is the nature of non-origination (utpatti-niḥsvabhāvatā); 3. The reality of all dhammas is empty and unattainable, this is the nature

29. 问:“三性三无性”的说法,与龙树的二谛有什么不同?

答:“三性三无性”的说法仍然是以缘起性空论为基础的,但以前龙树的“一切皆空”论只是就三无性的一边说的,瑜伽系则同时主张三性,而且详于阐说三性一边的道理,它大量采用了有部的“名相”(即术语)而加以组织来分析说明一切法的类别和关系,特别指出在依他起中应当认识一切法都是识所变现,所谓“万法唯识”的道理,这是中观系所没有的。

30. 问:佛教既认为根(眼、耳等)境(色、声等)相合,才有识的发生,如何又说万法唯识呢?

答:唯识家认为我们眼识所见的色,耳识所听的声,鼻识所嗅的香,舌识所尝的味,身识所触的坚、湿、暖、动等,都不是事物的本身,而是五识依着五根托外界事物为“本质”而变起的“影像”。所以识有两种功能:一种就是能够变起影像的功能,叫做“相分”;一种是能够了别影像的功能,叫做“见分”。我们的一切知觉无非是自己识上的见分对相分的了别而已。

of emptiness in the highest sense (paramārtha-niḥsvabhāvatā).

29. Q: How does the Theory of Tri-svabhāva and Trividhā-niḥsvabhāvatā compare with Nāgārjuna's Double Truth?

A: The theory of Trividhā-niḥsvabhāvatā and Tri-svabhāva is also based on the theories of Dependent-origination and the nature of emptiness. However, Nāgārjuna's theory that all is nothing but emptiness explains only one side in terms of Trividhā-niḥsvabhāvatā, while Yogācāra simultaneously stands for tri-svābhāva as well and elaborates this in detail. Yogācāras adopted a great deal of Sarvāstivādin terminology and fit them together to analyze and explain the classification and relation of all dhammas, pointing out in particular that all dhammas are mere transformations of consciousness and should be understood through the investigation of the Dependent-origination. This is what is meant by "All dhammas are nothing but consciousness" (Vijñapti-mātratā), which is not mentioned in Mādhyamika System.

30. Q: Since Buddhism believes that consciousness arises from the combination of sense organs (indriya: e.g. eye, ear etc.) and sense objects (visaya: e.g. colors, sound etc.), how can the theory of Vijñapti-mātratā hold true?

A: The Yogācāras believe that the color seen by the eye, the sound heard by the ear, the scent smelt by the nose, the flavor tasted by the tongue, and the hardness, wetness, warmth and action felt by touch do not constitute the things themselves, but are the mirror images of the five forms of consciousness transformed on the basis of the interaction between five faculties and external substance. Thus consciousness (viññāṇa) has two functions: the objective function which gives rise to changing images entitled "the conception of objects", and the other, the subjective function which discerns the images called "the capability of signifying". All our sensations are simply our differenti-

31. 问:这种说法,只能说明我们主观对客观世界的反映,并不能说明唯识的道理,因为照唯识家的说法,也必须先有外界事物才有相分,有了相分,才有见分,换句话说,仍然是根境相合才有识的发生,根与境都是离开识而存在的,倒是识不能离开根境而存在。

答:唯识家主张六识之外,还有两个识——第七末那识(mana)和第八阿赖耶识(ālaya)。末那意译为"意",是第六意识所依之根,它有一个单纯的作用,就是恒常不断地执持"我"的思想。由于"我"的思想,人们在接触外界事物时,便有爱憎、好坏、是非、彼此种种意识活动。阿赖耶意译为"藏识",它能保藏一切事物的"种子"不使失坏。"种子"在这里是一个借用的名词,它的实际意义是能力,或者是潜势力。阿赖耶藏的种子有两类:一是名言种子,"名言"用现代语说,就是概念。我们前七识所见闻觉知的东西留着印迹于阿赖耶识上面,用唯识家的术语,这叫做"薰习",好像用香薰衣服,衣服便留着香气那样。薰习所成的便是作为潜势力而存在的种子。二是业种子,就是我们的意识所造的善业、恶业熏在阿赖耶识上的种子。由阿赖耶所藏的二类种子变起现在的五官(根身),外界(器界)

ation of the subjective function from the objective one within consciousness itself.

31. Q: This can only explain our subjective reflection of the objective world, but not the principle of consciousness-only (Viññāṇavāda). Because, according to Yogācāras, the object of perception must be preceded by the existence of external matter, and the subject of perception must be preceded by the existence of the object of perception. In other words, it is true that consciousness originates from the combination of sense organs and environment, both of which exist independently of consciousness. Conversely, it is impossible for consciousness to exist without faculty and environment.

A: Besides the six consciousnesses the Yogācāras developed another two consciousnesses: the seventh, manas and the eighth, Ālaya-viññāṇa. Manas translates as "mental consciousness" and is the root on which the sixth consciousness depends. It has the single function of maintaining a constant presence of the ego-sense, which gives rise to varied mental activities in people, including love and hate, distinguishing of good and bad, right and wrong, this and that, etc., when they come into contact with external matter. Ālaya-viññāna means "storehouse consciousness", which can preserve the "seeds" of all dhammas from loss and deterioration. "Seed" used here is a metaphor which, in its true sense, refers to ability or latent force. There are two types of seeds in Ālaya. One is the conceptual type of seeds or what we call "concepts" in modern terms. The objects perceived by the seven senses leave traces in Ālaya-viññāna, in the way that clothes perfumed with incense retain a fragrance. So this is called, in a Yogācārin term, Vāsanā, meaning perfuming, the result of which is seeds in the form of latent forces. The other type is the Karmic Seeds accumulated through the former kusala and akusala kammas possessed from mental volition. These two types of seeds in Ālaya give rise (pariṇāma) to the five sense faculties (indriya), the external world (bhājana-loka)

以及现起前七识（所以根身、器界都是阿赖耶识所变现，它们是阿赖耶的相分）。这身心宇宙的变起，叫做“现行”（现在的活动）。于是再由现行薰习名言种子和业种子而有未来的身心宇宙的变现。这就是瑜伽系的“阿赖耶缘起论”。

32. 问：佛教是不承认灵魂的，但是阿赖耶识可否说是变相的灵魂？

答：佛教内部对这个问题也有争论，甚至后来瑜伽系的学者也有删去第七、第八识而只谈六识的。但主张阿赖耶缘起论的人认为阿赖耶不是一个常住不灭的东西，而是永远在迁流变化着的，这与一般灵魂的意义不同。好像远望中的瀑布，看上去以为是一片白布下垂那样，把极其急速而微细的迁流变化的阿赖耶识，认作是一个常住不变的“我”（或叫做灵魂）的存在，这是错觉。这个错觉，就是末那识。唯识家的目的仍然是破除我执，把有漏（烦恼）之识，转成为无漏之智。

33. 问：瑜伽系除建立了一套完整的唯心论体系之外，还有什么其他建树？

答：佛教的逻辑学——因明，到笈多时代有了很大成就。瑜伽系学者在这方面的贡献特别多。到了六世纪的陈那（Dinnāga）和七世纪的法称（Dhammakītti），因明更为

and the preceding seven forms of consciousness. (Thus both the five organs and the external world arise from Ālaya-viññāna, being the perceived Ālaya.) Such a genesis of sense-faculties, mind and universe is known as Abhisamskāra (presenting activity). The Abhisamskāra again perfumes the conceptual and karmic seeds to reach the future maturity (vipāka) of the faculties, mind and universe. This is the Yogācārin theory of genesis from Ālaya-viññāna.

32. Q: Buddhism does not acknowledge the existence of soul. But is it right to say that Ālaya is a soul in another guise?

A: There is controversy over this question in Buddhist circles. Even certain Yogācārin scholars in later times only referred to the six forms of consciousness while omitting the 7th and 8th ones. However, those who stand for Dependent Origination on Ālaya believe that Ālaya-viññāna is not an eternally unchangeable one but an ever-changing flux. It is thus different from the general meaning of soul. It would be wrong to regard the Ālaya-viññāna flux with its rapid and subtle changes as indicating the existence of a eternal ego or soul, just as it would be wrong to take a waterfall for a piece of white cloth hanging down when seen from a distance. Actually, this misconception is Manas (ego-centered mind). The Yogācārin theory also aims to eliminate the ego-grasping (P. atta-gāha, S. ātma-grāha) and to turn the defiled consciousness (sāsava-viññāna) into pure wisdom (anāsava-paññā).

33. Q: What else did the Yogācāra School accomplish apart from establishing a complete idealist system of thought?

A: The Buddhist science of logic "—" Hetuvidya – had also made considerable achievement by the Gupta Era (5th century AD). Special contributions were made by the Yogācārin scholars in this area. The further developments were attributed to Dinnāga in the 6th century and Dhammakītti in the 7th century,

发展。这两人都是瑜伽系的大学者。

34. 问:印度大乘思想除中观、瑜伽两系外,还有其他派系没有?

答:正式形成学派的是中观、瑜伽两系,它们是印度大乘思想的主流。两系之间固然有学说上的诤论,两系内部也各有不同流派的发展。此外,也还有不同于两系的思想上的支流,将来有机会再谈。

35. 问:笈多王朝以后的情况怎样?

答:笈多王朝后期(五世纪末)哌哒族(一说是匈奴族,未确。哌哒族又称白匈奴,但与匈奴不是一族。)由阿姆河南下,占领印度西北部,建立王国。西北印佛教受到严重的破坏。印度终因异族的继续入侵,笈多王朝的覆灭,而陷于分裂割据的局面。其时,东印度一个王国西侵中印度,中印度佛教又一度受到破坏。后来中印伐弹那王朝的戒日王(Śīlāditya)战胜了敌人,并统一了中印度,佛教始稍稍复兴。笈多时代已经开始兴建的那烂陀寺,在伐弹那王朝继续得到增建,规模日益宏大,大乘学者们集中在那里讲学研习,蔚为当时印度最高学府。大约六世纪中叶至七世纪中叶,这一百年左右是那烂陀寺的最盛时期。我国玄奘法师在这里留学时(公元七世纪三十年代),瑜伽系的大论师戒贤(Sīlabhadra)和中观系的大论师智光(Jñānaprabhā)都在那烂陀寺讲学。戒日王曾在他的首都曲女城(Kanyakubja 今名 Kanauj)开群众大会召集学者们辩论哲理,可见当时佛教讲学风气之盛。

both of whom were great Yogācārin scholars.

34. Q: Are there any other Mahāyāna schools of thought in India besides Mādhyamika and Yogācāra?

A: Mādhyamika and Yogācāra are the two that evolved into full-fledged academic schools of thought in main-stream Mahāyāna doctrine in India, though there were controversies pertaining to doctrines between the two sects and new trends of development within each of them. Besides, there were also doctrinal substreams different from the two major ones and this remains to be discussed later.

35. Q: What happened after the Gupta Dynasty?

A: In the later period of the Gupta Dynasty (end of the 5th century) the Ephtalites (Some take the Ephtalites to have been Huns, but this may not be correct. The Ephtalites were also known as the White Huns, but were not the same as the Huns) came down to the south from Amu Daria River, occupied the northwestern part of India and set up a kingdom. Buddhism in this area was severely disrupted. Eventually, with the collapse of the Gupta Dynasty and many invasions by other races, India was plunged into a phase of disunion or disintegration. In the meantime, an eastern Indian kingdom invaded Central India and also disrupted Buddhism in this part. Thus it was not until later, when King Śīlāditya of the Vardhana Dynasty in Central India defeated his enemies and unified Central India, that Buddhism made a slight revival. The Nālandā-saṅghārāma which had been in construction in the Gupta Era was further expanded, becoming increasingly larger in scale during the Vardhana Dynasty. Mahāyānin scholars used to assemble there for lectures and studies, making it the highest educational institution of that time in India. The one hundred years from the mid-6th century to the mid-7th century was the Golden age in the history of Nālandā. When Dhammācariya Xuan Zang from China went there to study (in the 30's of the 7th century AD), Ābhidhammika

36. 问：这以后的情况如何？

答：戒日王死后，中印度又陷于混乱局面。当时印度分据各地的王国都崇奉婆罗门教，佛教日益削弱。独有东印度的波罗王朝历代崇信佛教。这个王朝起于七世纪中叶，延续到十一世纪末。它统治着摩揭陀以东的地方，那烂陀寺在它的境内，它又在那烂陀附近另建一超戒寺，规模更大。这一时期，密宗逐渐兴盛起来，九世纪以后，更为盛行，但佛教在学术思想方面则逐渐衰落下去。

37. 问：密宗是怎样创立的？

答：密宗，或称为真言陀罗尼宗，或称为密乘（大乘其他宗派相对而称显宗或显乘），传说是龙树开南天竺铁塔，取出秘密经典而传出来的。事实上，自龙树以来，流行的大乘经典中，就杂有密乘的成分（密咒），但独立而成立所谓密宗，则是远在龙树之后的事。

38. 问：真言陀罗尼是什么意思？

答：真言陀罗尼就是密咒。根据密宗的说法，密咒是佛内证的智慧的语言，是能够显示诸法实相的真实语言，

Sīlabhadra of Yogācāra School and Ābhidhammika Jñānaprabhā of the Mādhyamika School were both teaching there. King Śīlāditya used to hold Pañca-vārṣikamaha (mass meeting) in his capital Kanyakubja (P. Kaṇṇakujja, today's Kanauji) to debate philosophical doctrines, such was the splendid atmosphere of Buddhist teaching at that time.

36. Q: What happened after that?

A: With the death of King Śīlāditya, Central India once again fell into a chaotic situation. The kingdoms in all parts of India turned to Brahmanism, and Buddhism gradually declined. However, in eastern India, the Pāla Dynasty which arose in the mid-7th century and lasted till the end of the 11th century believed in and patronized Buddhism. They ruled over the territory to the east of Magadha, with Nālandā-sanghārāma in their domain. They built another temple, Vikramaśīla, on a larger scale near Nālandā. During this period, Tantric Buddhism developed gradually and flourished after the 9th century, while Buddhism in general declined in the academic sphere.

37. Q: How did Tantric Buddhism arise?

A: Tantric Buddhism, or the Mantra-dhāraṇī Sect, or Tantrayāna (meaning Esoteric Buddhism, in contrast to other Mahāyāna sects which are termed Exoteric Buddhism or Pakāsaniyayāna), was said to have been founded by Nāgārjuna after he obtained secret scriptures when he opened up the Iron Pagoda in south India. In fact, ever since the time of Nāgārjuna, elements of Tantrayāna (dhāraṇī) have been creeping into the Mahāyānin classics, but it was not until long after Nāgārjuna that independent Esoteric Buddhism came into being.

38. Q: What is Mantra-dhāraṇī?

A: Mantra-dhāraṇī means mystical incantation. According to the Tantrayāna theory, these are words of wisdom demonstrating Buddha's own grasp of the truth, as well the genuine

所以叫做真言。陀罗尼(dhāraṇī)的意义是“总持”。密咒的一字一声,总含着无量教法义理,持有着无量威力和智慧,凭仗念诵密咒的威力,可以获得远比显宗迅速而伟大的成就。密宗着重在修习仪轨,按照一定的仪轨,结坛,设供,身结手印,口诵真言,意作观想等等,以求将自己的身口意三业,转成佛的身口意三密(佛的身口意作用微妙不可思议,所以称为三密),这样便可以迅速得到智慧、神通,乃至即身成佛。修习密法还有息灾、增福、降伏等作用。

39. 问:密宗佛像有许多是多头多手,有的是面貌狰狞,甚至不是人的形状,这是什么道理?

答:密宗的像都是表示一定的意义的,如观音像的四臂六臂表示菩萨行的四摄六度,大威德金刚的三十四臂加上身、口、意表示三十七道品,又如佛座上的莲花表示出离心,月轮表示菩提心,日轮表示空慧(通达一切皆空的智慧),又如手中执持的种种器具也都是表示佛菩萨的种种誓愿、智慧、功德等。面貌凶猛的一般是金刚(有大威力的神)像,表示降伏魔军的威力和作用。此外,还有其他许多天神的像。

language capable of demonstrating the reality of dhammas. Therefore, this language is named Mantra, meaning "true language". Dhāraṇī means "keep holding". Each word or sound of the secret incantation always contains the infinite truth of Dhamma, and possesses infinite might and wisdom. Through reciting the incantation, one can achieve far quicker and greater results than through the practice of the Exoteric sects. The Esoteric School emphasizes the practicing of rites. According to certain rituals, the practitioners set up maṇḍala, offer sacrifice, assume postures (mudrā) with hands or body, recite mantras and meditate etc., so as to unite their own physical, oral and mental kammas with those of the Buddha (whose functions are so subtle as to be unimaginable, and therefore called the three Mysteries), thereby quickly attaining wisdom (ñāṇa) and psychic power (abhiññā), or even sudden enlightenment. To practice Mantra-dhāraṇī also helps avert calamities, enhance happiness, overpower one's opponents, etc.

39. Q: Why is it that many statues of Esoteric School take the form of multi-headed and multi-handed figures, some of them having horrible appearances, even inhuman in form?

A: All statues of the Esoteric School denote definite meanings. For example, the image of Avalokiteśvara's four or six arms denotes Bodhisatta's Four All Embracing Virtues (catu-saṃgaha-vatthūni) and Six Transcendent Virtues (cha-pāramitā) and the Almighty Virtuous Vajra's 34 arms plus body, tongue and mind represent the 37 conditions (Bodhipakkhiya-dhamma) leading to enlightenment. Again, the lotus on Buddha's pedestal stands for nekkhamma-citta, the crescent (moon) for Bodhi-citta, the sun's disk for the wisdom leading to suññatā-ñāṇa (the awareness that all is emptiness). The various kinds of instruments held in their hands represent different vows, merits, etc. of Buddhas and Bodhisattas. The fierce faced ones are generally the images of Vajra deities with tremendous might representing

40. 问:密宗是否吸收了许多婆罗门教的内容和形式?

答:是的。从历史来看,佛教最初是反对婆罗门的教义和祭祀仪式的。佛教一度在孔雀王朝成为国教,大行其道,但不久即随王朝的更易而遭到排斥,其后虽得到某些地方王朝的护持,但一般说来是不断受到种种障难的。为了随顺时势与世俗,佛教不得不采取一些"方便",以推行其教化。同时婆罗门教虽在政治地位上居优势,但由于佛教哲学的发扬,不能不受到刺激而要求改进它的理论。因此双方在互相排斥中的互相影响,便成为自然的趋势。到笈多王朝,婆罗门教梵我论的建立,扩大和增强了它的影响。公元七世纪后期,婆罗门教学者鸠摩梨罗(Kumārila)和商羯罗(Śaṅkara)更吸收佛教的理论而大大发展它的神学,于是婆罗门教便以新的姿态大为兴盛起来(西方学者把这以后的婆罗门教称为印度教),而佛教当时则以人才廖落,相形见绌日见陵逼。适应这样时节因缘而兴起的密宗,在仪式上大量采取"方便",吸收了婆罗门教的许多东西而加以不同的解释,确是事实。但是在教义上仍是以空、无我的理论为根本的。

their ability to over power demonic forces. Besides these, there are many other images of devas.

40. Q: Did The Esoteric School assimilate much from the content and forms of Brahmanism?

A: Yes, historically, Buddhism was at first opposed to Brahmanic doctrines and sacrificial ceremonies. When Buddhism became the national religion of the Maurya Dynasty, it was the exclusive teaching of the day. However, soon after, with the changes of dynasties it met with rejection. In the subsequent years, despite the support rendered by certain local dynasties, it continually suffered from adversity. For the sake of accommodating itself to prevailing circumstances and customs, Buddhism was obliged to take certain "expedient measures" to facilitate the propagation of its doctrine. In the meantime, Brahmanism in spite of its political superiority, could not but be affected by the development of Buddhist philosophy and called for a reform of its theory. Therefore, it became a natural tendency that the two adversaries were affected by each other even while repelling each other. By the time of the Gupta Dynasty, with the creation of the Theory of Brahma-ātma Identity, Brahmanism expanded and augmented its influence. In the late 7th century, the Brahmanic scholars, Kumārila and Śaṅkara, absorbed Buddhist theories to develop its theology tremendously, so Brahmanism began to flourish with a new face (Western scholars refer to Brahmanism after this period as Hinduism). In contrast, owing to a shortage of intelligent apologists, Buddhism fell into an inferior position and became increasingly marginalized. Meantime, it is true that the Esoteric School, which emerged in response to these conditions, took many "expedient measures" in its ceremonies and assimilated a lot of Brahmanic elements, and endowed them with its own interpretations. Nevertheless, its doctrine continued to be based upon the theory of Emptiness and Selflessness.

41\. 问：佛教在印度的最后情况是怎样？

答：从七世纪中叶开始，便有信奉异教的突厥族由中亚细亚侵入印度的西北部。到十世纪后半期，他们逐渐进展到五河地区，并向内地侵略，所到之处，印度原有宗教均受到破坏。到十一世纪波罗王朝末期和继起的斯那王朝时期，侵略势力渐达东印各地。佛教上师们星散避难，多经历尼泊尔、迦湿弥罗等地来到西藏。最后斯那朝王室也改变了信仰，超戒寺等重要学府先后被毁，留存的僧人寥寥无几。于是佛教残余不久便绝迹于印度本土，这大约是在十二世纪末叶的时候。

42\. 问：近代印度佛教复兴的情况，可否介绍一些？

答：十九世纪末期，斯里兰卡一位达摩波罗（Dhammapāla）居士到印度瞻礼佛教圣地，看到那些地方的荒凉景象，他便努力从事复兴印度佛教的事业，于是印度又开始有了佛教的团体和活动。近几十年来，中国、缅甸、日本等国佛教徒也陆续在印度各佛教圣地——菩提伽耶、鹿野苑、拘尸那等处建立了一些佛寺。印度人民渐有归依佛教，而且也有到斯里兰卡出家受戒的，但是为数不多。直到 1956 年，突然有一个大规模的改宗佛教运动在“不可触种姓”的群众中发生起来，这是近代佛教史上一件大事。原来，有一位安贝德卡尔（B. R. Ambedkar）博士，是印度“不可触种姓”人民的领袖人物，1956 年 10 月，他在那伽浦尔一次群众大会上宣布他改信了佛教，并宣传“人不是神

41. Q: What happened to Buddhism in India finally?

A: Beginning from the mid-7th century, Turks following another religion invaded Northwestern India from Central Asia. By the 2nd half of the 10th century they gradually advanced to the Pañjāb area and began aggression to the central areas. Wherever they went, indigenous religions of India were devastated. By the 11th century, during the Pāla Dynasty and the following Sena Dynasty, the invaders' forces gradually reached all parts of Eastern India. The Buddhist high priests dispersed and took refuge in Tibet via Nepal, Kasmīra and other places. Finally, the royal family of the Sena Dynasty also changed their creed and important education institutions like Vikramasīlavihāra were demolished one after another, with very few monks remaining. Buddhism disappeared from Indian soil soon thereafter. This took place at about the end of the 12th century.

42. Q: Would you say something about the revival of Indian Buddhism in modern times?

A: At the end of the 19th century, a lay Buddhist of Sri Lanka named Dhammpāla visited the Buddhist holy-land in India on pilgrimage. Witnessing the spectacle of desolation in those places, he embarked himself on the task of rehabilitating Indian Buddhism. Buddhist organizations with their activities were started anew in India. In recent decades Buddhists from China, Burma and Japan have successively built a few monasteries in various holy places in India, such as Buddhagayā (Bodhimaṇḍa), Mṛgadāva (Sārnāth), Kusināra and elsewhere. Some Indian people gradually converted to Buddhism and some even went to Sri Lanka to take monasticism and receive ordination, but only in limited numbers. In 1956, all of a sudden, a large-scale movement to convert to Buddhism sprang up among the "untouchable" masses, and it was a great event in the modern history of Buddhism. It was made possible by Dr. B. R. Ambedkar, leader of India's untouchables, who at a mass meeting held in Oct. 1956 at Nagpur announced his conversion to Buddhism, and proclaimed the Buddhist doctrine that "human beings are not crea-

创造的”和“一切众生平等”的佛教教义。参加大会的五十万“不可触者”响应他的号召，同时宣布放弃印度教信仰而归依佛教。安贝德卡尔于1956年12月突然逝世，但是改宗佛教运动不但没有停止，反而掀起了澎湃浪潮，向印度全国各地发展，成千成万的人相率归依佛教。据1962年5月《世界佛教》杂志报道，印度七千万不可触种姓人民中已经有二千万人改宗佛教。这个运动目前还在继续发展。

ted by God" and that "all living beings are equal". Half a million untouchables taking part in the meeting responded to his call, and at the same time announced their conversion to Buddhism by giving up the Hindu creed. Ambedkar died abruptly in Dec. 1956, yet the movement to convert to Buddhism did not come to an end, but conversely brought forth a towering and tumultuous wave spreading all over India, with tens of thousands of people converting to Buddhism en masse. According to *World Buddhism* magazine of May 1962, 20 million out of 70 million untouchables in India have converted to Buddhism, and the movement is still keeping its momentum today.

# 第五章
# 佛教在中国的传播、发展和演变

## （一）佛教的传入和经典的翻译

1. 问:佛教是什么时候传入中国的?

答:佛教传入中国的具体时间和年代,现在很难考定。最初传入时,不过在少数人中奉行,未必为上层官府和史官之流所注意。公元前二年,大月支国(原居我国甘肃的一个强盛的少数民族西迁中亚后建立的国家)国王的使者伊存到了当时中国的首都长安(即今西安),他口授佛经给一个名叫景卢的博士弟子,这是中国史书上关于佛教传入中国的最早的记录。我们可推断,由于在此一百二十年前汉武帝开辟西域交通的结果,当时由印度传布到中亚细亚的佛教很可能早已通过行旅往来而向东方渐进。也有传说:在与印度阿育王(约公元前 272—226 在位)同时的秦始皇(公元前 246—210 在位)时代,已有印度的沙门室利房等十八人来到我国咸阳。阿育王时举行第三次结集约在公元前 250 年,会后派大德赴各国传教,前来中国很有可能。另外,也有认为宋玉《高唐赋》和《史记·始皇本纪》中的"羡门"即沙门的,但因无译述学说传世,无从确考。

# Chapter V
# THE SPREAD, DEVELOPMENT AND EVOLUTION OF BUDDHISM IN CHINA

## (I) The Introduction of Buddhism into China and the Translation of Buddhist Scriptures

1. Q: When was Buddhism first introduced into China?

A: It is difficult to ascertain the exact time of the introduction of Buddhism into China. In the early years of its introduction, its followers were few and may not have been noticed by the upper bureaucracy and historians. In the year 2 BC, Yi Cun, the envoy of the king of Great Kuṣana (a kingdom established by a powerful minority ethnic group after its migration from Gansu, China, to Central Asia), arrived in Chang'an (present day Xi'an), capital of the Han Dynasty. He recited Buddhist teachings to a high-ranking scholar named Jing Lu. This is the earliest record of the introduction of Buddhism into China. We may presume that 120 years before this, with the opening up of communications with the Western Regions by Emperor Wu of the Han Dynasty, Buddhism, which had spread from India to Central Asia, was probably already being carried eastward by travelers. According to another tradition, at the time of Emperor Qin Shihuang (who reigned 246-210 BC, contemporaneously with Asoka in India, who reigned 272-226 BC), 18 Indian samaṇas—Sri Fang and others—came to Xianyang (near present day Xi'an). After the Third Buddhist Council, held in about 250 BC during the reign of Asoka, Buddhist missions were sent to various countries, so it is quite possible that a mission came to

2. 问:佛教最初传入的年代既是传说纷云,很难考定,为什么一般公认是开始于汉明帝的求法呢?

答:史籍记载,汉明帝永平七年(公元64)派遣使者十二人前往西域访求佛法。公元67年他们同了两位印度的僧人迦叶摩腾和竺法兰回到洛阳,带回经书和佛像,开始翻译了一部分佛经,相传就是现存的《四十二章经》,是《阿含经》的节要译本。同时在首都建造了中国第一个佛教寺院,就是今天还存在的白马寺。这个寺据说也是以当时驮载经书佛像的白马而得名。根据这个传说来看,佛教的传入中国虽不始于汉明帝,而佛教作为一个宗教,得到了政府的承认崇信,在中国初步建立了它的基础和规模,可以说是始于汉明帝年代。公元73年班超使西域,以后三十六国内属,西域道路畅通,当时著名科学家和文学家张衡(78—139)写的《西京赋》就提到"桑门"(即沙门),可见那时佛教僧徒的存在已开始成为引起文人学士注意的社会现象了。

China. Besides, some identify the word "Xianmen" which appears in Song Yu's *Ode of Gao Tang* and the *Biography of Shi Huang* in the *Annals of History* with the word "Samaṇa". Yet this is hard to verify since there are no extant translations or other books on the matter.

2. Q: If there are so many views concerning the first introduction of Buddhism into China, why is it widely held to have been at the time of Emperor Ming of the Han Dynasty and his search for Dhamma?

A: According to historical records, in the 7th year of the Yongping Era (64 AD), Emperor Ming of the Han Dynasty sent 12 emissaries to the Western Regions in search of Buddha Dhamma. In 67 AD, they returned to Loyang together with two Indian monks, Kāśyapa-mātaṅga and Dharmaranya and also brought scriptures and statues of the Buddha back with them. They began to translate parts of Buddhist scriptures, one of these tranlations is believed to be the existing *Sutta of* 42 *Chapters*, an abridged version of the *Āgama*. At the same time, the first Buddhist temple in China was built in the capital, that is the Baima (White Horse) Temple which is still standing today. It was named after the white horse that carried the scriptures and statues of the Buddha to China at that time. In view of this tradition, even if the introduction of Buddhism into China predates Emperor Ming of the Han Dynasty, it can be said that Buddhism as a religion was first accepted and upheld by royal court and began to lay its foundations in scale in China during Emperor Ming's reign. In 73 AD, Ban Chao was sent as an envoy to the Western Regions, afterwards 36 kingdoms of this area were subjugated and communication with the Western Regions was made easy. Zhang Heng (78—139 AD), the famous scientist and writer at that time, mentioned "Sangmen" (samaṇa) in his work *Ode to the Western Capital*, which shows that the existence of Buddhist monks had already become a social phenomenon, attracting the attention of men of letters and learned scholars.

3. 问：佛教传入中国的途径除了最初由陆路从西域而到关中之外，有无经由海路到达吴楚的可能？根据汉明帝的弟弟楚王刘英信奉佛教的情况来看，可以证明这一点。

答：我同意这个看法。据史籍的记载看来，当时楚地佛教的传播比起中原，似乎更盛一些。

4. 问：中国佛教什么时候开始有自己的出家佛教徒的？

答：中国很早就有了本国出家佛教徒，汉明帝听许阳成侯刘峻出家是最早的记载。但最初那些僧人仅是从师出家，剃除须发，照戒律生活，还没有受戒的制度；到公元250年来自中印度的昙柯迦罗在洛阳白马寺正式建立戒坛传戒，中国才开始有了如法的比丘。由于没有外国比丘尼到来，最初女人出家为尼的也只是剃发罢了；稍后从大僧受戒，还不具备完全的受戒制度。到公元429年，由斯里兰卡先后来了以铁萨罗为首的十九位比丘尼，才使她们的受戒具备完全的条件；从此，中国才有了如法如律的比丘尼。

5. 问：佛经的翻译始于何时？

答：佛教在中国的弘传是和佛经的翻译事业分不开的。最早的翻译，前面已经提到，摩腾、竺法兰在汉明帝时开始翻译过《四十二章经》，据说还有一些别的经。这就是

3. Q: Is it possible that Buddhism spread to China not only by land route from the West to Central China, but also by sea to Wu and Chu (middle and lower Yangtse) area? This is suggested by the fact that the Prince of Chu, Liu Ying, who was Emperor Ming's brother, was an adherent to Buddhism.

A: I agree with this view. According to historical records, it would seem that Buddhism was more widespread in the Chu area than in Central China.

4. Q: When did native Chinese monks first appear in China?

A: Native Chinese monks appeared quite early in China. The earliest on record was Liu Jun, Marquis of Yangcheng, who got Emperor Ming's permission to adopt monasticism. However, the monks in the early days merely adopted monasticism by following their masters, shaving their beards and hair, and abiding by certain rules, there was yet no ordination system according to the Vinaya rules. Not until 250 AD, when Dhammakāla from Central India established a regular ordination altar at Baima Temple in Loyang to transmit the precepts, did China have genuine bhikkhus. Owing to the absence of foreign bhikkhunīs in China, women who renounced the world at first merely shaved their hair. Later on, their ordination was presided over by senior monks. A full system of ordination was not in place until 429 AD, when 19 bhikkhunīs headed by Devasara or Tissara came from Sri Lanka. It was then that fully ordained bhikkhunīs came into existence in China.

5. Q: When did the translation of Buddhist scriptures begin in China?

A: The propagation of Buddhism in China was closely associated with the translation of Buddhist scriptures. As mentioned before, Kāśyapamātaṅga and Dharmaranya began the translation of the "Sutta of Forty-two Chapters" at the time of Emperor

最早的翻译。

6. 问：以后，汉代还有哪些著名的翻译家？

答：在初期（公元二、三世纪）的译师中，我们不能不提到安息国（在今伊朗一带地方）的安世高，月支国的支娄迦谶，康居国（在今苏联吉尔吉斯地区）的康僧铠、康僧会，和一位有月支人血统的最早西行求法者之一的中国僧人竺法护，同时还有朱士行于公元 260 年西行求法。由于他们的努力，不少声闻乘的和大乘的经藉被翻译为汉文。

7. 问：这些译师所传译的经典有什么不同？

答：他们中间主要有两个系统：一是小乘学派，以《阿含经》和“禅数”之学为主，可以安世高为代表；二是大乘学派，以《般若经》和净土信仰为主，可以支娄迦谶为代表。两派同时并行。

8. 问：那时的翻译对后来的佛教有什么影响或作用？

答：当时翻译事业还在初创时期，限于各种条件，还未能进行有计划有系统的翻译，所译的经书很少是全译本，而翻译文体也还没有能够确立，但是他们已经出色地做到了开辟园地的工作，为佛教在中国思想界树立了地位，并且扩大了影响。

Ming of the Han Dynasty, together with some other suttas. These were the earliest translations.

6. Q: Were there other famous translators later in the Han Dynasty?

A: Among the translators at the initial stage (2nd-3rd centuries AD), we must not omit such names as An Shigao of Parthia (around present day Iran), Lokasema of Kuṣana, Saṃghavarman and Saṃgīti of Semeg-kand Kingdom (in today's Kirghizstan), as well as Dharmarakṣa, a Chinese monk of Kusana extraction, who was one of the earliest monks to go to the West in search of Dhamma. In addition, Zhu Shixing also went to the Western Regions in 260 AD to search for Dhamma. Owing to their endeavors, a large number of Sāvakayāna and Mahāyāna scriptures were translated into Chinese.

7. Q: Were there any differences in the scriptures translated by these translators?

A: The translations fall into two main systems: one was the Hīnayāna School represented by An Shigao, primarily focusing on the *Āgama* and *Dhyāna* teachings; and the other was the Mahāyāna School represented by Lokasema, concentrating mainly on the *Mahāprajñāpāramitā-sūtra* and the Sukhāvatī creed. The two schools existed side by side.

8. Q: What was the effect of these early translations on the later development of Buddhism?

A: Translation at that time was in the initial stage. Due to various limitations, it was not yet possible to carry out well-planned and systematic translations. As a result, only a few of the scriptures were translated completely, and a consistent style of translation was yet to be formulated. Nevertheless, they rendered a valuable service as pioneers, helped to establish Buddhism in Chinese intellectual circles and extend its influence.

9. 问：佛教传入后有不少人研习弘传，中国僧界出现过什么样的重要人物曾促进佛教的发展？

答：佛教在中国的广大流行，开始于四世纪，当时中国僧界道安法师是一位重要人物，是起了很大积极作用的佛教领袖。他是我国最早的热心传教者，曾经派遣徒众到各地大弘佛教。他又是我国第一个僧伽制度建立者。他努力寻求戒律，以补当时律藏不齐全的缺陷，并制定了当时全国风从的僧尼轨范（中国僧人出家后，废除原有姓氏，一律以“释”为姓，是由道安提倡并从他开始的）。他整理了已译出的经典，撰成了中国第一部“经录”；他极力奖励翻译事业，并第一次总结了翻译的经验。在他的主持下，翻出了许多重要经论，集中和培养了许多学者和翻译人才，为后来鸠摩罗什的大规模翻译事业准备了有利条件。

10. 问：佛教的确立，首先在于戒律，经过道安的努力，以后还有哪些律部的传译？

答：道安和他的弟子们寻求戒律的热心，对于律藏的充实起了很大的推动作用。道安在世时，已经得到大量的戒本，并且翻译了其中的一部分，可惜那些书已经失传了。之后不久，来自克什米尔的弗若多罗和昙摩流支，先后帮

9. Q: Since the introduction of Buddhism into China, a great number of people have been engaged in the study and propagation of Buddhism. Who were some of the important figures in Chinese Buddhist circles that contributed to the development of Buddhism in China?

A: The popularization of Buddhism in China dates from the 4th century AD. Ven. Dao An, a leader in Chinese Buddhist circles, was an important figure playing a very active role at that time. He was one of the earliest zealous propagators who sent his followers to various parts of the country to preach the Buddha Dhamma, and was the founding-father of the first Sangha institution in China. He made every effort in search of precepts to supply the deficiency in Vinaya Piṭaka, and regularized rules and rites for monks and nuns to follow throughout the country. (For example, upon taking up monasticism, Chinese monks and nuns adopt the surname "Shi" (Sākya) in place of their former surnames. This was first advocated by Ven. Dao An himself.) He collected and collated the texts already translated, and made the first bibliography of Chinese Buddhism— *Jinglu (Bibliography of the Suttas)*. He energetically promoted and rewarded translation work and for the first time summarized the experience of translation. Under his guidance, many important scriptures were translated and quite a number of scholars and translators were gathered and trained, which provided favorable conditions for the subsequent large-scale translation work of Kumārajīva.

10. Q: The establishment of Buddhism primarily rests upon Vinaya rules. What other texts of Vinaya were translated after Dao An?

A: The earnestness which Dao An and his disciples exhibited in search of disciplinary rules gave great impetus to the enrichment of the Vinaya Piṭaka. In his lifetime, Dao An collected a large number of books of disciplinary code (Pātimokkha) and translated some of them. Unfortunately these

助鸠摩罗什译出了萨婆多部《十诵律》，这部律得到鸠摩罗什的老师卑摩罗叉在江西大为弘扬；佛陀耶舍（也是克什米尔人）在公元 410 年又译出了昙无德部《四分律》；奉佛音尊者之命，由斯里兰卡来到中国的僧伽跋陀罗译出了《善见律毗婆沙》。五世纪初法显法师游历天竺，主要也是为寻求戒律而去的。法显法师是大家都知道的中国古代伟大的求法者和旅行家，他的不朽的“游记”和其它方面的成就，可能容易令人忽视他最初求律的动机和这方面的成就。他除带回许多书籍外，并且带回了《摩诃僧祇律》和弥沙塞部《五分律》，前者已由他自己和迦毗罗卫国（今尼泊尔）的佛驮跋陀罗译为汉文，后者则在他逝世后由佛陀什（克什米尔人）翻译了出来。另一位伟大的求法者，七世纪的义净，也是抱着学律的志愿而远游的。他带回了而且译出了一切有部的十一种著作，从而使律藏大为完备。因此汉文译出的律藏有《四分律》六十一卷，《一切有部律》一百五十七卷，《十诵律》六十一卷，连同各部的羯磨文和戒本及解释律文的诸论，先后译出而现存的约五百卷。后世中国高僧们关于律部的著作，现存的也有五百卷以上。至于中国比丘戒的传承，在南北朝时代，北方传《四分律》，南朝是《十诵律》，及隋朝统一中国，政治上以北统南，佛教戒律也是这样，从隋代起，一直只传北方昙无德部的《四分律》。藏语系佛教地区向来是传一切有部律，傣族地区则流传着与斯里兰卡、缅甸等国相同的上座部律，与《四分律》（法藏部律）同一源流。

have been lost. Afterwards, with the help of Puṇyatāra and Dharmaruci from Kasmīra, Kumārajīva translated the Sarvāstivāda Vinaya which was widely disseminated by Kumārajīva's teacher Vimalākṣa in the Jiangxi region. Buddhayaśas (another Kashmiri) translated the Dharmagupta Vinaya in 410 AD. Sanghabhadra, who came to China from Sri Lanka with a mission sent by Ven. Buddhaghoṣa, translated *Samantapāsādikā* (the Vinaya commentary). Also in order to search for Vinaya rules, Ven. Faxian (Fahsien) toured throughout India in the early 5th century, and became a great Dhamma-seeker and traveler of ancient China. His immortal Travelogue and other achievements might overshadow his initial motive of seeking for Vinaya as well as his other accomplishments in this respect. He brought back, in addition to many other books, the *Mahāsaṃghika Vinaya* and *Mahīśāsaka Vinaya*. The former was translated into Chinese by Faxian himself with help from Buddhabhadra of Kapilavastu (a part of Nepal today), the latter, by Buddhajīva (from Kashmir) after Faxian's death. Another great Dhamma-seeker, Yijing, of the 7th century also traveled abroad with the same aspiration of studying the Vinaya texts. He brought back and translated 11 works of the Sarvāstivāda School, thereby completing the Vinaya-piṭaka to a great extent. Thus, the Vinaya-piṭaka translated into Chinese includes the *Dharmagupta Vinaya* in 61 volumes, the *Sarvāstivāda Vinaya* in 157 volumes, another version of Sarvāstivāda Vinaya of 61 volumes, together with the texts of Kamma, Pātimokkha as well as commentaries on the various Vinayas, a total of about 500 volumes now exist. In addition, Chinese high monks wrote more than 500 volumes of treatises about Vinaya which are also extant. As to the lineage of Bhikkhu precepts in China, during the period of the North and South Dynasties (3rd - 4th centuries AD) *Dharmagupta Vinaya* prevailed in the North, *Sarvāstivāda Vinaya* in the South. When the Sui Dynasty united the whole of China, the North dominated over the South in politics and also in Buddhist disciplines, thus the *Dharmagupta Vinaya* of the North has dominated since the Sui

11. 问：关于律藏翻译流传的历史和情况，听到上面所谈，已经知道大概了，请再谈一谈经藏和论藏大规模有系统的翻译是从什么时代什么人开始的？

答：佛教经论大规模有系统的翻译，应该说是开始于五世纪初的鸠摩罗什。

12. 问：鸠摩罗什的翻译事业比以前有哪些特点？对后来的佛教和中国思想文化起了什么样的作用？

答：鸠摩罗什的翻译事业，有着前人所未有的优越条件，那就是当时政府（姚秦）的大力支持和有在道安影响下产生的具有高度文化修养的一大批义学僧人的辅助。但是他的伟大成就是由于他有丰富的学识和持久的努力。这一位有印度血统在今天中国西北（新疆库车）出生的智慧卓越的大师，是中印两大民族共同的光荣。他和后来的玄奘法师是翻译事业中两大巨匠，他所译出的三百多卷典籍，不仅是佛教的宝藏，而且也是文学的重要遗产，它对中国的哲学思想和文学上的影响非常巨大。在他的讲授和指导下，造就了成千的人才，使当时的佛教得到大大的提高和发展。

Dynasty. In the Tibetan Buddhist areas, the Sarvāstivāda Vinaya has always been in practice, while in the Dai-inhabited areas the Theravāda Vinaya spread. This is of the same origin as *the Dharmagupta Vinaya*, and identical with that of Sri Lanka, Burma and other Theravādin countries.

11. Q: Your talk above gives a fairly clear picture of the translation and spread of Vinaya Piṭaka. Could you please talk about the large-scale and systematic translation of the Sutta Piṭaka and Abhidhamma Piṭaka? When and with whom did the work begin?

A: The large-scale systematic translations of Sutta and Abhidhamma Texts of Buddhism should date back to Kumārajīva in the early 5th century.

12. Q: What were the special characteristics of Kumārajīva's translations when compared with previous attempts? What effect did they have on Buddhism, on Chinese thought and culture subsequently?

A: Kumārajīva's translation work enjoyed unprecedented favorable conditions, being supported by the government (Yaoqin Kingdom) and assisted by a large group of volunteer monks with high learning under the influence of Dao An. However, his great achievements were mainly owing to his profound knowledge and perseverance. This brilliant master, who was born in Northwest China (Kucha in Xinjiang), of mixed Chinese and Indian blood, is the pride of both Chinese and Indian peoples. He and the later Dhammācariya Xuanzang were the two giants in the cause of translation. The 300-odd volumes of canonical works translated by Kumārajīva are not only the treasure of Buddhism but also an important literary heritage, having tremendous influence on the philosophical thought and literature of China. Under his teaching and guidance, thousands of intellects were fostered, enabling the enormous leap forward of Buddhism at the time.

13. 问：前面说过，罗什的翻译是有系统的，不知是属于哪一个系统？

答：就佛学方面来说，鸠摩罗什最重要的贡献是在于对由龙树创立的中观系统典籍的介绍。由于他的努力，这一系的经论著作，如《中论》、《百论》、《十二门论》、《维摩经》、《法华经》、《大品般若经》、《小品般若经》、《金刚经》等，以及《大品般若经》的解释——《大智度论》，都传到中国来，为中国法性宗开辟了广大的基地。其次，鸠摩罗什还译有声闻乘中的一部重要论著——《成实论》，起初与中观三论（或"四论"，加《大智度论》）相辅流行，之后逐渐形成了独立学派，在南北朝期间盛极一时，后人称为成实师。这一学派在声闻乘中是比较接近大乘的一系。

14. 问：鸠摩罗什之后还有哪些著名的翻译大家，又是属于什么系统？

答：鸠摩罗什的译业进行于公元 401—413 年间，主要是全面系统地介绍了大乘空宗龙树、提婆的学说。罗什之后，重要译师来者相继，主要经论不断译出。如觉贤于公元 418—421 年译出《华严经》，昙无谶于 421 年译出《大般涅槃经》，求那跋陀罗于 443 年译出《楞伽经》等。这些经典的译出对中国佛教义学的发展产生了重大的影响。公元六世纪初菩提流支来华（508）创译大乘有宗无著、世亲

13. Q: You have said Kumārajīva's translations were systematic. Would you tell me about his system?

A: In the area of Buddhist studies, the most important contribution of Kumārajīva was his introduction of the books of the Mādhyamika School founded by Nāgārjuna. Owing to his effort, the Sutta and Abhidhamma texts of this school, such as the *Mūlamadhyamaka-kārikā*, the *Śataśāstra*, the *Dvādaśamukha-śāstra*, the *Vimalakīrti Nirdeśa*, the *Saddharma-puṇḍrīka-sūtra*, the *Mahāprajñāpāramitā-sūtra*, the *Cūlaprajñāpāramitā-sūtra* and the *Vajrachedikāprajñāpāramitā-sūtra* etc., as well as the *Mahāprajñāpāramita-śāstra* (the commentary on the *Mahāprajñāpāramitā-sūtra*) were introduced into China, thus laying a solid foundation for the Dharmatā School in China. Secondly, Kumārajīva translated the *Satyasiddhi-śāstra*, an important book of the Sāvakayāna, which was initially spread along with the three śāstras of the Mādhyamika School (or four śāstras if we include the *Mahāprajñāpāramita-śāstra*). Later this evolved into an independent school, known to posterity as the Satyasiddhi masters, which reached its climax during the period of North and South Dynasties. This sect of the Sāvakayāna was closer to the Mahāyāna tradition.

14. Q: Were there any other famous translators after Kumārajīva? What schools did they belong to?

A: Kumārajīva's translation work, which took place between 401-413 AD, mainly covered the doctrines of Mahāyānin Suñña Sect as advocated by Nāgārjuna and Āryadeva in a comprehensive and systematic manner. After Kumārajīva, many important translators came to China in a continuous stream, and major Suttas and Abhidhamma texts were translated one after another. For instance, Buddhabhadra translated the *Buddhāvataṃsaka-mahāvaipulya-sūtra* in 418-421 AD, Dharmrakṣa translated the *Mahāparinibbāna-sutta* in 421, Guṇabhadra translated the *Laṅkāvatāra-sūtra* in 443, etc. The introduction of these canons produced a significant effect on the development of Chinese

一系的论典，其中《十地经论》影响尤大，传习者形成地论师一派（分南北两道）。以后真谛三藏（498—569）于公元546年来华，563年译出无著的《摄大乘论》和世亲的《释论》，564年译出世亲的《俱舍论》，566年到567年又重译《俱舍论》。真谛不仅是翻译大家，而且也是一位义学大师，来华日久，擅长中国语言，所译经论，随翻随讲，弟子记述成为义疏，传习之者称为摄论师及俱舍师。真谛到中国后二十余年遭逢兵乱，于颠沛流离中仍能译出一百数十卷重要经论，形成中国佛教的重要义学派别，是罗什以后玄奘以前二百余年中贡献最大的译师。

15. 问：唐代玄奘是传译瑜伽学派的，真谛也是传译瑜伽学派的，对比之下，他们译传瑜伽学有什么不同？

答：据玄奘所传，戒贤生于公元528年，可以推定护法约生于530年。而真谛生于498年，故真谛长于护法三十余岁。又真谛译有陈那著的《无相思尘论》（即玄奘译的《观所缘缘论》）和《解拳论》（即义净译的《掌中论》）。陈那是世亲的弟子而为护法之师，可见真谛是介于陈那、护法

Buddhism. In the early 6th century (508 AD) Bodhiruci came to China and initiated the translation of Asanga and Vasubandhu's commentaries on the Yogācāra. Among their translations the *Daśabhūmika-sāstra* was particularly influential, and its students formed a school called the Daśabūmika School with Southern and Northern branches. Later on, Tipiṭakācariya Paramattha (498-569 AD) came to China in 546 AD. He translated Asanga's *Mahāyāna-saṃparigraha-sāstra* and Vasubandhu's *Mahāyāna-saṃgraha-bhāsya* in 563 AD, as well as the *Abhidharmakosa-śāstra* in 564 AD, which was retranslated between 566 and 567 AD. Paramattha was not only a great translator but also a master of Buddhist philosophy, and with his long sojourn in China, acquired an excellent command of Chinese Language. He could explain the sūtras and śāstras as he was translating them. His explanations were taken down by his students and resulted in good commentary books. The propagators and students of these texts were known as masters of the *Saṃparigraha-sāstra*, or masters of Kosa. Though Paramattha suffered hardships of war for more than 20 years after his coming to China he still managed to translate more than 100 volumes of important sūtras and commentary works, which formed an important sect of Chinese Buddhism. He was one of the translators who made the greatest contributions during the 200-odd years between Kumārajīva and Xuanzang.

15. Q: Xuanzang of the Tang Dynasty translated works of the Yogācāra School, so did Paramattha. Are there any differences between their translations of Yogācāra doctrines?

A: According to Xuanzang, Sīlabhadra was born in 528 AD, from which it may be inferred that Dhammapāla was born in about 530 AD. Paramattha was born in 498 AD, so Paramattha was 30-odd years older than Dhammapāla. Paramattha translated Dinnāga's *Ālam-banaparīksā* (which was also translated by Xuanzang) and *Hastavālaprakaraṇa* (also translated by

之间的佛教有宗大师。玄奘所传以护法的学说为正义，其门下传述以真谛之学及地论师之说为旧说或旧译，而称玄奘所传为新译，古人（唐灵润）归纳有十四义不同。如旧译认为一切众生悉有佛性，新译则认为有一分无性（佛性）有情；旧译认为佛果理智不二，新译则认为理智各别（即分断、智二果）；旧译于三性中遍计所执及依他起二性俱遮，新译唯遮遍计所执；旧译以缘起之本唯在第八识，新译则八个识及相应心所皆为缘起之本。又真谛译之《转识论》以阿陀那为第七识，新译则以为第八识。真谛所传之摄论宗更立第九识，新译则无此说。

总之，新旧两译同属有宗，宗旨相同，因时代先后，各成一家之言，义解稍有差异，也很自然。但真谛所译传之学在隋唐之际的中国佛教界曾激起很大波澜，因而引起了后来玄奘法师到印度去深入研究的动机。真谛来华后至玄奘赴印前的八十余年中（546—627），印度佛学也经历了

Yijing) into Chinese. Dinnāga was Vasubandhu's student and Dharmapāla's teacher. This suggests that Paramattha was a master of Yogācāra who lived between Dinnāga and Dharmapāla, while Xuanzang mainly dealt with Dharmapāla's theory. So Xuanzang's disciples regarded Paramattha's translation and scholars of the Bhūmiśāstra School as the old theory or the old translation, while regarding Xuanzang's as the new translation. The differences between them were summed up by Lingren of the Tang Dynasty (698-907 AD) into 14 points. For example, the former maintained that all beings possess Buddha-nature, whereas according to the latter, there is a part of living creatures without Buddha-nature (a-gotra); the former holds that the doctrines and wisdom (understanding and mind) of the fruit of Bodhi are identical, whereas according to the new theory they are different in that they result in momentary and permanent fruit respectively; according to the old theory, among the Three Characteristics, the parikalpita (illusory) and the paratantra (empirical) are relative truths, whereas according to the new, parikalpita alone is relative; the old holds that the root of Dependent-origination lies in the eighth consciousnesses, whereas the new holds that all eight consciousness and the corresponding cetasika (constituents of consciousness) form the basis of Dependent Origination. In Paramattha's translation of *Triṃśikā-vijñapti-mātratā-siddhi* ( or *Pravṛtti-vijñāna-śāstra* ), Ādānavijñāna was made the 7th consciousness, while in Xuanzang's the eighth. In addition, the Mahāyāna-saṃparigrahasāstra School founded by Paramattha created the 9th consciousness which was absent from the new translation.

In a nutshell, both new and old translations came from the same source—Yogācāra School, so they had similar basic principles. However, it is natural that there were slight discrepancies in interpretation due to the separation in time and later they each developed individual distinct doctrines. Paramattha's translation caused a great stir in Chinese Buddhist circles during the Sui and Tang periods and this motivated Xuanzang to go to India

剧烈的变化。最初护法和清辨兴起了空有之争,接着月称和清辨又同室操戈而使空宗分成为自续、应成两派,月称又和月官进行了长期的论战。护法的弟子法称也对祖师陈那的因明进行新的改革。学说总归是辨析日精后胜于前的,玄奘所承之学大体说来是较旧译更为精审的。

16. 问:你说到印度去深入研究法相瑜伽学的玄奘法师,是不是为大家所知道的那位到西天取经的“唐僧”或“唐三藏”?

答:是的。但“唐僧”、“唐三藏”用在一个人身上却是错误的。唐是当时我国的国号,这两个名词现代语来说就是中国僧人,中国的三藏法师。对佛教中人,这本来是常识问题,但社会上误解的人太多了,不能不解释一下。

17. 问:那么他的大概事迹请介绍一下好吗?

答:对于人人都知道的玄奘法师,是用不着详细介绍

to make more profound studies. In the 80-odd years (546-627) between Paramattha's arrival in China and Xuanzang's travel to India, Indian Buddhism also underwent radical changes. First there arose the controversies between Dharmapāla and Bhāvaviveka over Suñña (emptiness) of Mādyamika and Bhava (existence) of Viññāṇavāda. After that, strife between Buddhapālita (supported by Candrakīrti) and Bhāvaviveka led to the split of Suññatāvāda into two factions—Svātantrika (independent reasoning) and Prāsaṅgika (depending on opponent position). And then, Candrakīrti and Candragomin waged protracted polemics. Afterwards, Dharmakīrti, a disciple of Dhammapāla, also made revisions to the founding master Dinnāga's logic (Hetuvidya). As former theories are usually improved and surpassed by later ones through differentiation and analysis, the doctrines inherited by Xuanzang were in general more circumspect and accurate than the previous translations.

16. Q: The Ven. Xuanzang, who went to India for further study of the doctrines of Yogācāra, of whom you speak—was he identical to the well-known figure of "Tang Seng" (Tang monk) or "Tang Sanzang" (Tripiṭakācārya of Tang) who went to "Western Heaven" in search of Buddhist scriptures (as described in the novel *Pilgrimage to the West*)?

A: Yes. But it's a mistake to apply the terms "Tang Seng" and "Tang Sanzang" to a single person. Tang was the title of the reigning dynasty of China at that time. So these two in modern Chinese mean, simply, "Chinese monk" and "Chinese Tripiṭakācārya". This is common knowledge among Buddhists, but I feel I need to explain since too many people in China have misunderstood the terms.

17. Q: Then, could you please say something about his life?

A: Actually, it's not necessary to go into much detail about such a well-known figure as Dharmācārya Xuanzang. The great

的了。这一位孤征十七载、独行五万里、足迹遍于西域、印度百三十国而且留下一部不朽的游记——《大唐西域记》的伟大旅行家，这一位通达中印文字、洞晓三藏教理、由留学僧而最后主持当时印度最高学府——那烂陀寺的讲席，受到了印度及西域各国国王和僧俗人民欢迎敬重的伟大的佛教学者，他以毕生精力致力于中印文化交流事业，译出经论一千三百三十五卷（约五十万颂），他的系统的翻译规模、严谨的翻译作风和巨大的翻译成果，在中国翻译史上留下了超前绝后的光辉典范。他的成就和贡献不仅在佛教方面，而且在学术方面，都是非常重大的。他不仅比较全面地系统地译传了大乘瑜伽有宗一系的经论，而且把空宗的根本大经——《大般若经》二十万颂也完全翻译过来；又把小乘说一切有部的重要论典几乎全译过来。另外，他又独得印度一位罕有的佛教天才大师护法菩萨的秘传之作，如和会空有两宗的《广百论释》和编入《成唯识论》的护法正义，印度都无传本。由此可见，他实际上已成为印度佛学发展到最高峰的首屈一指的集大成者。故在戒日王为他举行的十八日无遮大会上，他高踞狮座，陈义立宗，无人敢出而与他对场争锋。因此，大乘学者共尊他为“大乘天”（Mahāyānadeva，即“大乘的神”），为祖国赢得了当时两大文明古国间学术上最高的荣誉。

traveler who made a pilgrimage of 17 years single-handed, traveling 50,000 li all on foot, traversing 130 countries throughout the Western Regions and India, left behind an immortal travelogue, *The Journey to the Western Regions of Great Tang*. A great Buddhist scholar, who had a good command of both Chinese and Indian languages, who thoroughly mastered the Tripiṭaka doctrines and elevated himself from a foreign student to the presiding lecturer position in Nālandā — the highest seat of learning in India at the time, he was warmly and reverently received and respected by kings and common people alike, by the monastics and lay of India and other countries of the western regions. He devoted his whole life to cultural exchange between China and India, and translated as many as 1335 volumes (about half a million odes) of sūtras and śāstras. For his large scale and systematic translation, rigorous scholarship and tremendous achievements, he holds a place forever unsurpassed in the history of translation in China. His achievements and contributions are great and significant not only in the sphere of Buddhism, but also in the academic world in general. He not only translated comprehensively and systematically the sūtras and śāstras of the Yogācāra School of Mahāyāna Buddhism, but also translated the cardinal sūtra of Suññatāvāda, the *Mahā-prajñāpāramitā-sūtra* with its 200,000 odes (or ślokas, each śloka consists of 32 syllables) into Chinese. In addition, he also translated almost all important śāstras of the Sarvāstivāda School. Besides, he had exclusive possession of the esoteric works written and handed down secretly by Bodhisatta Dhammapāla, an unusually gifted Buddhist genius of India, such as the works of *Catuhśatakavṛtti* which synthesizes the theories of Suññatāvāda and Bhavavāda, and *Vijñapti-mātratāsiddhi-śāstra* which was edited by Xuanzang based on Dharmapāla's view. Both original texts were lost in India. It is thus evident that Xuanzang, who brought the Indian Buddhist studies to their highest development, was second to none. Therefore, nobody could speak out and challenge him when he sat aloft on the Lion Pedestal to proclaim his tenets, and present his views at the 18-day assembly (pañca-

百余年后，日本僧人金刚三昧(公元818年前后在华)游印时看见中印的僧寺中都画有玄奘所着的麻履(即麻鞋)及所用的匙、筋，以彩云烘托，“每至斋日辄膜拜焉”(见段成式《酉阳杂俎·前集》卷三及《续集》卷二)。可知印度当时佛教界已把玄奘的麻鞋当作佛的足迹一样敬重、供养了。一个学者在外国享到这样高的尊敬，除了各大宗教的教主，历史上尚无第二人。直到现在日本佛教学者仍然认为玄奘法师这样的人才，只有中国这个伟大民族才能产生出来，玄奘法师确实是我们民族的光荣和骄傲。

18. 问：历史上像玄奘法师这类人物，可否再介绍一、二？

答：再举法显和义净法师。前面提到，法显法师于公元399年，以六十五岁高龄发迹长安，涉流沙、逾葱岭，徒步数万里，遍游北印，广参圣迹，学习梵文，抄录经典，历时多年，复泛海至师子国(今斯里兰卡)，经耶婆提(今印度尼西亚)而后返国。时年已八十岁，仍从事佛经翻译。他著有《佛国记》，成为重要的历史文献。义净法师稍晚于玄奘，取道南海去印度求法，经时二十五载，凡历三十余国，寻求律藏，遍礼圣迹。回国后翻译经律五十多部二百多卷，撰有《南海寄归传》及《大唐西域求法高僧传》。法显、

vārṣikamaha) which was convoked in honor of Ven. Xuanzang by Śīlāditya (Harsa). He was haled as the Mahāyānadeva (meaning the Deity of Mahāyāna) by Mahāyāna scholars, earning the highest academic honor of two ancient civilizations.

About a century later, a Japanese monk named Vajrasamādhi (who visited China about 818 AD), during his tour in India, found that in Buddhist monasteries in central India, the jute sandals worn by Xuanzang as well as the spoon and chopsticks he used were painted against the background of colorful clouds, and were worshipped on occasions of fast days (Uposatha) (see Vol. III of Part I of *Anecdotes of You Yang*, and Vol. II of Part II of same, by Duan Chengshi). Apparently Xuanzang's jute sandals were already honored and worshipped as venerably as Buddha's footprints in India at the time. There is scarcely a parallel in history that a scholar enjoyed such high respect abroad except for the founders of various religions. Up to the present, the Japanese Buddhist scholars still assert that such a genius as Dharmācārya Xuanzang could only be produced by a great nation like China. Indeed, the great master Xuanzang is the pride and glory of the Chinese people.

18. Q: Can you tell us about some other historical figures similar to Dharmācārya Xuanzang?

A: Yes, Dharmācāryas Faxian and Yijing may be cited. As mentioned before, Ven. Faxian set forth on his pilgrimage from Chang'an in 399 AD at the advanced age of 65. He traveled on foot over tens of thousands of kilometers, across deserts, trekking through the Hindu Kush mountains, left his footprints throughout North India, visiting holy places, studying Sanskrit and copying Buddhist scriptures for many years. Then he embarked for Ceylon (Sri Lanka of today), and returned to China via Java (now Indonesia). At the age of 80, he continued to translate the Buddhist scriptures with perseverance. His masterwork *Records of Buddhist Kingdoms* became an important historical document. Soon after Ven. Xuanzang, Ven. Yijing

义净和玄奘法师一样，都是以大无畏的精神，为法忘身，冒九死一生的艰险，为求真理而百折不挠，鲁迅称赞他们为中华民族的脊梁确非过誉。他们为我们伟大民族争得了荣誉，为灿烂的东方文化增添了异彩，为佛教的发扬光大建立了不世出的奇勋。他们是不朽的翻译家、思想家和旅行家，他们对祖国文化的发展和提高都有不可磨灭的贡献。

19. 问：除前面所讲的几点之外，历史上曾有许多人从事佛典的翻译弘传，还有哪些著名的代表人物？

答：中国汉语系佛教翻译事业持续了十个世纪(二至十一世纪)，翻译过来的经律论三藏共有一千六百九十余部，六千四百二十余卷，著名的本国和外国来的译师不下二百人。除前面提到的诸人之外，如印度的昙无谶、佛驮跋陀罗、菩提流支，巴基斯坦的阇那崛多和施护，阿富汗的般若，柬埔寨的曼陀罗仙和僧伽婆罗，以及斯里兰卡的弘传密教的不空三藏等都是大家所熟悉的。通过这样多的人持久不懈的辛勤努力，把佛教的声闻乘、性、相、显、密各

made his pilgrimage for Buddha Dhamma by sea to India. In the course of 25 years, he visited more than 30 countries, searching for Vinaya-piṭaka and paying homage to the holy places. After returning home he translated more than 50 texts of Sūtra and Vinaya texts totaling more than 200 volumes, and wrote two books, namely *A record of the Buddhist Religion as Practiced in India and the Malay Archipelago* (another version is titled *A Journey to the South Seas and Back*) and *Biography of Eminent Monks of Great Tang Who Went to the Western Regions in Search of Dhamma*. Both Faxian and Yijing were like Ven. Xuanzang in indefatigably searching for truth with no thought of themselves, taking chances and risking death. Therefore, Lu Xun did not exaggerate when he eulogized them as the backbone of the Chinese nation. They have brought high honors for our great nation, added bright color to the magnificent oriental culture and scored unparalleled feats for the promotion of Buddhism. They are immortal translators, thinkers and travelers who made indelible marks on the development and enhancement of Chinese culture.

19. Q: There were a lot of people in history engaged in the translation and propagation of Buddhist scriptures aside from those mentioned above. Who were some of the more prominent figures?

A: The course of translating Buddhist scriptures into Chinese lasted 10 centuries (from the 2nd to the 11th century), and resulted in over 1690 texts of Tripiṭaka being translated, totaling more than 6420 volumes, with no less than 200 famous Chinese and foreign translators involved. In addition to the above mentioned characters, Dharmarakṣa, Buddhabhadra, Bodhiruci of India, Jñānagupta and Dānapāla of Pakistan, Paññā of Afghanistan, Mandra and Sanghapāla of Kampuchea, as well as Tripiṭakācārya, Amoghavajra from Sri Lanka who propagated Tantric Buddhism, are well-known. Through the persevering, industrious efforts of so many people , the Buddhist theories of

系统的学说都介绍到中国来，从而形成了中国佛教的巨大宝藏。1954 年中国全国文学翻译工作者会议上，作家协会主席茅盾在他的报告中说："我国的翻译事业，是有悠久历史和光荣传统的。我们的先辈在翻译佛经方面所树立严谨的科学翻译方法，及其所达到的卓越成就，值得我们引以为骄傲，并且奉以为典范。"毫无疑问，中国古代的翻译事业，给灿烂的汉民族文化创造了巨大的精神财富，在世界上是无可匹敌的。它是我们足以自豪的优秀文化传统之一。

但是，我们还必须指出常常容易忽略然而非常重要的另外一面。我国自古以来就是一个多民族的大家庭，各个兄弟民族在创造全民族的文化中都做出了重大的贡献和出色的成绩，在佛教方面尤其如此。西藏在吐番王朝时期，由于文成和金城两公主的下嫁，引进了盛唐文化和佛教的信仰，并创制了通用至今的文字。到持松德赞时期，迎请了印度当时最著名的显教学者寂护、莲花戒和密宗大师莲华生等建寺立僧，从事系统的翻译；同时又由沙州和向唐朝请去汉僧传授禅宗，讲经说法；到赤热巴中(即巴黎可足或彝泰赞普，815—836 在位)时，又迎请印度大德多人和西藏学者一起厘定译名，校正旧有译文，补译大量经论。公元十世纪以后西藏开始了佛教后弘期。直到 1203 年印度超戒寺及各大寺被入侵军破坏，三四百年间印度和西藏两地传法求法的大德往来不断。

Sāvakayāna, Dharmatā, Lakṣaṇa, Exoteric and Esoteric Schools were introduced into China, thereby forming the enormous treasures of Chinese Buddhism. In 1954, Mao Dun, Chairman of the Chinese Writers' Association, in his address to the All-China Conference of Literary Translation Workers, said, "The translation work of our country has a long history and glorious heritage. The conscientious scientific approach of translation created by our predecessors in translating the Buddhist scriptures and their outstanding achievements are worthy of our pride and should be acknowledged as our models." Undoubtedly, the translation work of ancient China created a great spiritual heritage in the magnificent culture of the Chinese people which is beyond compare in the whole world. It is one of the splendid cultural traditions of which we are proud.

However, one very important aspect, which is often neglected and must not go unnoticed, is that China has been a multinational community from ancient times, and each nationality has made significant and remarkable contributions to the creation of the culture of the nation as a whole, particularly in the sphere of Buddhism. During the period of the Tibetan kingdom, thanks to King Sroṅ-bstan-sgam-po's marriage with the two Princesses, Wen Cheng and Jin Cheng of Tang, the culture of the great Tang Dynasty and the Buddhist faith were introduced into Tibet, and Tibetan writing, in use to this day, was created. During the Reign of Khri-sroṅ Ide-btsan, the most eminent Exoteric scholars Śānta-rakṣita and Kamalasīla, and Tantric master Padma-saṃbhava and others were invited to Tibet from India to build monasteries, to establish the Sangha Order, and to make systematic translations. At the same time, monks of the Han nationality were invited from Sha Zhou of the Tang Dynasty to teach Zen Buddhism and the sūtras. During the reign of Khri-Ral Pa-can (815-836 AD), a number of Indian high priests (Bhadantas) were invited to standardize the nomenclature, revise the old translations and add new ones of sūtras and

举其最著名者，如出生于孟加拉的阿底峡尊者（982—1053），是印度当时学德最高的大师，于1042年应请至藏，创立迦当派。其学说为后来宗喀巴大师（1357—1419）所继承，创立了格鲁派（即黄教），遍传藏、汉、蒙广大地区。又西藏的玛尔巴曾三度赴印学法，创立了迦举派（即白教），此派在明代曾长期掌握西藏地方政权。世界知名的西藏圣人弥拉日巴即此派的第二代祖师。其余译经传法的大德难以备举。自公元八世纪中叶至十三世纪中叶五百年间，西藏译出的三藏经籍就已收入甘珠、丹珠两藏计算，部数五千九百余种，分量约合三百万颂，约当汉译一万卷。在藏译藏经中重译甚少，故实际内容大大超过汉译藏经。其中尤以空有两宗的论典以及因明、医方、声明的著作和印度晚期流行的密教经论，数量庞大，为汉译所未有。由于藏文翻译照顾到梵语语法的词尾变化和句法结构，因而极易还原为梵语原文，所以受到现代佛学研究者的高度重视。

śāstras, with the help of Tibetan scholars. After the 10th century there was another period of Buddhist promulgation in Tibet. Great monks came and went in succession propagating or seeking Dhamma between India and Tibet. This continued for 3 or 4 centuries until the year 1203 AD when the Vikramasīlavihāra and all other large monasteries in India were destroyed by invading troops.

Take, for example, an outstanding one among them, Ven. Ārya Atīśa (982-1053 AD). Born in Bengal, he was a master with the highest learning and moral integrity in India at that time. He went to Tibet in 1042 AD on invitation and founded the Bkah-gdam-pa Sect. His doctrine was later carried on by Master Tsoṅ-kha-pa(1357-1419AD) who founded the Dge-lugs-pa Sect (or the Yellow Sect), which spread over wide areas inhabited by Tibetans, Hans and Mongolians. Then there was Mar-pa of Tibet, who three times went to India to study Buddha Dhamma and founded the Bkah-brgyud-pa Sect (or White Sect) which ruled Tibet for a long time during the Ming Dynasty. The world-famous Tibetan sage Mi-la Ras-pa was the second patriarch of this Sect. Other Bhadantas engaged in translating the scriptures and preaching Buddha Dhamma are too numerous to mention. In the 500 years from mid-8th to mid-13th century, the Tripiṭaka scriptures translated into Tibetan, which are collected in Bkah-hgyur and Bstan-hgyur, number more than 5900 texts, consisting of approximately 3, 000, 000 lines, roughly equivalent to 10,000 volumes in the Chinese version. Since there are very few duplicate translations of the same text in Tibetan Tripiṭaka, the total contents must be far more than that in Chinese version. In particular, the śāstras of Suññatāvāda and Bhavavāda as well as books on Hetu-vidyā (logic), Cikitsā-vidyā (medicine) and Śabda-vidyā (linguistics), and Esoteric sūtras and śāstras which were popular in the late period of Indian Buddhism, are numerous in Tibetan but absent from the Chinese Tripiṭaka. Because it takes into account the inflectional endings and syntactic structures of Sanskrit grammar, the Tibetan version is easier to convert back into the original Sanskrit version,

另外，在清代曾进行满文大藏经的翻译。近代还发现西夏文大藏经以及回鹘文佛经的残卷。还有，我国的傣族文化一向不为人所知，解放后才发现傣族有非常丰富的傣文著作，其中即包含有南传巴利三藏的傣文译本。由此可见，我国各族文字的大藏经是人类文化史上极为罕有的巍峨丰碑，其中凝聚了多少世代人的聪明智慧和辛勤劳动，体现了我们民族的坚韧精神和伟大气魄，这是我们可引以自豪的无价的精神宝藏。现在我国决定校勘出版《大藏经》作为整理古籍的重要项目之一。这是我们佛教界值得引以为庆的大喜事，也是国际文化学术界所衷心仰望、企盼已久的大喜事。

therefore, contemporary Buddhist scholars attach great importance to Tibetan translations.

In addition, the translation of Tripiṭaka into Manchurian language was carried out in the Qing Dynasty. In modern times, remnants of the Tripiṭaka in Bactrian Language and in Ancient Uighur Language have been discovered. Furthermore, the culture of Dai nationality of China was not known to the outside world for a long time, not until after liberation was Dai found to have a very rich literature of its own, including the Dai translation of Pāli Tripiṭaka of Southern tradition. Thus it can be seen that the Tripiṭakas in the various minority languages in China are very rare lofty monuments in the cultural history of mankind, presenting the wisdom and toil of people of generations, embodying the perseverance and grandeur of our nation. This is an invaluable spiritual treasure worth our pride. Now, China has decided to collate and republish the Tripiṭaka as one of the important projects in re-editing the classical works. This is an event worth celebrating, not only by Chinese Buddhists, but also in international cultural and academic circles, which have been eagerly awaiting the event for so long.

## （二）佛教各宗派的兴起

20. 问：佛教传入中国，经过长期的弘扬和传播，有哪些发展变化，又有哪些学术成就？

答：随着大量经论的传来，印度佛教各部派思想与我国民族文化相接触，经过长时期的吸收和消化，获得了创造性的发展。公元六世纪末至九世纪中叶的隋唐时期，是中国佛教极盛时期，在这时期，思想理论有着新的发展，各个宗派先后兴起，呈现百花争艳的景象。

21. 问：中国佛教有哪些宗派，可否请简单介绍一下？

答：过去中国佛教出现过许多派别，现在流行的主要有八宗：

一是三论宗又名法性宗，

二是瑜伽宗又名法相宗，

三是天台宗，

四是贤首宗又名华严宗，

五是禅宗，

六是净土宗，

七是律宗，

## (II) The Emergence of Various Buddhist Schools

20. Q: Over the long course of propagation of Buddhism after its introduction into China, what developments and transformations have taken place? And what academic achievements have been made?

A: With the introduction of numerous canonical works into China, the doctrines of various schools of Indian Buddhism came into contact with the national culture of China, and after a long period of assimilation and digestion, gave rise to creative development. In the span of Sui and Tang Dynasties from the end of the 6th century to the mid-9th century, Chinese Buddhism underwent a period of florescence in which new developments took place in doctrine and theory and various schools emerged one after another, displaying a spectacle of a hundred flowers in blossoming.

21. Q: How many schools or sects are there in Chinese Buddhism? Could you give a brief description?

A: In the past many schools have existed within Chinese Buddhism. Nowadays there are 8 main schools:

(1) the Three Śāstras School (Mādhyamika School), also called the Dhamma Pakati School,
(2) the Yogācāra School or the Dhamma Lakkhaṇa School,
(3) the Tiantai School,
(4) the Xian Shou (or Hua Yan) School, the Avataṃsaka School,
(5) the Chan School (the Zen or Dhyāna School),
(6) the Pure Land School (the Sukhāvatīvyūha School),
(7) the Disciplinary School (the Vinaya School),

八是密宗又名真言宗。

这就是通常所说的性、相、台、贤、禅、净、律、密 八大宗派。

22. 问：这八宗各有哪些不同的主要宗义，想请您简略地分别介绍一下。首先请问，三论宗为什么要叫“三论”宗，它的主要教义是什么？

答：此宗主要依据鸠摩罗什译的《中观论》、《百论》、《十二门论》研究传习而形成的宗派，因为是依据中观派三《论》立的宗，所以叫做三论宗。它的教义以真俗二谛为总纲，以彻悟中道实相为究竟。

23. 问：什么是真俗二谛？什么叫中道实相？

答：二谛的“谛”字是真实的意思，从法性理体边说的叫真谛，从缘起现象边说的叫世俗谛。从俗谛说事物是有，就真谛说诸法是空，所以真俗二谛也叫空有二谛。色即是空，空即是色，色空不二，真俗不二就是中道，也叫诸法实相，这就是此宗的中心思想。此宗着重从真空理体方面揭破一切世出世间染净诸法缘起无自性，五阴十二处等虚妄不实，彻底破除迷惑，从而建立起无所得的中道观，以求实现其无碍解脱的宗旨。这一宗，实际就是印度龙树、

(8) the Esoteric School (the Tantra School) also called the Mantrayāna School.

These eight major schools are commonly referred to in Chinese as: Xing, Xiang, Tai, Xian, Chan, Jing, Lü and Mi.

22. Q: Would you briefly describe what major distinctive theories each of them upholds? May the first question be why the Three Śāstras School is so named? What are its main doctrines?

A: This School was formed primarily on the basis of studying and transmitting the *Mūlamadhyamaka-kārikā*, the *Śata-śāstra*, and the *Dvādaśamukha-śāstra* translated by Kumārajīva. Because its basis is the Three Treatises (śāstras) of Mādhyamika Sect, it is called the Three Śāstras School. The general principle of its doctrines is the double truth—the Ultimate Truth (P. Paramattha-sacca, S. Paramārtha-satya) and the Conventional Truth (P. Sammuti-sacca, S. Saṃvṛti-satya). The ultimate end is to perceive the reality of the Middle Path (P. Majjhima-paṭipadā, S. Madhyamā-pratipad).

23. Q: What is meant by the two truths – Ultimate Truth and Conventional Truth? What is the reality of the Middle Path?

A: The Chinese here use the word "di" to mean truth. The truth that refers to the nature of reality is called the Ultimate Truth (Paramattha-sacca), and the truth that refers to worldly phenomena originated according to the Paṭiccasamupāda is the Conventional Truth (Sammuti-sacca). According to the Conventional Truth, all things exist (bhava), and in terms of the Ultimate Truth, all dhammas are empty (suññatā), thus the two kinds of truth, ultimate and conventional, are equated with that of existence and non-existence. Matter (Rūpa) is Emptiness (suññā) and Emptiness is Matter, they are identical. Seeing the two truths as one is the Middle Path or the reality of all dhammas. This is the core of the theory of this school. According to

提婆中观学说的直接继承者。

24. 问:瑜伽宗为什么叫瑜伽宗,它的主要教义是什么?

答:瑜伽宗是由印度弥勒、无著、世亲创立的宗派。此宗主要依据有《解深密经》、《瑜伽师地论》、《成唯识论》等,因为是依弥勒说、无著记录整理的《瑜伽师地论》为根本教典而立的宗,所以叫瑜伽宗。我国玄奘法师译传此宗并糅译十师之说为《成唯识论》,故此宗又称法相唯识宗,亦称慈恩宗。它的教义以五法三自性,八识二无我为总纲,以转识成智(转依)为宗旨。

25. 问:什么叫五法三自性、八识二无我?

答:五法是:一名、二相、三分别、四正智、五如如;三自性是:遍计所执性,依他起性,圆成实性;八识是:眼识、耳识、鼻识、舌识、身识、意识、第七末那识、第八阿赖耶识;二

the ultimate emptiness of reality, this school lays stress on revealing that all dhammas, worldly or transcendental, defiled or pure, have no self-nature because of Dependent Origination, that the Five Aggregates (Pañca-khandha), the Twelve Spheres or bases (āyatana) etc., are nothing but illusions. Accordingly, one can thoroughly break with confusion, build up the view of the Middle Path on the base of nothing obtainable, and finally reach the goal of deliverance without obstacle. This school is in fact the direct succession of the Mādhyamika doctrine advocated by Nāgārjuna and Deva in India.

24. Q: Why is the Yogācāra School so called? What is the main doctrine of this school?

A: The Yogācāra School was founded by Maitreya, Asaṅga and Vasubandhu of India. The main bases of this school are the *Saṃdhinirmocana-sūtra*, the *Yogācārya-bhūmi-śāstra* and the *Vijñānamātratā-siddhi-śāstra*, it is so called on account of its basic text of *Yogācārya-bhūmi-śāstra* dictated by Maitreya and recorded and compiled by Asaṅga. The Chinese Dharmācārya Xuanzang translated and propagated its doctrine and made an abstract of the theories of ten masters and compiled it as one book, the *Vijñāptimātratā-siddhi-śāstra*. It is also called the Dharma Lakṣana Vijñānavāda School or Ci En Zong. The general program of its doctrine is of Five categories of dhammas, Three natures (Tri-svabhāva), Eight kinds of Consciousness and Two-fold Egolessness, and the purpose is to convert consciousness into wisdom (āśraya-parivṛtti).

25. Q: What are the Five categories of dhammas, Triple-nature doctrine, Eight kinds of Consciousness and Two-fold Egolessness?

A: The Five categories of dhammas (Pañca-dhammā) are: (1) Name (Nāma) (2) Form (lakkhaṇa) (3) Discrimination (vikalpa) (4) Right wisdom (sammā-ñāna) (5) Ultimate Reality or suchness (Tathā). The triple-nature (tri-svabhāvatā) consists

无我是人无我和法无我。“五法”是对世出世间一切法的概括，“名”和“相”指世间有为法皆有名有相，称为名相之法；“分别”指人们的主观能对事物分别认识；“正智”指圣人清净(无漏)实智；“如如”指如实智所对真如理境。“五法”不出染净和主客观，是以总括诸法。

三自性：

一是二取执着，无而谓有，起惑造业，名遍计所执；

二是三界心法，依他缘生，名依他起；

三是依他起上除遣二取所显二空真如为圆成实。

事物的性质不出此三种，所以叫三自性。

八识：

“识”是了别认识的意思，又叫心或意，每个有情都有

of: the illusory (parikalpita), the dependent (paratantra) and the perfected (pariniṣpanna) aspects. The eight consciousnesses consist of visual, auditory, olfactory, gustatory, tactile, mental, manas, and ālaya forms (or eye vijñāna, ear vijñāna, nose vijñāna, tongue vijñāna, body vijñāna, mind vijñāna, the 7th manas and the 8th ālaya). The two-fold egolessness is the non-existence of self (pudgala-nairātmya) and the non-existence of dhammas (dharma-nairātmya). The Pañca-dhamma includes all dhammas, both of this world and other worlds. Name and form refer to the fact that all worldly conditioned dhammas (Saṅkhata-dhamma) have their names and forms, and are thus called "dhammas bearing names and forms". Discrimination explains how people as subjects can differentiate and recognize objects. Right Wisdom refers to the pure (anāsava) and genuine wisdom of the saints. Suchness implies the intuitive wisdom towards the true reality. Therefore, the Pañcadhamma is the general catalogue of all dhammas, pure (anāsava) or impure (āsava), subjective or objective.

The Three Self-natures (Tri-svabhāva) are the following:

The first one indicates the two kinds of grasp (abhinivesa) of subjective and objective things (grāhaka and grāhya), the false attribution of existence to the non-existent and the fact that illusion produces kamma. So this is called Illusory Obsession (parikalpita).

The second refers to the dhammas of three spheres (kāma-loka, rūpa-loka and arūpa-loka) which originate from causes and conditions. So this is named the Dependence upon Others.

The third is the perfect wisdom corresponding to reality which is achieved by getting rid of the two kinds of grasp and by understanding of the emptiness of ultimate reality with the view of dependence upon others.

The nature of all things falls into the above three categories. Therefore, they are called the Three Self-natures.

The eight forms of consciousness:

Consciousness (viññāna) means conception and recognition,

这种心意识的认识作用，共有八种，就是前面列举的八种识。

二无我：每个有情或众生都没有永恒不变的实体（即一般所说的自我或灵魂）叫人无我；客观事物也没有恒常不变的实体（即自性或绝对的真实）叫法无我。二无我也叫作我、法二空。此宗教义深入分析诸法性相，阐明心识因缘体用，修习唯识观行，以期转识成智，成就解脱、菩提二果。此宗由玄奘法师译传而成立，是印度无著、世亲学说的直接继承者。

26. 问：天台宗的主要教义是什么？

答：此宗是以罗什译的《法华经》、《大智度论》、《中论》等为依据，吸收了印度传来的和中国发展的各派思想，重新加以系统地组织而形成的思想体系，因为创始人智顗，住在浙江天台山，所以叫天台宗。它的宗义以五时八教为总纲，以一心三观、三谛圆融为中心思想。

27. 问：什么叫五时？

答：此宗把释迦如来所说的经教，划分为五个不同的

and is also called mind (mano or citta). Every sentient being possesses a perceptive mind or consciousness, displaying eight kinds of consciousness as mentioned above.

The two-fold egolessness (anattā) means that neither individual sentient beings, nor the whole mass have any unchangeable or eternal entity (commonly known as ego or soul). This is called non-existence of self. Nor do objective things have perpetual entity as self-nature or absolute reality. This is called non-existence of dhamma. The two-fold egolessness is also known as emptiness of both human beings and things. The theories of this school analyze the inherent nature and form of all dhammas in depth to expound the cooperation of mind, consciousness and causality. This school practices meditation on Consciousness (Viññāna-vipassanā) in order to convert consciousness into wisdom and attain the fruits of liberation and enlightenment (bodhi). This school was founded by Dhammācārya Xuanzang with his translation and transmission, and is the direct successor of the doctrines of Asaṅga and Vasubandhu of India.

26. Q: What is the main doctrine of the Tiantai School?

A: The basis of this school is the *Saddharmapuṇḍarīka-sūtra* (Lotus Sūtra), the *Mahāprajñāpāramitā-śāstra* and the *Mādhyamika-śāstra* translated by Kumārajīva. Its doctrine was formed through the assimilation of the ideas of various schools introduced from India and developed in China by systematic reorganization. Since the founder of the school, Zhi Yi, lived in the Tiantai Mountains, Zhejiang Province, it was called Tiantai School. It takes the theory of Five Periods and Eight Teachings as its main creeds, and the Three-fold Contemplation with one's mind and the Perfect Harmony of Three Truths as its central idea.

27. Q: What are the Five Periods?

A: This school divides the preaching time of Sākyamuni Tathāgata into five different periods, and speaks of the "Teach-

时期，称为五时教，就是华严时、阿含时、方等时、般若时、法华涅槃时。五时的名称都是佛经的名称，主张佛陀所说的经教不出这五个时期的范畴，所以叫五时。

28. 问：什么是八教？

答：此宗从教理的内容上把佛教分为浅深不同的四个级别，就是藏教、通教、别教、圆教，称为“化法四教”。藏教是声闻小乘教；通教，通前小乘，通后大乘，通大小乘的大乘初级名为通教；别教是纯大乘教，但分别诸法各别有碍名为别教；圆教是大乘圆融无碍、圆满无缺的法门称为圆教。藏、通、别、圆就是以从浅至深为次第的四教。此宗又从佛陀说法的机感不同，将佛的教法分为顿、渐、秘密、不定四种，称为“化仪四教”。

29. 问：什么叫一心三观和三谛圆融？

答：三观是修行的观法，即空观、假观、中道观。此三观可以于一心中获得，名为一心三观。三谛圆融：真谛、俗谛、中道谛叫做三谛。此三谛举一即三，虽三而常一，说三说一是圆融无碍的，所以叫圆融三谛。一心三观，三谛圆

ings of Five Periods", namely, the Avataṃsaka Period, the Āgama Period, the Vaipulya Period, the Prajñā Period, the Saddharmapuṇḍrīka and Nirvāna Period. The name of each period corresponds to a Buddhist text. They assert that all sermons preached by Buddha fall within the categories of these five periods. Hence the term "Five Periods".

28. Q: What are the Eight Teachings?

A: This school divides the Buddha's Teachings into four different grades according to the profundity or simplicity of the contents, namely, the Tripiṭaka Teaching, the Intermediate Teaching, the Differentiated Teaching and the Highest Perfect Teaching. These four are collectively known as the "Fourfold Converting Teaching". The Tripiṭaka Teaching is the Hīnayāna teaching for sāvakas; the Intermediate Teaching is the medium interconnecting the earlier Hīnayāna with later Mahāyāna, and contains doctrines of Hīnayāna, Mahāyāna or the elementary Mahāyāna, hence the name; the Differentiated Teaching is the pure Mahāyāna doctrine with different approaches to various dhammas as its name implies; the Highest Perfect Teaching is the Mahāyāna doctrine, tactful without impediment, consummated without imperfection. These four grades of teaching are arranged in order from simple to profound. Then, on the basis of the Buddha's techniques of instruction, it differentiates between four modes of instruction, namely: Direct Teaching, Gradual Teaching, Esoteric Teaching and Indeterminate Teaching. These four together are called the "Four Modes of Instruction".

29. Q: What are the Three-fold Contemplation with One Mind and the Perfect Harmony of Three Truths?

A: The Threefold Contemplation (Ti-vipassanā) is a system of meditation practice, consisting of the contemplation of Emptiness, Illusion and the Middle Path. These three contemplation can be attained within one mind. Hence the term "Three - fold Contemplation within One Mind". The three Truths are the

融是圆教的教义，说明诸法无碍，事理圆融。天台宗以自宗为圆教，别的宗属前三教。此宗总结了以前各派的思想，将佛教教义加以精密的调整，发展了大乘圆教理论，展示了中国独创的大乘思想。

30. 问：贤首宗的主要教义是什么，为什么名为贤首宗？

答：此宗以《华严经》为根据，对《华严经》有深入的研究和精辟的阐发，是在前人（三论、天台、慈恩、地论师，摄论师等）学说发展的基础上形成的一个思想体系。创始人是七世纪末的贤首国师（法藏），所以叫贤首宗，又名华严宗。此宗以五教来判摄整个佛教，以六相、十玄、三观为它的中心思想。

31. 问：五教是哪五教？

truths of Paramattha, Sammuti and Majjhima-paṭipadā (ultimate, conventional and middle path) which are in perfect harmony. Though they are three, they are three in one, so, saying three or saying one means the same, thus they are regarded as the Perfectly Harmonious Threefold Truth. The Threefold Contemplation within One Mind and the Perfect Harmony of Threefold Truth are the tenets of the Highest Perfect Teaching which holds the view that all dhammas are basically the same, the truths are consummated without impediment. The Tiantai School identifies its own doctrine with the Highest Perfect Teaching and regards other schools' as affiliations to the former three teachings. This School sums up the theories of all previous schools, makes an elaborate arrangement of Buddhist doctrines, and creates the Mahāyāna theory of Highest Perfect Teaching which exemplifies the indigenous development of Mahāyāna doctrine in China.

30. Q: What is the main doctrine of the Xian Shou Sect (Avataṃsaka School)? Why is it so called?

A: This School takes the *Avataṃsaka Sūtra* as its foundation and makes a comprehensive study and a penetrating elaboration of it. Its ideological system is formed on the basis of the development of the theories of previous scholars and schools (such as the Three Śāstras School's, the Tiantai's, the Viññānavāda's, the Masters of Daśabhūmika-śāstra School and Masters of Mahāyāna-saṃparigraha School etc.). Its founder was the Imperial Preceptor, Xian Shou (Fazang) in the late 7th century, so it was named Xian Shou School, or Hua Yan (Avataṃsaka) School. This school asserts that the whole of Buddhism has Five Components of Teachings, the gist of which is the Six Features, Ten Metaphysical Entrances (doors) of thought and Three Contemplations.

31. Q: What are the Five Components of Teachings?

A: The first is the Small Teachings, i. e. the Hīnayāna

答：一是小教，即声闻小乘教；

二是始教，即大乘开始初级阶段的教义；

三是终教，即大乘终极阶段的教义；

四是顿教，即大乘中顿超顿悟的法门；

五是圆教，即圆满无缺，圆融无碍的理论。

此宗把佛教分作浅深不同的五种教义，比前天台宗多加一种顿教，所以称为五教。

32. 问：什么是六相？

答：六相是：总相、别相、同相、异相、成相、坏相。这六相既同时表现在一切事物中，也同时表现在一个事物中；无论在一切事物中或在一个事物中，都是相反相成、同时具足、互融互涉、彼此无碍的，从此可以揭示出法界缘起的道理。

33. 问：什么叫十玄门？

答：十玄门是：

一、同时具足相应门，

二、因陀罗网境界门，

三、秘密隐显俱成门，

四、微细相容安立门，

Teachings for Sāvakas.

The second is the Initial Teachings, i. e. the Teachings of the initial stage of Mahāyāna.

The third, the Terminal Teachings, i. e. the Teachings of the Terminal Stage of Mahāyāna.

The fourth is the Teachings for Immediate Comprehension, applied in Mahāyāna as the key to sudden enlightenment.

The fifth is the All-round Teachings, which means The Perfect Teachings, harmony without impediment, consummated without imperfection.

This School classifies the Buddhist doctrine into five parts from simple to profound with one more level than Tiantai School i. e. the Teaching for Immediate Comprehension. Hence the term "Five Components of Teachings".

32. Q: What are the Six Features?

A: The Six Features are: whole and part, unity and diversity, entirety and individuality (individuation). These six are manifest in all things simultaneously, as well as in each single thing simultaneously. Whether in all things or in a single one, they always oppose each other and also complement each other, are present at the same time, with harmony and mutual penetration without mutual disruption. In this way, the principle of Dependent Origination of dhamma world is revealed.

33. Q: What are the Ten Metaphysical Entrances of thought?

A: The Ten Entrances are:

(1) All phenomena are present simultaneously and correlate with each other.
(2) The relationship between them is like the endless Indra Net.
(3) The visible and the invisible phenomena exist within one unit.
(4) Even the smallest particles retain their own nature while mutually penetrating.

五、十世隔法异成门，
六、诸藏纯杂具德门，
七、一多相容不同门，
八、诸法相即自在门，
九、唯心回转善成门，
十、托事显法生解门。

这十玄门总的意义是显示华严大教关于一切事物纯杂(染净)无碍、一多无碍、三世无碍、同时具足、互涉互入、重重无尽的道理。

34. 问：什么叫三观？

答：一是真空绝相观，二是事理无碍观，三是周遍含融观。六相、十玄、三观的建立，阐发了《华严经》的法界缘起、理事无碍、事事无碍、无尽圆融的教义。六相、十玄是就所观的法界之境说的，圆融三观是约能观之智说的。这种重重无尽、法界圆融的思想，虽说导源于《华严经》，而实际为中国所独创，它的法界缘起、一切无碍的学说大大发展了印度传来的大乘思想。

(5) Dhammas in ten epochs are manifest without separation.

(6) Dhammas in all traditions have virtues whether pure or impure.

(7) Each thing and all other things inter-penetrate, but do not lose their own character.

(8) Various Dhammas exhibit phenomenal identity, free from resistance.

(9) All Dhammas exist as the reflection of the Tathāgata's mind.

(10) Profound theory can be illustrated and perceived with things.

The general significance of the Ten Metaphysical Entrances is to demonstrate Hua Yan's theory, demonstrated by all phenomena, that all things are present simultaneously, with endless mutual interaction, regardless of whether things are pure or impure, one or many, of the past, present, or future.

34. Q: What are the Three meditations ?

A: The first is the meditation on the ultimate reality of voidness. The second is the meditation on the unity of forms and substance without separation and hindrances. The third is the meditation on the universal harmony in which all dhammas abide. The establishment of the theories of the Six Features, Ten Metaphysical Entrances, and Three Meditations expounds the gist of the *Avataṃsaka-sūtra* such as the Dependent Origination of the dhamma world, the unity of phenomena and truth without hindrance, no separation and hindrances among things or forms, all in infinite harmony. The Six Features and the Ten Metaphysical Entrances are used in meditation on the basis of dhamma world, while the Three all-round Meditations are used in the insight gained through wisdom. This view that the dhamma world is endlessly multi-meshed and in infinite harmony is in fact a unique creation of China despite its source from the *Avataṃsaka-sūtra*. Its doctrine of the Dependent Origination of the dhamma world without hindrances is an enormous develop-

35. 问:禅宗的教义是什么?禅是什么意思?

答:禅是禅那(Jhāna)的简称,汉译为静虑,是静中思虑的意思,一般叫做禅定。此法是将心专注在一法境上一心参究,以期证悟本自心性,这叫参禅,所以名为禅宗。禅的种类很多,有声闻禅、有菩萨禅、有次第禅、有顿超禅。禅学方面,在中国有一支异军特起,那就是所谓“教外别传”的禅宗。这个宗所传习的,不是古来传习的次第禅,而是直指心性的顿修顿悟的祖师禅。

36. 问:此宗是否也有典籍依据?

答:相传此宗的禅法是在六世纪初由印度的菩提达摩传来的。过去说:禅宗单传心印,不立文字,称为“教外别传”。但初祖达摩以四卷《楞伽经》传于二祖慧可作为印心的准绳,弘仁、慧能又教人诵持《金刚般若》,这样,《楞伽》、《般若》便是此宗的经典依据。以后更有《六祖坛经》和许多“语录”的出现,不能说禅宗没有经典依据。

ment on the Mahāyāna doctrines introduced from India.

35. Q: What is the doctrine of the Chan (or Zen) School? what is the meaning of "Chan"?

A: "Chan" is short for "Channa", the Chinese transliteration of Jhāna (S. Dhyāna), meaning meditation or contemplation in tranquillity, also known as Chanding (Samādhi practice). This practice is to make the mind concentrate on one point of an object, and keep contemplating in order to become aware of the true nature of one's own mind. It is known as "Can Chan" in Chinese, so this school is called Chan School, or Jhāna School. There are a number of types of "Chan", including Sāvaka Jhāna, Bodhisatta Jhāna, Step by Step Jhāna and Jhāna of Immediate Enlightenment. In Jhāna studies, there is a special subsect different from others that is the Chan Sect who claim "transmission of Dhamma without recourse to the scriptures". It is not the traditional gradual Jhāna, but the Jhāna of the Patriarch which emphasizes "Direct pointing at the mind of the man, and the attainment of immediate enlightenment".

36. Q: Does this school have some specific suttas as its theoretical basis?

A: It is believed that the meditation practice of this school was introduced into China by Bodhidharma from India in the early 6th century. It used to be said that the Chan School (Dhyāna School) was passed on through mind to mind transmission one by one, without recourse of language, words and writing, thus it was known as "a special transmission without use of the scriptures". However, the first Patriarch of the School, Bodhidharma, handed down the 4-volume *Laṅkāvatāra-sūtra* to the second Patriarch Hui Ke as the criterion of its seal or essential idea. Besides, Hong Ren and Hui Neng taught their followers to uphold and preach the *Vajracchedikā-prajñāpāramitā-sūtra*. Thus the *Vajracchedikā* and the *Laṅkāvatāra* sūtras became the canonical basis of the School, and subsequent to

37. 问：我曾见到过一些寺庙，都叫作某某禅寺，是不是禅宗在中国很兴盛？

答：是的，禅宗在中国是很兴盛的。在八世纪间，此派曾分为南北两宗，北宗神秀（约606—706）一派主张渐修，盛极一时，但不久便衰歇；南宗慧能（638—713）主张顿悟，后世尊为六祖，弘传甚盛。从唐到宋，南宗的禅师辈出，在此三、四百年中又分为五家七派，可想见其兴旺的景象。此宗和净土宗一样，一直是中国流传最广的宗派。

38. 问：南宗后来的五家七派是哪五家七派？

答：南宗六祖慧能弟子中，有南岳怀让（667—744）和青原行思（？—740）两大支系，由这两大支系又分成五宗七派。从南岳先分出一派外沩仰宗，次又分临济宗。青原行思一系分出三派：曹洞宗、云门宗、法眼宗。由两系分为五宗，以后又从临济宗分出黄龙、杨岐两派，合前五宗名为七派，都曾兴盛一时，经过一段时期有的就衰绝不传了。后来的禅宗只有临济、曹洞两派流传不绝，临济宗更是兴旺。近代所有的禅宗子孙，都是临济、曹洞两家后代。

this, appeared the *Platform Sūtra* of the 6th Patriarch and many other recorded utterances. So it is impossible to say that Chan School is without canonical basis.

37. Q: I have seen quite a few temples named such and such Chan monastery. Does it indicate that the Chan School has been flourishing in China?

A: Yes, it does. In the 8th century the School was divided into two subsects, named the Northern Sect and the Southern Sect. The Northern Sect headed by Shen Xiu (circa 606-706) which advocated gradual cultivation was in fashion for a time, but declined before long. While the Southern Sect headed by Hui Neng (638-713), who advocated Immediate Enlightenment and was venerated as the 6th Patriarch by later generations, became prosperous and carried on. From the Tang Dynasty to the Song Dynasty, masters in the lineage of the Southern Sect succeeded one after another. Over the course of 3-4 centuries, it further branched into 5 subsects and 7 subgroups, which gives some indication of how the school flourished. This school, like the Pure Land (Sukhāvatī) School, has flourished long and wide in China.

38. Q: What were the later five subsects and seven subgroups of the Southern School?

A: Among the disciples of Hui Neng, the 6th Patriarch of the Southern School, were the two branches led respectively by Huai Rang (667-744) in Nan Yue, and Xing Si (?-740) in Qing Yuan, which gave rise to the five subsects and the seven subgroups. From Nan Yue branch first emerged the Wei Yang Subsect and then the Lin Ji Subsect. From the lineage of Qing Yuan, three subsects evolved, namely Cao Dong, Yun Men and Fa Yan. These are the five subsects from the two branches. Later on, Huang Long and Yang Qi subgroups emerged from Lin Ji. These two together with the previous five subsects formed the seven subgroups. All of them thrived for a time but some

39. 问:听说参禅打坐可以健康身体,却病延年,是这样的吗?

答:佛教在修习禅定的过程中,有一些调身调气、息心静坐的方法,是有强健身体、却病延年的作用的,但这不是佛教参禅静坐的目的。佛教修习禅观(包括各宗的修观),是为的制心一处,参究真理,以期显发智慧,彻见法性,此即所谓明心见性,解脱自在。至于静坐气功,只是修禅的形式或基础,却病延寿,也不过是修习禅观实践中的副产品,佛教并不专门提倡这些并以之为目的。但初学静坐的人必须懂得这些调身调气的基本方法,使身心保持健康状态,避免禅病的发生,才能保证修习禅观的顺利进行。

40. 问:净土宗的宗旨教义是什么?

答:此宗是依《无量寿经》等提倡观佛、念佛以求生西方阿弥陀佛极乐净土为宗旨而形成的宗派,所以名为净土宗。此宗分佛陀说的法门为二道,即难行道和易行道,并

waned and became extinct after a period. Only Lin Ji and Cao Dong subsects have survived, with the former more flourishing. All descendants of the Chan School in modern times are the offspring of the Lin Ji and Cao Dong subsects.

39. Q: Some believe that Dhyāna practice (Can Chan or Da Zuo in Chinese) has the effect of helping people keep in good health, avert illness and attain longevity. Is it true?

A: In Buddhist meditation, there are certain ways to adjust posture and breath, to rest the mind and sit down in tranquillity which have the positive effect of promoting good health, averting illness and attaining longevity. However, this is not the purpose of Buddhist Dhyāna practice. Buddhist meditation (including contemplation of various schools) is aimed at concentration of mind on one point, thoroughly understanding the truth, and finally manifesting wisdom (paññā) and perceiving the nature of Dhammas. This is known as illuminating the mind (citta), revealing the true nature and obtaining freedom. As to sitting in quiet and Qigong, these are merely the form or base for practicing meditation, while keeping from illness and attaining longevity are merely the byproduct of dhyāna practice. Buddhism does not particularly encourage these effects or set them as its goal. Nevertheless, it is necessary for the beginners of meditation to know these basic methods of adjusting postures and breath in order to keep the body and mind in a proper state and to avoid ailments arising from meditation practice, only then can the smooth approach of the dhyāna-contemplation be safeguarded.

40. Q: Could you please summarize the theories of the Pure Land (Sukhāvatīvyūha) School?

A: This school was formed on the basis of the *Sukhāvatīvyūha (Amitāyus-sūtra)* and other texts, with the aim of advocating a practice of meditating and intoning Amita Buddha so as to gain rebirth in the Western Pure Land where Amita Buddha

说别的宗依戒定慧修六度万行，需经三大阿僧祇劫为难行道，说修净土法门一生至诚念佛，临命终时，仗承阿弥陀佛的愿力往生安养净土永不退转为易行道。因此，此宗主张劝人念佛求生西方净土极乐世界。

41. 问：此宗有哪些特点？

答：此宗的特点，简单易行，普能摄受广大群众。修学此宗不一定要通达佛经，广研教乘，也不一定要静坐专修，行住坐卧皆可称念“南无阿弥陀佛”，只要信愿具足，一心念佛，始终不怠，临命终时，就可往生净土。当然平时也要持戒诵经，广行众善以作助行。由于法门简便，所以最易普及。别宗的学者，也多兼修此法，因而使净土法门在中国得到特殊广泛的流行。

resides. Hence the name Pure Land School. This school divides the Buddha's methods into two courses, the difficult course and the easy course. They point out that those schools who observe the Six Perfections (cha-pāramitā) and practise numerous exercises requiring discipline (sīla), concentration (samādhi) and wisdom (paññā) over three long periods of time (asaṅkhya), belong to the difficult course; that the Pure Land School practice, on the other hand, is to devote one's heart and soul to recitation of the Buddha's name, and in this way one can go to the peaceful Pure Land at the moment of death by the power of Amita Buddha's vow, so it falls under the category of easy course. Therefore, this school advises people to recite Amita Buddha's name in order to attain rebirth in the Western Pure Land.

41. Q: What are the characteristics of this School?

A: This school is characterized by its simplicity in practice and its strong appeal to the broad masses. According to this school it is necessary neither to master the Buddhist scriptures and study the doctrines extensively, nor to adopt meditation and special cultivation, but to keep reciting "Namo Amita Buddha" while walking, standing, sitting or lying down. With sufficient faith and devotion to recite the Buddha's name whole-heartedly and unremittingly, one can be reborn in the Pure Land at the time of death. Of course one should, too, observe the precepts, chant the suttas, and widely do good in daily life, so as to assist one to reach the goal. Since the manipulation is so simple and thus easy to popularize, even scholars of other schools practice this method, thereby enabling the Pure Land School to command particular popularity in China.

42. 问:律宗,顾名思义是着重学习和研究戒律的宗派吧?

答:是的,律宗主要是学习和研究戒律的。由于此一宗的盛行,中国僧人们在修学大乘的戒定慧三学中,仍然重视出家声闻乘的戒律。

43. 问:戒律都有哪些内容?

答:简单的说:戒律有声闻戒、有菩萨戒,这里所讲的律宗,是依声闻律部中的《四分律》,由终南山道宣律师一系所立的律宗。就戒条戒相说,有五戒、十戒、具足戒之分。五戒是出家,在家佛弟子共持的戒;十戒、具足戒是出家弟子的戒,这些在前面已经叙述,这里不多重复。各部律藏不只是戒相和制戒因缘,更大的部分是僧团法规、各种羯磨法(会议办事)、出家法、授戒法、安居法、布萨法、衣食法,以及日常生活小事,都有详细规定。因为时代的关系,环境的不同,许多戒律的规定,早已废弛不行了。菩萨戒有在家菩萨戒,出家菩萨戒。出家菩萨戒如《梵网戒经》有十重四十八轻戒,在家菩萨戒如《优婆塞戒经》有六重二十八轻戒。又总摄菩萨戒为三聚,三聚是三类的意思,称为三聚净戒。一是摄律仪戒,是戒相,是“诸恶莫作”;二是摄善法戒,是“众善奉行”;三是饶益有情戒,是“利益一切众生”。中国主要是大乘佛教,所以这里也简单提一提菩萨戒律。以上是大小乘戒律的内容。

42. Q: Judging by its name, one would say the Vinaya School is a school placing emphasis on learning and research of the Vinaya Piṭaka. Is that right?

A: Yes, the Vinaya School mainly pays attention to Vinaya studies. Due to the popularity of this School, Chinese monks, in the course of their learning and practice of Mahāyāna's Three Categories of Studies (tisso sikkhā)—discipline, contemplation, and wisdom (adhisīla, adhicitta and adhipaññā), also attach importance to the Vinaya Piṭaka of Sāvakayāna.

43. Q: What are the contents of the Vinaya rules?

A: In brief, Vinaya rules consist of Sāvaka-vinaya and Bodhisatta-vinaya. The Vinaya School mentioned here refers to the lineage founded by Vinayācārya Dao Xuan of the Zhongnan Mountains on the basis of Dharmagupta Vinaya of Sāvakayāna. In terms of the precepts and features of discipline, there are respectively the Five Precepts, the Ten Precepts and the Full Commandments (upasampadā). The Five Precepts are observed by both monastic and lay Buddhists, while the Ten and the Full Commandments are observed by monastic disciples. These have been mentioned before and need not be repeated. The Vinaya Piṭaka of each sect does not merely include the precepts and the reasons for their being laid down, (or enacted), but also, in greater portion, the regulations (kamma, or the procedures of meeting) for Sangha Order, such as the institution of renunciation, ordination, rainy retreat (Vassa), fortnightly assembly (Uposatha), robes and alms begging as well as other daily routines, each in detail. With the lapse of time and the change of circumstances, many rules of the Vinaya have long fallen into laxity. The Bodhisatta Vinaya consists of precepts for lay followers and for monks and nuns respectively. The monastic Bodhisatta Vinaya stipulates, as in *Brahmajāla-sīla-sutta*, 10 major and 48 minor precepts, while that for lay followers stipulates 6 major and 28 minor rules as contained in the *Upāsaka-sīla-sutta*. Again, the Bodhisatta-vinaya is generally summed up into Three Aggregates or three categories of purifying sīla. They

44. 问:《四分律》是声闻戒,八大宗里为什么有小乘宗?

答:《四分律》虽属小乘戒,但其文义通于大乘,自古就有“分通大乘”的说法。中国盛行大乘,以大乘教义解释律藏,摄小入大,就是大乘戒的组成部分,出家菩萨三聚净戒中的摄律仪戒就是以声闻戒为基础的。如杀、盗、淫、妄四根本戒,是大小乘共同遵守的。对于律学的研究,最重要的是善于分辨开、遮、持、犯,就是在出家戒条中,本来是不得触犯的,但在某种情况下可以开许,这叫开;在通常情况下又不得违犯的,就叫遮。在某种情况下,本人也不知是持戒还是犯戒,这就需要研究律学。律师根据律藏分辨清楚确定开、遮、持、犯的界限。在声闻戒中除四根本戒(杀、盗、淫,妄),或者还加十三僧残(尼戒是八根本十七僧残)必须严格遵守,不得违犯外,其它绝大部分的戒条,在特殊情况和必要情况下是可以开许的。例如“非时食”这一条戒,即通常过午就不许吃东西,而在劳作以后就允许吃东西。但如何开许,要依戒律来判定。可见佛教戒律不是死板的,除根本性戒外,都是具有灵活性的。

are: first, Saṃvara-sīla which refers to the moral precepts, meaning "the Avoidance of all evils"; second, Kuśala-dharma-saṃārāhaka-śīla, meaning "the acquisition of all good"; and third, Sattvārtha-kriyā-śīla, meaning "benefiting all sentient beings". Since China essentially belongs to Mahāyāna Buddhism, the Bodhisatta Vinaya has to be briefly referred to here. The aforesaid are the contents of the Vinayas of both Mahāyāna and Hīnayāna.

44. Q: Since the Dharmagupta Vinaya belongs to Sāvakayāna, why is this Hīnayāna School listed among the eight major schools of China?

A: Though it belongs to Ṣāvakayāna, the essence of Dharmagupta Vinaya is in common with Mahāyāna; as the saying from early time goes, "There is something applicable also to Mahāyāna". With the prevalence of Mahāyāna in China, the Vinaya-piṭaka can be explained in terms of Mahāyāna and the "small vehicle" can be included as a constituent part of "great vehicle", so the Dhammagupta Vinaya forms part of Mahāyāna Vinaya. It is on the basis of Sāvaka Vinaya that the Restraint of Senses (Saṃvara-sīla) in the three aggregates of purifying sīla of monastic Bodhisatta Vinaya was established. As to the four most fundamental precepts (Pārājika), abstaining from killing, stealing, improper sex, and lying about one's spiritual achievements, these are followed by both Mahāyāna and Hīnayāna. The most important thing in the study of Vinaya rules is to distinguish the purview of flexibility and constancy, abidance or deviation. Flexibility means that certain Vinaya precepts, being inviolable in normal times, may be breached under certain circumstances, while constancy refers to those that can not be violated at any time. In certain circumstances, one may not be certain oneself whether a rule has been violated , so it is necessary to consult the Vinaya rules. Then the Vinaya masters can determine the demarcation line between flexibility and constancy, abidance or violation. Of the sāvaka precepts, the four fundamental rules (to abstain from taking life of people, stealing, sexual miscon-

45. 问：密宗的教义是什么？

答：八世纪时印度的密教，由善无畏、金刚智、不空等传入中国，从此修习传授形成密宗。此宗依《大日经》、《金刚顶经》建立三密瑜伽，事理观行，修本尊法。此宗以密法奥秘，不经灌顶，不经传授不得任意传习及显示别人，因此称为密宗。

46. 问：什么叫三密瑜伽？什么叫本尊法？

答：本尊（S. Satyadevatā，P. Saccidevatā）是学者选择自己最敬爱最尊崇的一尊佛、一位菩萨或者一位明王，作为学习成就的对象或榜样，就叫本尊。要成就本尊的所有功德智慧，就要修习三密瑜伽法。三密就是身、口、意三

duct and lying about one's spiritual achievements), plus the thirteen rules of saṅghādisesa (Bhikkhuni pātimokkha includes 8 fundamentals and 17 Saṅghādisesa rules), must be strictly followed without infringement, while most of the rest are permitted to be relaxed under special and necessary circumstances. Take the precept of "abstaining from eating at an inappropriate time" for example, it is observed in normal times, yet eating after physical labor is permissible. However, the flexibility is determined according to the Vinaya. It can be seen that Buddhist Vinaya precepts are not rigid, but are flexible except for the fundamentals.

45. Q: What is the doctrine of the Esoteric School (the Tantra School)?

A: In the 8th century, Esoteric Buddhism of India was introduced into China by Śubhakarasiṃha, Vajrabodhi, Amoghavajra and others. After that it gradually grew into the Esoteric School in China along with practice and dissemination. Based on the *Mahāvairocana-sūtra* and the *Vajraśikhara-sūtra*, this school established the Three Secret Yoga, performing contemplation to culminate in the four peaks of view and cultivation in order to achieve integration with a specific Buddha or master (guru-yoga). This school, in order to preserve its secret nature, does not permit those who have not undergone the ceremony of pouring water on the head (abhiṣeka) from freely displaying and passing down to others the instruction. Hence the name Esoteric School.

46. Q: What are the Three Secret Yoga? What does Guru-yoga mean?

A: A Guru, or Satyadevatā, is a most venerable and honored Buddha or Bodhisatta or wise spirit (vijjā-rāja) chosen by a practitioner as an object or a model to learn from to enable his own attainment. In order to integrate oneself with the merits, virtues and wisdom of the Honored One, the practitioner has to

业，瑜伽（yoga）译为相应。三密瑜伽，就是三业相应。与谁相应？就是修行者自己的身口意与本尊的身口意三业相应。修法时，修行者要身作本尊的姿态，手结印契，口诵本尊真言，意作本尊观想或种子字，务使自己的三业与本尊的三密相应，名为瑜伽修法。此法如果修成，可以即身成就本尊之身。密教的修法很多，这只是举一个例证。此宗最高理论还是以性空无相的法性理体为基础，所谓阿字本不生，不生就是空义。

47. 问：听了您的介绍，我对佛教八宗有了一点简单的了解。八宗以外，还有哪些别的学派？这既称为八大宗派，是不是还有什么小宗派？

答：八宗以外还有以《俱舍论》为主的学派叫俱舍宗；专讲《成实论》的学派称成实宗。成实、俱舍都属小乘教，唐以后不甚流行。八宗之外若加这两派便成十宗。此外，还有弘扬《涅槃经》的涅槃师，专讲《摄大乘论》的摄论师，专讲《十地经论》的地论师。这些学派初兴都曾盛极一时，但为时不久便失去传承，或者汇入其它宗派。

study and practice the Three Secret Yoga which means the union of the three kammas. The "Three Secret" are physical, oral and mental kammas, and "yoga" means connected and identical in each of the three. Connected and identical with whom? That is to say the practitioner's actions of body, speech and mind should connect and identify with the Honored One's. To practice this method, the practitioner should embrace the Guru's postures, hand signs (mudra) and recite the honored One's spell (mantra), keep contemplating on his own Guru or bīja (seed) words, ensure that his own three kammas correspond to that of the Guru. That is called yoga practice. If this practice proves a success, the practitioner's own body would become one with the body of the Guru. There are many methods of practice in Esoteric Buddhism. This is but one example. The ultimate principle of this school is still based on the theory of the emptiness (Suññatā) of nature and formlessness of Dhamma; just as this School claims " There is no origination of 'A' at all" (akāra-ādyanutpādaḥ), no origination is the same as emptiness.

47. Q: From your discussion I've got a preliminary understanding of the eight schools of Chinese Buddhism. Are there any other schools besides these eight? Since they are called eight major schools, are there any minor schools?

A: Besides the eight, there are the Abhidharma-kośa School, mainly upholding the *Abhidharma-kośa-śāstra,* and the Satyasiddhi School specifically dealing with the *Satyasiddhi-śāstra*. Both of them belonged to Hīnayāna Buddhism and waned after the Tang Dynasty. With the addition of these two schools, there are a total of ten schools. In addition, there are masters, called Nibbāna Teachers, who propagated the *Mahāpari-nibbāna-sutta*, masters who taught the *Mahāyāna-saṃparigraha-śāstra*, and Masters of the *Daśabhūmika-sūtra-śāstra*. These schools flourished for a time and soon lost followers or merged into other schools.

48. 问:各宗派兴起后,在弘传的过程中有些什么样的曲折变化?

答:各宗的发展情况是不平衡的,发展变化也不一样。有的宗派初兴起时流传很盛,而后来渐衰,这就是三论宗。此宗经过陈隋兴皇法朗和嘉祥吉藏的大力弘扬,在隋、陈、初唐时,流传之广,几乎遍及全国,但以后便逐渐衰落。有的起初流传不广,后来却很盛行,如天台宗。此宗在天台智者和章安成宗之后,流传地区仅限于浙江东南一带,师资传承不绝如缕,一百多年后到荆溪湛然始号称中兴。有的宗派一直在发展流传,从未有衰歇过,这便是禅宗。此宗有大成就的人多住在山林中,自耕自食,对于社会的依赖性不大,也不需要太多的典籍,所以虽遭会昌之难,影响不大,一直传承下来,并有很大的发展。有的宗派绝而复苏,很多的宗派都是这样,在会昌灭法之前,各宗先后都已兴起,相比之下,虽各有兴衰的不同,但都同时流行于世。到九世纪后期唐武宗会昌(845)年间灭法,所有的经书佛像毁坏殆尽,各宗的章疏典籍大都丢失无存。十世纪时天台宗的著作又从朝鲜传回来,贤首宗的典籍也恢复一部分。所以从五代以来,天台、贤首二家又算复兴。其余中观、瑜伽以及密宗的许多著作流传域外,到了清末,性相二宗的章疏才由日本重返故国。近半个多世纪以来,上述八宗都有人研究讲说,有复苏的趋势。总观诸宗历史,隋唐是各宗兴起和极盛时代,会昌法难后,除禅宗外,是诸宗衰亡时代。稍后有天台、贤首的复兴和禅宗的大发展,这可算是佛教复兴的时代,但也没有初唐中唐那样的盛况。自元代起西藏佛教传入内地,很受朝廷的崇奉,但未普及民

48. Q: Were there any twists and turns or evolution among the schools in the course of their spread after inception?

A: The developments of different schools were uneven, as were their variations. Some schools flourished upon their inception and waned afterwards. This was the case with the Three Śāstras School. This school, through energetic propagation by Fa Lang of Xinghuang Temple and Ji Zang of Jia Xiang Temple in the Chen and Sui Dynasties respectively, spread widely over nearly the entire nation until early Tang Dynasty, but gradually declined afterwards. Some schools, such as the Tiantai School, were not initially popular, but thrived later. This School was founded by Zhi Zhe and Zhang An in the Tiantai mountains and was just confined to Southeastern Zhejiang province, lingering on like a thread from teacher to disciple. But 100 years later, at the time of Zhan Ran of Jing Xi, it blossomed. And some schools kept on flourishing and disseminating without decline. This was the case with the Chan School. Many masters of this school who made great achievements were recluses residing in forests or mountains and subsisting alone without much reliance on the outside world. Nor did they need many canonical books. That is why this School could survive the Hui Chang Extermination of Buddhism and carry on with significant developments. Some other schools seemed to die out and then revive. Prior to the attempted Extermination of Buddhism during the Hui Chang era, various schools had successively arisen and flourished, though attaining different levels in prosperity. During the Hui Chang years (845 AD), Emperor Wuzong of the Tang Dynasty attempted to exterminate Buddhism. Nearly all Buddhist scriptures and statues were demolished and most of the canonical works of each school were lost. By the 10th century, the works of Tiantai School were regained from Korea, as were parts of the works of the Xianshou Sect (or Avataṃsaka School). This was considered the revival of the two schools after the time of Five Dynasties. Many works of the remaining schools, like Mādhyamika, Yogācāra and Esoteric Schools, were scattered

间，而汉地原有佛教则不及宋时兴盛。有清一代，汉地佛教没有什么起色，仅可保持原有的余绪。

49. 问：唐末已来，佛教逐渐衰落，直到清代还是如此，但从清已来，佛教似乎有复兴之势，出了不少人才，不知近代佛教有哪些著名人物？

答：近代的佛学提倡者首推杨仁山（1837－1911）。为了培养人才和扩大佛典流通，便利佛学研究，他用了几十年的光阴，致力于讲学和刻经事业。他所创办的金陵刻经处曾经刊印了由日本取回的我国已经遗失的性、相诸宗的重要著作，因而使性、相两宗的教义得以复兴。金陵刻经处同时又是讲学场所，谭嗣同、章太炎等都在那里听过他的讲，在他的培育影响下产生了一些佛教学者，其中特出的是欧阳竟无居士，专治法相唯识之学，他在南京举办的

abroad. Not until the end of the Qing Dynasty, were certain texts of Dhammapakati and Dhammalakkhaṇa Schools brought back to China from Japan. In the last half century, all the eight schools have been revived with their doctrines being studied and preached. To sum up the history of Buddhist schools in China, Sui and Tang Dynasties saw the heyday of all schools, following the Hui Chang Persecution came the period of their decline and extinction, with the exception of the Chan School. Not long afterwards, the revival of Tiantai and Xianshou Schools and the momentous development of Chan School brought about a period of Buddhist revival, but still it never regained its grandeur of the early and middle Tang Dynasty. After the Yuan Dynasty, Tibetan Buddhism spread over central China, and was favorably accepted by the imperial court, but was not popular among the people there. The original Buddhism in the Han-inhabited area was not as prevalent as in the Song Dynasty. During the Qing Dynasty, Buddhism in the Han region showed no sign of increase, but was able to maintain itself.

49. Q: From the end of Tang Dynasty till the Qing Dynasty Buddhism declined gradually. After the Qing Dynasty, Buddhism appeared to revive with the emergence of many Buddhist talents. Who were some of the distinguished personalities in recent times?

A: One of the most distinguished advocates of Buddhism in modern times was Yang Renshan (1837-1911), who, in order to nurture Buddhist scholars and facilitate the circulation and study of Buddhist texts, dedicated decades of his time to lecturing on and printing Buddhist scriptures. He was the founding father of Jinling Scripture Publishing House which published many important works of the Dhammapakati and Dhammalakkhaṇa Schools which had long been missing in China and were brought back from Japan. This enabled the revival of these two schools. At the same time, the Jinling Scripture Publishing House was also an educational center where Tan Sitong, Zhang Taiyan and

支那内学院，成为当时法相学的重要研究场所。与欧阳齐名的法相研究的提倡者有北京三时学会的韩清净居士。

50. 问：听了上面的介绍，了解这几位德高望重的居家大士对于近代佛教的贡献确实巨大，是值得后学称赞学习的。但同时在出家菩萨中有哪些著名高僧弘传佛教？请略为介绍。

答：近代高僧中著名人物有月霞、谛闲、印光、弘一、虚云等，他们分别弘扬贤首、天台、净土、律宗、禅宗。还有积极从事整理僧伽制度，提倡僧伽教育，宣扬大乘精义，发扬佛教文化事业最有力的圆瑛法师和太虚法师。圆瑛是一位宗说兼通，禅净双修，精研《楞严》的大德，他热爱祖国、热爱佛教，一生讲经、建寺、兴办各种福利事业，奖掖引导后学，不遗余力。太虚是一位教海渊深的佛学通家和弘扬佛教的积极活动家，在他的倡导带领下，涌现了一大批弘法的僧伽人才。他们对我国近代佛教事业的发展做出了不可磨灭的贡献。我国佛教自唐武宗毁法(844)以来义学凋敝，达千余年，经过近百年中僧俗大德学者的努力而渐有起色，这是值得庆幸的。但是，和目前国外的佛教学术研究事业的兴旺情况相比，我们还有很多工作亟待进行。

others used to go to hear Yang Renshan's lectures. Among the Buddhist scholars he nurtured, the most outstanding personality was Ouyang Jingwu, a lay Buddhist, who devoted his life to the study of Dhamma-lakkhaṇa or Viññānavāda and established the China Buddhist College in Nanjing which became an important research center of Viññānavāda studies at that time. Another promoter of the study of Dhamma-lakkhaṇa was the lay Buddhist Han Qingjing of the San Shi Society in Beijing who enjoyed a reputation equal with that of Ouyang Jingwu.

50. Q: From your description, I understand why these highly-acclaimed lay Buddhists who have made very significant contributions to modern Buddhism deserve eulogy and emulation by succeeding generations. Besides these, were there famous monks who have contributed to the spread of Buddhism? Could you please give a few examples?

A: Famous monks in contemporary times include Ven. Yuexia, Dixian, Yinguang, Hongyi, Xuyun etc. who propagated the doctrines of the Xianshou (Avataṃsaka), Tiantai, Pure Land (Sukhāvatī), Vinaya and Chan schools respectively. Then, there were the powerful propagators, Masters Yuanying and Taixu, who energetically set about consolidating the Sangha Order, promoting Sangha education, demonstrating the Mahāyāna tenets and uplifting Buddhist culture. Ven. Yuanying was a paragon with profound learning in the *Śūraṃgama-mahāsūtra* and the practice of both Chan and Pure Land schools, who, throughout his life, did his utmost to preach Dhamma, build monasteries, start all kinds of welfare services and encourage and promote the coming generations with his deep love for his country and Buddhism. Ven. Taixu was an erudite Buddhist scholar with vast knowledge comparable to abyss and ocean and a noted activist in propagating Buddhism. Under his advocacy and guidance emerged a large number of Sangha talents for the promulgation of Buddhism who made indelible contributions to

如何恢复我国佛教在盛唐时期波澜壮阔声华腾蔚的光荣地位，以与祖国当前的伟大时代相适应，还需要佛教界有识有志之士发大愿心，继承先德未竟之业，作出艰苦卓绝的努力。

以上就是中国汉族佛教各宗的兴起、弘传和盛衰变化的大概情况。

the development of contemporary Buddhist cause in China. In the past 10-odd centuries since Emperor Wuzong's attempted the Extermination of Buddhism in the Tang Dynasty (844 AD), Buddhist learning has been at low ebb. So it is a matter for rejoicing that there have been some signs of restoration owing to the efforts of both lay and monastic Buddhists in the past 100 years. However, compared with the vigorous growth of Buddhist academic research outside China at present, much work awaits our prompt action. How can we restore the magnificence and glorious position occupied by Chinese Buddhism in the Tang Dynasty and make Buddhism keep pace with the great contemporary development of our country? It invites the far-sighted aspirants in Buddhist circles to carry on the unfinished work of the pioneers and to exert their utmost endeavors with zeal.

So much for a brief summary of the origin, dissemination, and vicissitudes of various Buddhist Schools of the Han nationality in China.

## （三）少数民族地区的佛教

51. 问：听了您的介绍，知道了汉地佛教的大概轮廓，不知我国西藏佛教是什么时期传入的，是经什么人弘扬起来的？

答：我国藏语系佛教开始于七世纪中叶。当时的西藏松赞干布（Sroṅ-bstan sgam-po）藏王，在他的两个妻子，唐文成公主和尼泊尔毗俱胝（Bhṛkuṭi，藏名尺尊 khri-btsun）公主共同的影响下皈依了佛教。他派遣大臣端美三菩提（Thonmi sambhoṭa）等十六人到印度学习梵文和佛经，回来后创造了藏语文字并开始翻译了一些佛经，到了八世纪中叶藏王持松德赞（Khri-sroṅ-lde-btsan）迎请莲华生（Padmasaṃbhava）由印度入藏，折服了原来盛行的本教（Bon-po），佛教于是得到了弘扬。

52. 问：后来发展的情况怎样？

答：莲华生入藏之后，首先建立了桑耶寺，度僧出家，成立僧伽，并请译师从梵文翻译大批佛典，同时也从汉文翻译一些佛经。据现在的登嘎尔目录（布敦认为是持松德赞王府所编），当时译出的大小显密经律论有 738 种（内从汉文转译的 32 种），故当时佛教流传是很兴盛的。但在九世纪中叶，西藏佛教曾一度遭到破坏，即所谓朗达玛灭法，曾有一段时间（842—978）佛教沉寂了。后来由原西康地

## (III) Buddhism in Minority-inhabited Regions of China

51. Q: After your explanation, I have got a rough outline of Buddhism in the Han regions. Could you tell me when Buddhism was introduced into Tibet and who were the propagators?

A: The Tibetan Buddhist tradition dates back to the mid 7th century. The Tibetan ruler at that time, Sroṅ-btsan-sgam-po, was converted to Buddhism under the influence of his two wives, Princess Wencheng of Tang and Princess Bhṛkuṭi (or Khri-btsun in Tibetan) of Nepal. He dispatched his Minister Thon-mi-sambhoṭa to lead a 16-person envoy to India to learn Sanskrit and Buddhist scriptures. On their return they created the Tibetan writing system and began to translate Buddhist texts. In the mid-8th century, the Tibetan Ruler Khri-sroṅ Ide-btsan invited Padmasaṃbhava to come to Tibet from India. The indigenous religion—Bon was subdued and Buddhism, thereupon, spread in Tibet.

52. Q: What about subsequent developments?

A: After his arrival in Tibet, Padmasaṃbhava first built the Bsam-yas Temple, ordained monks and then established the Sangha Order there. He also invited masters to translate many Buddhist scriptures from Sanskrit, as well as some from Chinese. According to the existing catalogue of translated Buddhist works called Ldan-dkar-ma in Tibet (compiled in the royal house of Khri-sroṅ Ide-btsan, according to Bu-ston), works of all kinds—Mahāyāna, Hīnayāna, Esoteric and Exoteric—translated at that time totaled 738, (including 32 translated from Chinese). Such was the prevalence of Buddhism at the time. How-

区再度传入，西藏佛教又得复苏。十一世纪时有孟加拉佛教大师阿底峡（Atīśa）入藏（1042），又大弘佛法，同时藏族比丘仁钦桑波（rin-chen bzaṇ-po，宝贤）等翻译了很多的经论。西藏史上称朗达玛灭法之前为前弘期，之后重兴的佛教为后弘期。

此后印度的佛教学者，特别是遭遇变乱时期（1203 年印度比哈尔省的佛教各大寺庙被入侵军全部毁坏）的那烂陀寺、超戒寺等的学者，来到西藏的很多，传译事业因而很盛，藏文大藏经近六千部中绝大多数是直接由梵文翻译的，少数是从汉文转译的。因此，印度后期佛教的论著保存在藏文藏经里的，极为丰富。尤其是因明、声明、医方明等论著数量庞大，非常重要。西藏的佛法以密教最为普遍，最为突出，这是大家所熟知的。在显教方面，西藏格鲁派（黄教）各大寺都推行以因明、俱舍、戒律、中观、瑜伽（现观）五科佛学为中心的教学制度，从玄奘、义净的记载来看，可以说这是继承了当初印度那烂陀寺遗留的学风和规范。

ever, in the mid-9th century, Tibetan Buddhism suffered a setback, which was known as Glaṅdar-ma Persecution of Buddhism, thus for a while (828—978AD), Buddhism subsided. Later on, with the reintroduction of Buddhism from Xikang region Tibetan Buddhism revived. In the 11th century (1042AD), a Bengali Buddhist, Mahānāyaka Atiśa came to Tibet and energetically promulgated Buddha Dhamma. Meanwhile, the Tibetan Bhikkhu Rin-chen Bzaṅ-po (Bao Xian) and others translated numerous sūtras and śāstras. Tibetan history uses the Glaṅdar-ma Persecution as the dividing line, referring to the period before as the Early Spreading Period, and the period after the restoration of Buddhism as the Later Spreading Period.

Afterwards, Indian Buddhist scholars, especially those of Nālandā, Vikramaśīla and other great monasteries came to Tibet in large numbers, especially at the time of turbulence (all great Buddhist temples in Bihar Pradesh in India were completely demolished by the invading troops in 1203). The translation work grew rapidly as a consequence. Most of the 6,000 volumes of the Tibetan Tripiṭaka were directly translated from Sanskrit and a small portion were translated from Chinese. Therefore, a very rich collection of later works of Indian Buddhism are preserved in the Tibetan Tripiṭaka, particularly those of Logic (Hetu-vidyā), Linguistics (Śabda-vidyā), Medicine (Cikitsā-vidyā) are great in number and importance. It is well known that the most popular and salient feature of Tibetan Buddhism is Esoteric Buddhism. As for Exoteric Buddhism, all large monasteries of the Dge-lugs-pa School (Yellow Hat) in Tibet adopted an educational system centered on the 5 subjects of Buddhist studies: Hetu-vidyā, Abhidharmakośa, Vinaya, Mādhyamika and Yoga, which, to judge by the accounts of Xuanzang and Yijing, may be the academic standards and style handed down from Nālandā.

53．问：前面提到过，我国还有巴利语系佛教，其弘传情况怎样？

答：巴利语系佛教（上座部佛教）流传于我国云南省傣族、布朗族等地区，那里人民的佛教传统信仰与南方佛教国家（泰国、缅甸等）大致相同，属巴利语系佛教。因为他们直接读诵巴利语文经典，所以用不着有翻译之劳。那里，若干世纪来能保持如法如律精进修学的原始佛教的优良传统，还是值得欣喜赞叹的。

54．问：汉语系佛教有许多宗派建立，藏语系佛教是否也有不同的宗派？

答：藏语系佛教先后也有不同的宗派产生。由于传承、传译、讲说和依据的不同，也逐渐形成了若干大小的教派。有从前弘期传承下来的宁玛派，有阿底峡传给敦巴一系的迦当派，有玛巴译师传给弥拉日巴一系的迦举派，有卓弥译师传给昆宝王一系的萨迦派，有由宗喀巴改革创建的格鲁派（又名嘎登派）。此外还有些传布不广，影响不大的派别，如觉曩派、希结派、觉宇派、霞鲁派等。这些教派，各有他们自己特殊的学说和修持方法。尤其是格鲁派，是十四世纪末宗喀巴大师（1357—1419）继承上代的传承，在学说上加以整理和发扬，在僧伽制度上加以整顿和改革而创立的教派——黄教，在当前蒙藏族地区最为盛行。

53. Q: You have mentioned before, there exists in China, too, a Pāli tradition of Buddhism. What about its development?

A: The Pāli tradition of Buddhism (Theravāda Buddhism) prevails in the areas inhabited by Dai and Bulang nationalities in Yunnan Province, where the traditional Buddhist belief among the people is similar to that in Southern Buddhist countries. All of them belong to the Pāli system of Buddhism. As they can directly read the scriptures in Pāli, there is no necessity to labor on translation. It is worthy of delight and praise that the good tradition of primordial Buddhism—practice with effort according to Dhamma and Vinaya—has been preserved in this area for centuries.

54. Q: Are there different schools of Tibetan Buddhism as there are different schools of Buddhism in Han inhabited areas?

A: Within Tibetan Buddhism too there emerged different schools at different times. Due to the diversity in evolution, translation, and sūtras preached or favored, there gradually appeared a number of schools, large or small, such as the Rñiṅma-pa Sect which survived from the Early Spreading Period, the Bkaḥ-gdam-pa Sect, which was passed down from Atīśa to Ston-pa, the Bkaḥ-brgyud-pa Sect handed down from the translator Mar-pa to Mi-la ras-pa, the Sa-skya-pa Sect passed down from Master Ḥbrog-mi to Dkon-mchog rgyal-po; and the Dge-lugs-pa Sect established by Tsoṅ-kha-pa (1357-1419) during his religious reform. In addition, there were minor sects that were not widespread and had limited influence, such as Jo-naṅ-pa, Shi-byed-pa, Good-yul-pa, Sa-ru-pa and other sects. Each of them upheld its own peculiar doctrine and method of cultivation. A particularly note-worthy sect, the Dge-lugs-pa, was founded by Master Tsoṅ-kha-pa in the late 14th century on the basis of an earlier tradition, along with his further elucidation of doctrine, and congregational reform in Sangha system. This School is known

55. 问:巴利语系佛教在我国是否也有派别的不同?

答:中国巴利语系的佛教也有几个不同的派别,但这些派别只是在持戒律仪方面要求有所不同,而不是学说教义上的派别。

as the Yellow Sect, and is widespread throughout Mongolia and Tibet.

55. Q: Are there different sects, too, within the Pāli system of Buddhism in China?

A: There are different sects within the Pāli Buddhist system in China, but the differences are only in the requirements of discipline and rituals, rather than differences in theories and doctrines.

## （四）佛教对中国思想文化的影响

56. 问：佛教传来中国将近两千年，思想体系发展演变成十多个派别，可说是学术成果灿烂辉煌，这对中国的思想文化起过什么样的影响和作用？

答：佛教各宗派学说，经过长期的研究和广泛的弘扬，对中国思想界曾起了不可磨灭的影响。举宋明理学为例，很明显，它是在很大程度上受了华严、禅宗和另一部分佛教理论的刺激和影响而产生的，这是思想界公认的历史事实。在晚清时期，中国知识界研究佛学成为一时普遍的风气。一些民主思想启蒙运动者，如谭嗣同、康有为、梁启超、章太炎等学术名流，都采取了佛教中一部分教理来作他们的思想武器。佛教的慈悲、平等、无常、无我的思想，在当时的知识界中起了启发和鼓舞的作用。

57. 问：佛教对文化艺术有什么样的影响，比如说，对中国文学起过什么样的作用？

答：数千卷由梵文翻译过来的经典，本身就是伟大、富丽的文学作品。其中如《维摩诘经》、《法华经》、《楞严经》特别为历代文人们所喜爱，被纯粹地为着文学目的而研读着。我国近代文豪鲁迅曾捐款给金陵刻经处，刻印了一部

## (IV) The Impact of Buddhism on Chinese Thought and Culture

56. Q: Buddhism has had a presence in China of nearly twenty centuries, developed 10-odd schools and has made significant, even splendid academic achievements. How has it influenced and affected Chinese thought and culture?

A: The theories of various Buddhist schools, through long-term research and widespread propagation, have had lasting influence on Chinese thinking. For instance, it is commonly acknowledged in philosophical circles that the Neo-Confucianism of Song and Ming Dynasties was obviously generated, to a great extent, by the impetus and impact of the doctrines of Avataṃsaka, Chan, as well as other Buddhist schools. In the late Qing Dynasty, the study of Buddhism became fashionable among Chinese intellectuals. A number of leading scholars and pioneers of democratic movements, such as Tan Sitong, Kang Youwei, Liang Qichao, Zhang Taiyan and others made good use of some Buddhist ideas. Buddhist theories of love and compassion (Mettā-Karunā), equality (Upekkhā or samānatta), impermanence (Anicca) and egolessness (Anattā) inspired and encouraged the intellectuals at that time.

57. Q: What is the impact of Buddhism on culture and the arts? In particular, what role has it played in Chinese literature?

A: Thousands of volumes of Buddhist scriptures translated from Sanskrit are themselves great and magnificent literary works. Among them, such works as *Vimalakīrti-nirdeśa*, *Saddharma-puṇḍarīka-sūtra* and *Śūraṃgama-mahā-sūtra* have been particularly attractive to literature lovers through the dynasties. They read and study them specifically out of literary interest. Lu

《百喻经》。这部经所叙的譬喻故事,常常被译为语体文发表在今天的报刊上,作为文学作品来欣赏。佛教为中国的文学带来了许多从来未有的、完全新的东西——新的意境、新的文体、新的命意遣词方法。马鸣的《佛所行赞》带来了长篇叙事诗的典范,《法华》、《维摩》、《百喻》诸经鼓舞了晋唐小说的创作,《般若》和禅宗的思想影响了陶渊明、王维、白居易、苏轼的诗歌创作。

58. 问:佛教对我国文学的发展有所影响已如上说,但不知对中国文体的变化起了哪些作用?

答:为佛化普及的目的而盛行于古代的歌呗产生一种特殊的文学——变文,这就是把佛经内容演为便于讲唱的通俗文词。敦煌石窟发现的各种变文,都是文词酣畅想像力都非常丰富的大众化的文艺作品。从这些作品中,可以看出后来的平话、小说、戏曲等中国俗文学的渊源所自。此外还有由禅师们的谈话和开示的记录而产生的一种特殊文体——语录体。这种朴素而活泼自由的口语文体,后来被宋明理学家仿效而产生了各种语录。此外还有音韵学,如过去中国字典上通行的反切,就是受梵文拼音的影响而发展起来的。总之,佛教在中国文学领域中的表现是丰富多彩的。

Xun, the great writer of modern Chinese literature, donated funds to the Jinling Scripture Publishing House for carving and publishing *Sata-upamā-sutta*, the admonitory stories which are still often translated into modern Chinese, published and enjoyed as literary works today. Buddhism has brought to Chinese literature numerous entirely new things unknown before—new spheres of meaning, new writing styles and new rhetorical methods. Aśvaghoṣa's *Buddha-carita* set a model for long narrative poetry. The *Saddharmapuṇḍrīka-sūtra*, the *Vimalakīrtinirdeśa* and the *Sata-upamā-sutta* inspired the writing of novels in Jin and Tang Dynasties. The thought of the *Prajñā-pāramitā-sūtra* and of the Chan School influenced the poetry writing of Tao Yuanming, Wang Wei, Bai Juyi and Su Shi.

58. Q: While Buddhism has exerted influence on the development of Chinese literature as mentioned above, what effects has it had on the development of Chinese literary styles?

A: To meet the need to extensively spread Buddhism, a peculiar style of literature, "Bianwen", evolved. It actually springs from a style of songs and odes popular in ancient times. Bianwen is the expression of Buddhist scriptures in common words for easily narrating and singing. Various Bianwen discovered inside the Dunhuang Caves are popular literary works whose ease, verve and richness of imagination contributed to the subsequent popular Chinese literature forms such as Pinghua, novels and plays. Besides, another special style, named Recorded Utterance, arose out of the records of conversations and inculcations of the Chan masters. This simple and lively oral style was later followed by the Neo Confucianist scholars in Song and Ming Dynasties and many such works were produced. In addition, in the field of Chinese Phonology, a system of phonetic letters known as "Fanqie" developed under the influence of the Sanskrit alphabet. This was popularly used in the old Chinese dictionaries. Generally speaking, the Buddhist manifestations in Chinese literary sphere are varied and colorful.

59. 问：建塔造像，大家知道，多数来源于佛教，佛教在这方面的艺术成就是举世闻名的，可否请重点介绍一下？

答：随着佛教的传入，建塔造像的艺术很快地便风行于中国各地。现存的上海龙华寺塔和苏州报恩寺塔，都是在公元二世纪三国时代创建而经后人重修的。四世纪到六世纪，全国各地都有壮丽的塔寺建筑。世界闻名的佛教石窟寺，如敦煌、云冈、龙门以及其它同等重要的石窟寺——这些古代雕塑壁画艺术的宝库，西至新疆，东到辽宁，南到江南，都是在这一时期开始动工的，随后继续了数世纪之久。在中国，塔的形式很多，大致可归纳为两类：一类是印度式的，但也有许多变化；一类是中国式的，主要是采用中国原有的楼阁形式而建筑的。研究中国建筑艺术，寺塔是其中主要部分。至于佛教造像，在取材与造法上种类也很多，有石窟造像，有木、石、玉、牙的雕刻像，有金、银、铜、铁的铸像，有泥塑像，有锤鍱像，有夹纻像，有砖像，有瓷像，有绣像，有画像。它吸收了犍陀罗和印度的作风而发展成为具有中国民族风格的造像艺术，是我国伟大的文化遗产。

60. 问：佛画艺术也很著名，都有哪些类别？

答：佛教绘画主要是壁画。现存于敦煌石窟中的壁

59. Q: As is well known, the construction of pagodas and statues in China mostly originated from Buddhism. The achievements of Buddhist arts in this respect are world famous. Could you give a brief account ?

A: With the introduction of Buddhism into China, the arts of pagoda construction and statue-making rapidly spread over every part of China. Early in the Three Kingdoms Period (2nd century A.D.) the pagodas standing in the Longhua Temple in Shanghai and in the Baoen Temple in Suzhou were erected and rebuilt later. From the 4th to the 6th century, magnificent pagodas and temples appeared all over the country. The world-famous Buddhist grottos of Dunhuang, Yungang, Longmen and others equally important, are a treasure trove of ancient sculpture and murals. Ranging from Xinjiang in the west to Liaoning in the east, to the south beyond the Yangtze, these grottos were also begun during this period and the work lasted for centuries. In China, there are numerous forms of pagodas, but they largely fall into two categories: one is the Indian style with many variations, and the other is the Chinese style, adapted from the traditional style of pavilion. The study of temples and pagodas is a major part of the study of Chinese architecture. As for Buddhist images, they are made from many types of materials and with many techniques, including carved and engraved images of wood, stone, jade and ivory, statues cast in gold, silver, bronze and iron, clay sculptures, beaten metal plate statues, ramee tapestries, brick statues, ceramic statues, as well as embroidered and painted images. With the assimilation of Gandhāra and other Indian styles, the Buddhist art of sculpture has become a great cultural legacy that is distinctly Chinese.

60. Q: Buddhist painting is world famous. How many types are there?

A: Buddhist paintings are mainly murals. The mural paintings preserved in Dunhuang Grottos furnish us with a wealth of

画，供给我们非常丰富的艺术和历史的资料。值得注意的是，最初盛行的佛陀本生故事画，发展到唐代，逐渐为“经变”画所代替。正如文学中有变文一样，佛画中的“经变”，也就是将佛经中的故事譬喻演绘成图，如敦煌石窟中的演绘《维摩经》的“维摩变”，演绘净土经的“净土变”等，都是十分精彩生动的伟大作品。经变画的兴起，使壁画内容大为丰富起来，因而唐代佛寺壁画之盛，达到极点。当时名画家辈出，在姓名有记载的数十人中，如阎立本、吴道子等，大多是从事于佛画的。由此可见佛教对当时绘画艺术所起的作用。中国画学中由王维一派的文人画而发展到宋元以后盛行的写意画，则与般若和禅宗的思想很有关系。佛教版画，随着佛经的刊印而很早就产生了，现在所看到的中国最早的版画是在大藏经上面的佛画。房山石经中有唐代的石刻线条佛画。宋元以来的观音画、罗汉画以及水陆画等都是很流行的。

61. 问：佛教是否也有音乐、天文、医药等技艺的传习？

答：伴随佛教俱来的也有天文、音乐、医药等的传习。1955 年我国发行邮票纪念的古代天文学者一行，就是八世纪初的一位高僧，是由印度来华弘传密教的善无畏的弟子。他在天文学方面著有《大衍历》和测定子午线等，对天文学有着卓越的贡献。至于医药，隋唐史书上记载由印度

information about the arts and their history. It is worth noting that the paintings of Buddha's Jātaka story prevailing at the initial period gradually gave rise to the "Jingbian" paintings of the Tang Dynasty. Like Bianwen, its counterpart in literature, "Jingbian", was representation of Buddhist stories and metaphors in paintings. the "Vimalakīrti-nirdeśa Jingbian" and the "Sukhāvatī-sūtra Jingbian", in the Dunhuang Caves for examples, are splendid and vivid works. "Jingbian" paintings greatly enriched the contents of murals and mural art reached a climax in the Tang Dynasty (618-906 AD). Famous painters came forth in large numbers. Among the dozens whose names have come down to us, Yan Liben, Wu Daozi and others, were mostly engaged in Buddhist paintings, which shows the role Buddhism played on painting at the time. The development of Chinese paintings from scholar-painters' works represented by Wang Wei's group to freehand brush works prevailing from Song and Yuan Dynasties is closely associated with the thought of Paññā and Chan schools. Buddhist etchings also came into existence very early on, along with the printing of Buddhist texts. The oldest etchings existing today in China are illustrations seen in Tripiṭaka texts. Buddhist images engraved in stone, dating from the Tang Dynasty, can be seen in the stone-carved scriptures in Fang shan county today. Besides, since the Song and Yuan Dynasties, paintings of Avalokiteśvara, Arahats, as well as landscape paintings have also been very popular.

61. Q: Does Buddhism also have its own tradition in such areas as music, astronomy, medicine etc.?

A: Yes. Along with Buddhism there came a tradition of astronomy, music and medicine. Ven. Yixing, an ancient astronomer who was commemorated in 1955 with a special issue of stamps in his honor, was a Buddhist monk in the early 8th century. He was a disciple of Śubhakarasiṃha, who came to China from India to propagate Esoteric Buddhism. Yixing made remarkable contributions to astronomy by writing the famous

翻译过来的医书和药方就有十余种，藏语系佛教中并且有医方明之学。再说音乐，公元二世纪时，中国已有梵呗的流行。七世纪初，在今缅甸境内的骠国赠送给中国佛曲十种，并派来乐工三十二人。中国唐代的音乐中吸收了天竺乐、龟兹乐、安国乐、康国乐、骠国乐、林邑乐等来自佛教国家的音乐，唐代音乐至今还有少部分保存在某些佛教寺庙中。

62. 问：佛教主张利益众生，不知在社会公益事业中从事哪些种类？有过哪些成就？

答：佛教徒从事公益事业的面是很广泛的，也是多种多样的，如有的僧人行医施药，有的造桥修路，有的掘义井、设义学，有的植树造林，这在古人记载中是屡见不鲜的。特别是植树造林，成就卓越。试看我国各地，凡有佛教塔寺之处，无不翠枝如黛，碧草如茵，环境清幽，景色宜人。一片郁郁葱葱之中，掩映着红墙青瓦，宝殿琼阁，为万里锦绣江山平添了无限春色。我国许多旅游胜地，其风景自然之美与寺僧的精巧建筑和植树造林显然是分不开的。

这些事实说明佛教在中国不仅其本身发扬光大开出灿烂的花朵，而且延伸到民族文化的各个领域结出丰硕的

Astronomic book *Da Yan Calendar*, and determining the meridian etc.. While in the field of medicine, according to the records of Sui and Tang dynasties, more than ten Indian works on medicine and pharmacology were translated. The Tibetan Buddhist canon includes Cikitsā-vidyā (science of medicine). With respect to music, Buddhist singing — Bhāṣā — was already current in China as early as in the 2nd century. At the beginning of the 7th century, the Piao Kingdom (located in the present-day Burma) presented to China 10 pieces of Buddhist bhāṣās, together with a troupe of 32 players. Chinese music in the Tang Dynasty absorbed elements from Buddhist countries including India, Kucīna (today's Kucha), Kasmīra, Samarkand, Piao and Champa. Some Tang music is still preserved in Buddhist temples today.

62. Q: Buddhism advocates the benefit of all sentient beings, What kinds of social welfare are Buddhists engaged in? And what achievements have been made?

A: Buddhists are engaged in a wide range of social welfare work, some monks took up the medical profession and distributed medicine; some built bridges and roads, some dug wells voluntarily and established free schools; some planted trees — all these are frequently mentioned in records made by the ancients. Planting of trees, especially, was a remarkable success. Take a look at places throughout our country where Buddhist pagodas and temples stand. Always there are green trees and grassy meadows presenting a tranquil and exquisite environment as well as attractive scenery. Red walls and green tiles, magnificent monasteries and pavilions against the luxuriant-green background add to the beauty of our splendid land. The natural beauty of many tourist resorts in China is enhanced by the exquisite architecture and verdure of these monasteries.

These facts show that Buddhism has not only come, itself, to blossom in China, but has contributed bountifully to all spheres of our culture. We Buddhists should all feel proud of the

果实。我们佛教徒应该为我们的先辈的卓越成就和贡献感到光荣和自豪。他们不仅在佛教事业上，而且在人类文化事业上，人类友好事业上都建立了不可磨灭的功绩。他们不仅翻译了几千卷的经论和写下了许多不朽的著作，为中国和印度及其他民族留下了宝贵的共同遗产，而且热心地相互传播了各自民族的劳动和智慧的花果，从而丰富了各自民族的文化宝藏。特别是在亚洲各国的友好合作日益恢复发展的今天，我们佛教先辈们辛勤努力所做出的许多历史业绩，不但重新显发了它的光辉，并且继续起着新的积极作用。

glorious achievements and contributions made by our predecessors. They advanced not only the cause of Buddhism, but also the cause of human culture, as well as friendship among mankind. They not only translated thousands of volumes of sūtras and śāstras, and wrote numerous immortal works, preserving the very precious common cultural legacy of China, India and other peoples, but also enthusiastically spread and exchanged the fruits of the labor and wisdom of different nations, thereby enriching the culture of their respective nations. Today, particularly with the ever-increasing development of friendly cooperation among the Asian nations, the historic achievements resulting from the arduous endeavors of the Buddhist predecessors, have not only revived their splendor, but are constantly playing new positive roles.

## （五）发扬人间佛教的优越性

63. 问：佛法教理，博大精深，义理幽玄，文化不高和悟解力差的人很难学习领会，怎样才能使佛法结合人们生活实际，有补于社会道德，精神文明的建设？

答：诚然，佛法博大渊深，不易为人们所了解接受，但也不能一概而论。佛经早已明言，大乘教理不是一般人都能信解的。佛法有浅深程度不同的各种法门，有适应各种根基的修持方法，各乘、各宗、各派都有引摄世间的教法适合一般人的需要，是合理契机的。

64. 问：什么是五乘佛法？什么是世间法和出世间法？

答：人乘、天乘、声闻乘、缘觉乘、菩萨乘这叫五乘。其中后三种叫出世间法，教理深奥，比较难学；前二人天乘教是世间法。世间法是世人易学而能够做到的也是应该做到的，前人名之为人间佛教。人间佛教主要内容就是：五戒、十善。五戒是：不杀生、不偷盗、不邪淫、不妄语、不饮酒。佛教认为，这类不道德的行为应该严格禁止，所以称

## (V) Carrying Forward the Advantage of Popular Buddhism

63. Q: Buddhist theory is broad and profound, and its metaphysical philosophy is difficult for those who have an average education and comprehension to learn and understand. So how can we combine the Buddha Dhamma with the realities of people's daily life and benefit the construction of social morals and spiritual civilization?

A: Though the Buddha Dhamma is too extensive and profound to be understood and accepted by ordinary people, it can be comprehended on different levels. Just as the early Buddhist scriptures proclaimed: the Mahāyāna doctrines were not to convince and be mastered by average people. The Buddha Dhamma has different levels of approach and numerous modes of practice which can be adapted to suit different gifts. Thus it is reasonable and practical for various yānas, schools and sects to have their own ways of teaching to meet the needs of the ordinary people.

64. Q: What is the Five-vehicle (Pañcayāna) Buddha Dhamma? What are the Worldly Conditions or things (Loka-dhamma) and the Super-mundane Conditions or things (Lokuttara-dhamma)?

A: The Five Vehicles (Pañcayāna) consist of Human Vehicle, Heavenly Vehicle, Sāvaka Vehicle, Pacceka-buddha Vehicle and Bodhisatta Vehicle. The last three are referred to as the Super-mundane conditions or Lokuttara-dhamma, its doctrines are comparatively profound and difficult to learn; the former two, Human and Heavenly Vehicles, are the Worldly conditions or Loka-dhamma. The Worldly Conditions or theories are easy to study and should be followed by the common people. So it

为五戒。十善是在五戒的基础上建立的，约身、口、意三业分为十种。身业有三种：不杀、不盗、不邪淫；口业有四种：不妄语欺骗，不是非两舌，不恶口伤人，不说无益绮语；意业有三种：不贪、不嗔、不愚痴。这就叫十善，反之就叫十恶。

65. 问：不杀生戒，应不许杀好人，假使有杀人放火，罪大恶极，负有命债的坏人，这种人依法应当抵命，难道这种恶人也不许杀他吗？

答：对罪大恶极，负有命债的杀人犯，应当绳之以法。这是因为触犯国家法律，应按法律制裁，而不是哪个人要杀他。法官虽有判决权，那是依法判决，不是法官个人的事。释迦牟尼为弟子制戒，不许弟子们杀生害命，这是就个人说的，同时也是为了避免触犯国家法律。佛陀从来没有说过国家法律对坏人的制裁有什么不对，总是教诫弟子遵守所在国的法律的。这是根本不同的两回事，不能混为一谈。佛教讲因果律时常说：善有善报，恶有恶报，杀人一定要偿命。这就说明了佛教是不会违反世间法律的，而是承认世间法律的。不杀生是这样，不贪、不嗔也是这种精

was named Popular Buddhism by the predecessors. The main contents of the Popular Buddhism are the Five Precepts (Pañcasīlā) and Ten Good Acts or Ten Virtuous Deeds (Dasa Kusala). The former involves abstaining from killing, stealing, sexual misconduct, lying and drinking intoxicants. Buddhism holds that these immoral conducts must be strictly prohibited. Hence the term Five Precepts. The Ten Good Acts, based on the Five Precepts, regulate the Three Kammas (body, speech and mind) in a total of ten ways. Pertaining to the body kamma, there are three items: avoidance of killing, stealing, sexual misconduct; pertaining to the verbal kamma are four items: avoidance of lying, slandering, rude speech and foolish babble; and to the mental kamma are three items: avoidance of covetousness, hatred and ignorance. These are Ten Good Acts, and the opposite is known as the Ten Bad Acts or Ten Unwholesome Deeds.

65. Q: The precept of abstaining from killing sentient beings should be understood to mean one should not kill good people. If there are felons who have committed atrocious crimes such as murder and arson, by law these are capital offenses. Should they be exempted from the punishment?

A: Felons who commit murder or other atrocious crimes should be brought to justice for sure, because anyone who violates the law of the state must be punished according to law. This is nothing to do with any personal will. While the judge holds the power to pronounce sentences, he merely acts according to law, it is nothing personal. When Sākyamuni decreed that his followers abstain from taking life of beings he did it in terms of individuals. It was also intended to keep them from breaking the laws of the state. The Buddha never argued the state should not punish criminals, but always admonished his disciples to abide by laws of the state. Here are two things of different nature, which must not be confused. When referring to the law of causality (hetu-phala), Buddhism often claims that good

神，若是为国家生财，为人民谋利，这是利益众生的事，是大好事。若是为个人贪财，为私人泄忿而害人，那就为戒律所不许。总之，假使人人依照五戒十善的准则行事，那么，人民就会和平康乐，社会就会安定团结，国家就会繁荣昌盛，这样就会出现一种和平安乐的世界，一种具有高度精神文明的世界。这就是人间佛教所要达到的目的。

66. 问：据闻，大乘佛法说一切众生都能成佛，这种人间佛教，和成佛有什么关系？

答：大乘佛教是说一切众生都能成佛，但成佛必需先要做个好人，做个清白正直的人，要在做好人的基础上才能学佛成佛。这就是释迦佛说的，

"诸恶莫作，
众善奉行，
自净其意，
是诸佛教。"

怎样叫学佛？学佛就是要学菩萨行，过去诸佛是修菩萨行成佛的，我今学佛也要修学菩萨行。

yields good returns while evil yields bad returns and that any debt of murder should be paid off. This shows that Buddhism doesn't run counter to temporal laws, but recognizes them. Such a spiritual principle not only applies to abstention from killing sentient beings, but also applies to abstention from covetousness and hatred. As to making wealth for the whole country and do good for the people, it is a great merit for the interest of mankind. However, it would be against the precepts for one to thirst for personal gain or do harm to others to revenge personal grudge. In brief, if everybody conducts him/herself according to the codes of the Five Precepts and the Ten Good Acts, people would live in peace and health, society would be stable and united, and the nation would prosper and thrive, leading to a world of peace and happiness with high spiritual civilization. This is the goal pursued by popular Buddhism.

66. Q: It is said that according to Mahāyāna doctrine, every sentient being is able to attain Buddhahood. Is there any connection between Popular Buddhism and the attainment of Buddhahood?

A: Mahāyāna Buddhism, indeed, believes that every sentient being is able to attain Buddhahood, but first, one must be a good and pure person. Only on the basis of being a good person, can one learn from Buddhas and attain Buddhahood. Just as Sākyamuni puts it,

Do no evil,

Do all that is good,

Purify your own mind,

This is all Buddhas' teaching.

What is meant by learning from Buddhas? It means to follow the Bodhisatta code of conduct. This is how preceding Buddhas attained their Buddhahood. For us too, to learn from Buddhas is just to follow the Bodhisatta code of conduct.

67. 问:什么是菩萨行?

答:菩萨行总的来说是上求佛道,下化众生,是以救度众生为己任的。修学菩萨行的人不仅要发愿救度一切众生,还要观察、认识世间一切都是无常无我的,要认识到整个世间,主要是人类社会的历史,是种不断发生发展、无常变化、无尽无休的洪流。这种迅猛前进的滚滚洪流谁也阻挡不了,谁也把握不住。菩萨觉悟到,在这种无常变化的汹涌波涛中顺流而下没有别的可做,只有诸恶莫作,众善奉行,庄严国土,利乐有情,这样才能把握自己,自度度人,不被无常变幻的生死洪流所淹没,依靠菩萨六波罗蜜的航船,出离这种无尽无边的苦海。《华严经》说,菩萨以"一切众生而为树根,诸佛菩萨而为花果,以大悲水饶益众生,则能成就诸佛菩萨智慧花果"。又说,"是故菩提属于众生,若无众生一切菩萨终不能成无上正觉。"所以,只有利他才能自利,这就是菩萨以救度众生为自救的辩证目的,这就是佛教无常观的世界观和菩萨行的人生观的具体实践,这也是人间佛教的理论基础。

68. 问:什么是六波罗蜜?

答:布施、持戒、忍辱、精进、静虑、智慧六种就叫六波

67. Q: What is the Bodhisatta code of conduct?

A: The Bodhisatta code of conduct is to take the deliverance of all living beings as one's own responsibility, so, generally speaking, it is to learn the way of Buddha above, and to convert all beings below. The practitioners of Bodhisatta Code are required not only to vow their willingness to save all living beings, but also to see through and realize the impermanence and egolessness of everything in the world, to see that the whole world, particularly the history of human society, is an ever-flowing, changing and developing current without end. Nobody can stop or control this swift current in its torrential advance. Bodhisattas are aware that nothing can be done while drifting along this torrential tide of impermanent changes, but to do no evils, uphold all good, glorify the land and benefit sentient beings. Only thus can one take one's own destiny in hand, liberating oneself as well as others without being drowned in the ever changing current of life and death, and finally leave the ocean of boundless suffering by the boat of Bodhisatta's Six Perfections (cha pāramitā). The *Avataṃsaka-sūtra* reads that the Bodhisattas "compare all living beings to the root of a tree, all Buddhas and Bodhisattas to its flowers and fruits, they benefits all beings with the water of compassion (Karunā), and thus they attain the flowers and fruits of wisdom as Buddhas and Bodhisattas". It adds, "therefore, Bodhisattas belong among living beings, and without the latter all Bodhisattas would be unable to attain perfect Enlightenment (anuttara sammā-sambodhi)." So, only through benefit to others can one benefit oneself, this is the Bodhisatta's goal, in a dialectical point of view, of delivering all living beings for the sake of self-deliverance. This is also the concrete practice of the Buddhist world outlook of impermanence (anicca) and life outlook of the Bodhisatta code. This is the theoretical basis for Popular Buddhism.

68. Q: What are the Six Perfections (cha pāramitā)?

A: Charity (Dāna), Morality, or Abiding by discipline

罗蜜，也叫六度。这六度是菩萨万行的纲领。

69. 问：请略解说六波罗蜜的内容和意义。

答：根据佛陀的教导，修学菩萨行的佛弟子，不但不贪求分外的财物，还要以自己的财法施给别人，这叫布施；一切损害别人不道德的行为严禁去作，这叫持戒；不对他人起嗔害心，有人前来嗔害恼我，应说明情况，要忍辱原谅，这叫忍辱；应该作的事情要精勤努力去作，这叫精进；排除杂念，锻练意志，一心利益众生，就叫静虑；广泛研习世出世间一切学问和技术，就叫智慧。这六种法门通常也叫作六度。这六件事做到究竟圆满就叫波罗蜜，波罗蜜意为事究竟，也叫到彼岸，古译为度。佛陀叫弟子依这六波罗蜜为行动准则以自利利人，就叫菩萨行。菩萨以此六波罗蜜作为舟航，在无常变化的生死苦海中自度度人，功行圆满，直达涅槃彼岸，名为成佛。菩萨成佛即是得大解脱、得大自在，永远常乐我净。这就是大乘佛教菩萨行的最后结果。菩萨成佛之前，学佛度众生，以度众生为修行佛道的中心课题，成佛之后还是永远地在度众生，这就是大乘佛教的中心思想。菩萨行的人间佛教的意义在于：果真人人能够学菩萨行，行菩萨道，且不说今后成佛不成佛，就是在当前使人们能够自觉地建立起高尚的道德品行，积极地建设起助人为乐的精神文明，也是有益于国家社会的，何况以此净化世间，建设人间净土！

(sīla), Forbearance (Khanti), Effort, or energy (variya), Contemplation (bhāvanā) and Wisdom (paññā) are known as the Six Perfections or the Six Ferries. They form the guidelines for the entire Bodhisatta code of conduct.

69. Q: Please explain briefly the contents and significance of the Six Pāramitās.

A: Following the Buddha's teachings, the Buddhist disciples practising Bodhisatta Conduct not only have no desire for extra property, but give of their own wealth to others — this is called Charity; all immoral behavior detrimental to others is strictly prohibited — this is Morality, or Abiding by the Precepts; bearing no malice to others, yet enduring malice or hatred directed against oneself with patience or necessary explanations — this is called Forbearance; work with energy on what should be done — this is called Effort; to banish all wrong views, to train one's mind to the state of whole-heartedly benefiting living beings is Contemplation; broadly learning and studying all knowledge and technology within or beyond the world is called Wisdom. These Six gate-ways are also known as the Six Ferries. When all these six are perfectly accomplished, it is called Pāramitā, meaning ultimate perfection, or reaching the other shore. Hence the ancient translation Ferry. The Buddha admonished his disciples to act according to the codes of the Six Perfections so as to benefit others as well as oneself, i.e. Bodhisatta Conduct. Bodhisattas take the Six Perfections as a ferryboat to deliver themselves and others across the ever-changing ocean of sufferings of birth and death, to reach the other shore of nibbāna with meritorious service. This is known as attaining Buddhahood, or the attainment of great salvation, great freedom, and eternally unchangeable enlightenment, happiness, ease and purification. This is the final outcome of the Bodhisatta Conduct of Mahāyāna Buddhism. Prior to attainment of Buddhahood, Bodhisattas learn from the Buddha to liberate living beings, which is the cardinal practice for the attainment of Buddhahood. After attaining Buddhahood one's task is to continue to deliver living beings.

70. 问:你对今后佛教前途的发展是怎样看的?

答:存在了将近两千年的中国佛教,是拥有内容丰富绚丽多采的文化遗产的。论它的典籍文化,论它的成绩经验,论它的国际影响,无论作为宗教或学术来看待,中国佛教在全人类的文化发展和文明进步的历史中都有不容忽视的地位。但是另一方面,由于过去长期的衰落,中国佛教也存在着不少的缺点和局限。如何克服历史所给予的污染和困难,积极发扬自己的优良传统,主要在于当前中国佛教徒本身的努力。如培养传灯人才,管好重点寺庙,开展学术研究和国际交流等等都是要立即抓好的大事。我们是共产党领导的社会主义国家,党和政府保护宗教信仰自由政策是长期不变的,坚定不移的,毫不含糊的。解放以后全国佛教从奄奄一息的状态中得到复苏和发展,宝镜重光,法炬复燃,像设严饰,气象万千。尤其是粉碎“四人帮”以来,一切恢复整顿工作顺利进行,短短数年之中取得了有目共睹的巨大成绩。所有这一切都是和党的宗教信仰自由政策的正确贯彻,党和政府的亲切关怀和大力支持分不开的。

This is the focal point of Mahāyāna Buddhism. The significance of Bodhisatta Conduct of Mahāyāna Buddhism lies in that, if everybody learns from the Bodhisatta code of conduct and walks on the Bodhisatta's way, no matter whether or not it will result in Buddhahood later, it certainly will be good for the nation and human society as it enables the people to consciously build up lofty moral virtues and actively build a spiritual civilization in which to serve the people is a pleasure. Let it serve to purify the human world, and build the Pure Land in the human world.

70. Q: How do you see the prospects of Buddhism in the future?

A: Chinese Buddhism, with its history of nearly 2000 years is a rich and splendid cultural heritage. In terms of its canonical culture, its achievements and experience and its international influence, Chinese Buddhism occupies a position that can hardly be ignored in the history of cultural development and progress of civilization of mankind as a whole, whether in the religious or academic field. However, on the other hand, it has quite a few shortcomings and limitations due to the prolonged period of decline in the past. To overcome the contamination and difficulties it has inherited from history and actively develop its own fine traditions requires mainly the endeavors of Chinese Buddhists themselves. Training up successors, taking good care of key temples, promoting academic research and international exchange, all these are areas where urgent work needs to be done. Ours is a socialist country led by the Communist Party where the policy of freedom of religious belief, pursued by the Party and government, is unchangeable, steadfast and unambiguous. After Liberation, Chinese Buddhism has revived and developed from the verge of extinction to the present, with its mirror of Dhamma shining once again, its torch rekindled, the image of Buddha repainted, presenting all its majesty. Especially after the fall of the "Gang of Four", all work of restoration and consolidation is running smoothly, achieving great success within a short span of time. All this is inseparable from the cor-

抚今思昔，我深为中国佛教庆，深为中国佛教徒庆。我深信，作为灿烂的民族古典文化的绚丽花朵，作为悠久的东方精神文明的巍峨丰碑，中国佛教必将随祖国建设事业的发展而发展，并在这一伟大事业中，为庄严国土，为利乐有情，为世界人类的和平、进步和幸福作出应有的贡献。瞻望未来，前程似锦，春回大地，万卉争妍，佛教的前途是无限光明的。

rect implementation of the Party's policy of religious freedom, from the deep concern and strong support of the Party and government.

Reflecting on the past in the light of present, I rejoice for Chinese Buddhism as well as Chinese Buddhists. I am firmly convinced that, as a beautiful flower of the classical Chinese culture and as a magnificent monument to the time-honored spiritual civilization of the Orient, Chinese Buddhism will certainly keep pace with the reconstruction of our motherland, and will contribute a great deal to glorifying the land, benefiting the people, and peace on earth, progress and happiness for all mankind. Looking ahead I see a splendid future with millions of flowers contending in beauty in the warmth of spring, the future of Buddhism is infinitely bright.

## 附录：巴、英、汉佛教术语对照表

## Appendix: Buddhist terms in Pāli, English and Chinese

（按章排列。章内按问题排列）

(By chapter and question number)

# Chapter I

| | Pāli | English | 汉语 |
|---|---|---|---|
| 1. | Sangha | Monastic Order | 僧团 |
| | Buddha | Enlightened One | 佛 |
| | Dhamma | Dharma, Buddhist Doctrine | 佛法 |
| 2. | dhamma | every thing | 法 |
| | pakati | attribute | 性质 |
| | lakkhaṇa | appearance | 相状 |
| | Pāli | Pali language | 巴利语 |
| 3. | Siddhattha | Siddhartha (person) | 悉达多 |
| | Gotama | Gautama (family name) | 乔达摩 |
| | Sākya | the Sākya clan | 释迦族 |
| | Sākyamuni | title: sage of the Sākya | 释迦牟尼 |
| 4. | Sambodhi | enlightenment | 正觉 |
| | Sammā-sambodhi | Perfect enlightenment | 等觉或遍觉 |
| | anuttara Sammā-Sambodhi | Supreme enlightenment | 圆觉或无上觉 |

| | | | |
|---|---|---|---|
| 6. | tathatā | suchness | 真如 |
| | Yathābūtaṃ | according to the reality | 如实 |
| | Tathāgata | coming according to the reality | 如来 |
| 7. | Amita | Boundless | 无量 |
| | Amitābha (S.) | boundless light | 无量光 |
| 8. | namo | salutation or homage | 敬礼 |
| 9. | Kapilavatthu | Kapilavastu (Kingdom) | 迦毗罗卫国 |
| | Suddhodana | Suddhodana (person) | 净饭 |
| | Māyā | (mother of the Buddha) | 摩耶(佛的生母) |
| | Lumbinī | Lumbini Grove (birthplace of the Buddha) | 蓝毗尼花园 |
| 10. | Tipiṭakācariya | Triple-Text Master | 三藏法师 |
| | Asoka | King Asoka | 阿育王 |
| 11. | Prajāpati (S.) | Princess Prajapati | 波阇波提夫人 |
| | Rāja Cakkavattin | a king who can unify the world, or a "wheel-turning king" | 转轮王 |
| 12. | Veda | Veda (scriptures) | 吠陀书 |
| 13. | Yasodharā | Princess Yasodhara | 王女耶输陀罗 |
| | Rāhula | (the Buddha's son) | 罗怙罗 |

| | | | |
|---|---|---|---|
| 14. | Koṇḍañña | Kauṇḍinya (S.) (person) | 憍陈如 |
| | Bhaddiya | Bhadrika (S.) (person) | 跋提 |
| | Vappa | Vāṣpa (S.)(person) | 跋波 |
| | Mahānāma | Mahānāma (S.)(person) | 摩诃男,大名 |
| | Assaji | Aśvajit (S.)(person) | 阿说示,马胜 |
| | Nerañjarā | Lilaian River | 尼连禅河 |
| | Bārāṇasī | Benares City (Varanasi) | 波罗奈城 |
| | pippala | pippala tree | 毕钵罗树 |
| | kusa | auspicious grass | 吉祥草 |
| | Kilesa | moral affliction | 烦恼 |
| | Māra | eril | 魔障 |
| 15. | Buddhagayā | (the place of Buddha's enlightenment) | 菩提伽耶 |
| | Pippala | Pippala tree | 毕钵罗树 |
| | Bodhi (tree) | Bo-tree | 菩提树 |
| | Gayā | Gaya City | 伽耶城 |
| | Vajirāsana | diamond pedestal | 金刚座 |
| | thūpa | pagoda | 塔 |
| | Mahābodhi Ārāma | Mahabodhi Monastery | 大菩提寺 |
| 16. | Dhammacakkappa-vattana | turning the wheel of Dharma | 转法轮 |
| 17. | cakka | wheel | 轮 |
| | Rāja | king | 国王 |
| | Dhammacakka | the wheel of Dharma | 法轮 |

| | | | |
|---|---|---|---|
| | Sārnāth | Deer Park (place) | 鹿野苑 |
| | Asoka | King Asoka | 阿育王 |
| | Kusināra | place where Buddha passed away | 拘尸那伽 |
| 18. | Tiratana | the Three Gems | 三宝 |
| 19. | ratana | gem | 宝 |
| | sangha | buddhist order | 僧团 |
| 20. | Tisaraṇa | the Three Refuges | 三归依处 |
| | Saraṇaṃ gacchāmi | abiding | 归依 |
| 21. | Magadha | Magadha Kingdom | 摩揭陀国 |
| | Kassapa | Kāśyapa (S.) (person) | 迦叶 |
| | Rājagaha | Rājagṛha (S.) (place) | 王舍城 |
| | Sāriputta | Śāriputra (S.) (person) | 舍利弗 |
| | Mahāmoggallāna | Mahāmaudgalyāyana (S.) (person) | 摩诃目犍连 |
| | Mahākassapa | Mahākāśyapa (S.) (person) | 摩诃迦叶 |
| | Nanda | Nanda (person) | 难陀 |
| | Ānanda | Ānanda (person) | 阿难陀 |
| | Devadatta | Devadatta (person) | 提婆达多 |
| | Rāhula | Rāhula (person) | 罗怙罗 |
| | Upāli | Upāli (person) | 优波离 |
| | Vinaya bhānaka | master of Buddhist disciplines (title) | 佛教戒律学大师 |
| | Prajāpati | (person) | 波阇波提 |

| | | | |
|---|---|---|---|
| | bhikkhu | monk | 比丘 |
| | bhikkhunī | nun | 比丘尼 |
| | upāsaka | male lay follower | 邬波索迦（信男） |
| | upāsikā | female lay follower | 邬波斯迦(信女) |
| 22. | Sāvatthī | Śrāvastī (S.) (place) | 舍卫城 |
| | Kosala | Kośala (ancient State) | 拘萨罗国 |
| | Bimbisāra | King Bimbisāra | 频毗娑罗王 |
| | Veḷuvanārāmaya | Bamboo Grove Monastery | 竹林精舍 |
| | Sudatta | Sudatta (person) | 须达多 |
| | Jeta | Prince Jeta | 祇陀王子 |
| | Jetavanārāmaya | Jeta Grove Monastery | 祇园精舍 |
| | Gijjhakūṭa | Gṛdhrakūṭa Hill | 灵鹫山 |
| | Vesālī | Vesali (place) | 毗舍离城 |
| | Kusiṇāra | Kuśinagara (S.) (place) | 拘尸那伽 |
| | Parinibbāna | (Buddha's) passing away | 涅槃 |
| | nibbāna | nirvana | 涅槃 |
| 24. | Vassa | the Rainy Season Retreat | 雨安居 |
| | Cunda | Cunda (person) | 纯陀 |
| | sala | sala tree | 娑罗树 |
| | Subhadda | Subhadra (person) | 须跋陀罗 |
| | sarīra | the remains of the dead after cremation | 舍利 |

| | | | |
|---|---|---|---|
| 27. | Theravadin | Elders' | 上座部佛教的 |
| 28. | Vesākha (S. Viśākha) | the Buddhist Holy Day | 佛教节日(三吉祥日) |
| 30. | Madhya Desa (S.) | the Middle Kingdom of ancient India | 中国(古印度一国家) |
| 31. | Vajji | Vṛji (Kingdom) | 跋耆国 |
| 33. | varṇā (S.)(P. vaṇṇa) | caste | 种姓 |
| | Brāhmaṇa (S.) | Brahmin (caste) | 婆罗门 |
| | Kṣatriya (S.) | Ksatriya (caste) | 刹帝利 |
| | Vaiśya (S.) | Vaisya (caste) | 吠舍 |
| | Śūdra (S.) | Sudra (caste) | 首陀罗 |
| | Caṇḍāla | Candala (caste) | 旃陀罗 |
| 39. | Manu-Smṛti (S.) | Manu Code | 《摩奴法典》 |
| | Sarvadarśana Saṃgraha (S.) | Manuals of Public and Domestic Rites | 述记氏法论 |
| 40. | dāna | offering | 供,布施 |
| 41. | aniccā | impermanence | 无常 |
| 43. | Veda | Veda (scriptures) | 吠陀经 |
| | Atta | Ego | 我 |
| | saṃsāra | rebirth | 轮回 |

| | | | |
|---|---|---|---|
| 44. | Nirgrantha-jñātaputra (S.) (person) | | 尼乾子 |
| | Jaina (S.) | Jainism | 耆那教 |
| | Purāṇa-kassapa | (person's name) | 富兰那迦叶 |
| | Makkhali-gosāla | (person's name) | 末迦梨 |
| | Ajita-kesakambala | (person's name) | 阿耆多 |
| | Pakudha-kaccāyana | (person's name) | 婆鸠多 |
| | Sañjaya-belaṭṭhiputta | (person's name) | 散若夷 |
| | Mahābhūta | great elements | 大种 |
| 45. | paṭiccasamuppāda | dependent origination | 缘起 |
| | kamma | karma | 业 |
| | Hetu-phala | Cause and effect | 因果 |
| | Tayo addhā | Three periods of time (past, present, future) | 三世 |
| | Gati | realm world | 道、界 |
| | Deva-gati | the realm of deities | 天界 |
| | Manussa-gati | human realm | 人界 |
| | Asuratta | asura realm | 阿修罗界 |
| | Naraka-gati | hell | 地狱 |
| | Peta-gati | ghost realm | 饿鬼道 |
| | Tiracchāna-yoni | animal world | 畜生道 |
| | Cattāri mahābhūta | the blending components of four elements | 四大 |
| | Brahmā | Brahma | 梵天 |

# Chapter II

| | **Pāli** | **English** | **汉语** |
|---|---|---|---|
| 1. | Dhamma | Doctrine | 法 |
| | Cattāri-ariya-saccāni | Four Noble Truths | 四圣谛 |
| | Dukkha-sacca | The Truth of Suffering | 苦谛 |
| | Samudaya-sacca | The Cause of Suffering | 集谛 |
| | Nirodha-sacca | The Extinction of Suffering | 灭谛 |
| | Magga-sacca | The Way Leading to Cessation of Suffering | 道谛 |
| | Paṭiccasamuppāda | Dependent origination | 缘起 |
| 2. | Hetu | Cause | 因 |
| | Paccaya | Conditions | 缘 |
| 4. | dhamma | phenomenon | 现象 |
| 6. | sarīrika-thūpa | relic pagoda | 舍利塔 |
| | gāthā | verse or ode | 偈颂 |
| | kalasa | water-dish crest | 露盘 |
| | Dhammakāya-sarīra Gāthā | Ode of Sarīra | 法身舍利偈 |
| 7. | Assaji | Aśvajit, one of Buddha's first five disciples | 阿说是，最初五比丘之 |

| | | | |
|---|---|---|---|
| | | (The name literally means" victory of horse") | 一，意译是"马胜" |
| | bhikkhu | monk | 僧 |
| | Sāriputta | Sāriputra (person) | 舍利弗 |
| | Moggallāna | Maudgalyāyana (person) | 目犍连 |
| | Samaṇa | | 沙门 |
| 8. | Khaṇa | an instant — a brief unit of time | 刹那 |
| 12. | Anattā | Egolessness | 无我 |
| | Satta | Sentient being | 有情 |
| | Atta | Ego, equivalent to "soul" | 自我，灵魂 |
| | cha dhātuyo | the Six Great Elements | 六大 |
| | Paṭhavī | Earth | 地 |
| | Āpo | Water | 水 |
| | Tejo | Fire or heat | 火 |
| | Vāyo | Air | 风 |
| | Ākāsa | Space | 空 |
| | Viññāṇa | Consciousness | 识 |
| | Khandha | Heap or group | 蕴 |
| | Rūpa | Corporeality | 色 |
| | Vedanā | Feeling or sensation | 受 |
| | Saññā | Perception | 想 |
| | Sankhāra | Mental formation | 行 |
| | Pañc' indriyāni | The Five Roots | 五根 |
| | Pañcāyatana | The Five Objective Sources of Sensation | 五境 |

| | | | |
|---|---|---|---|
| | Sukha | Happiness | 乐 |
| | Dukkha | Pain | 苦 |
| | Adukkha-m-asukha | Neutral feelings | 不苦不乐 |
| 13. | Nāmarūpa | name and form | 名色 |
| | Dhātu | sphere, realm | 界 |
| | Mahā-bhūta | great element | 要素 |
| 14. | Phala | effect, fruit | 果 |
| | Samsāra | cycle of birth and death | 轮回 |
| 15. | Anicca | Impermanence | 无常 |
| | Aniccā vata saṅkhāra | All things are impermanent | 诸行无常 |
| | Uppādavaya dhammino | They are subject to birth and death | 是生灭法 |
| | Uppāda (or jāti) | Origination | 生 |
| | Ṭhitika | Maintenance | 住 |
| | Jarā (or aññathatta) | Destruction | 异 |
| | Nirodha | Cessation | 灭 |
| | Sāssata diṭṭhi | Belief in eternity | 常见 |
| 16. | Saddhamma | The Period of True Dhamma | 正法时期 |
| | Saddhamma-paṭirūpaka | The Period of Image Dhamma | 像法时期 |
| | Saddhamma-vippalujjati | The Period of Termination | 末法时期 |

| | | | |
|---|---|---|---|
| 18. | Abhidhammakosa-śāstra | Commentary of Abhidhamma | 阿毗达磨俱舍论 |
| | Mahāprajñā-pāramitā-śāstra | Treatise on the Great Perfection of Wisdom Sūtra | 大智度论 |
| | Kumārajīva | (person) | 鸠摩罗什 |
| 19. | Sabbe sankhārā aniccā | All phenomena are impermanent | 诸行无常 |
| | Sabbe dhammā anatta | All dhammas are devoid of self | 诸法无我 |
| | Lakkhaṇa | Characteristics of Dhamma | 法印 |
| 20. | Sāsava | Defiled dhammas | 有漏 |
| 21. | Āsava | Taint or canker | 漏 |
| | Kilesa | Affliction | 烦恼 |
| | Rāga | Greed | 贪 |
| | Dosa | Anger or hate | 嗔 |
| | Moha | Delusion | 痴 |
| | Avijjā | Ignorance | 无明 |
| | Māna | Arrogance | 慢 |
| | Vicikicchā | doubt | 疑 |
| | Micchā-diṭṭhi | Wrong views | 恶见 |
| | Uccheda-diṭṭhi | Annihilation-view | 断见 |
| | Kāya-kamma | Actions of the body | 身业 |
| | Vacī-kamma | Actions of speech | 语业，口业 |
| | Mano-kamma | Actions of the mind | 意业 |

| | | | |
|---|---|---|---|
| | Kamma | Actions | 业 |
| 22. | Saṃkhāra | Mental formation | 行 |
| | Saḷāyatana | Six sense bases | 六入 |
| | Phassa | Contact between sense organs and sense objects | 触 |
| | Taṇha | Desire | 爱 |
| | Upādāna | Grasping | 取 |
| | Bhava | Coming into existence | 有 |
| | Jāti | Birth | 生 |
| | Jarā-maraṇa | Old age and death | 老死 |
| | Upekkhā | Neither pleasant nor unpleasant | 不苦不乐 |
| | Atta-abhinivesa | Affirmation of self | 我执 |
| 23. | Anāsava | No flux，no-defilement | 无漏 |
| | Suddha-ñāna | Undefiled，pure wisdom | 不染污的清净智 |
| | Sopadhi-sesa-nibbāna | Nirvana with corporal remainder | 有余涅槃 |
| | Nirupadhi-sesa-nibbāna | Nirvana without remainder | 无余涅槃 |
| 24. | Ti-sikkhā | The Threefold Learning | 三学 |
| | Sīla | Morality | 戒 |
| | Samādhi | Concentration | 定 |
| | Paññā | Wisdom | 慧 |
| | Upasampadā | the higher ordination | 具足戒 |

| | | |
|---|---|---|
| Sāmaṇera | Novice | 沙弥 |
| Bhikkhunī | Nun | 比丘尼 |
| Sangha | Congregation of Monks and Nuns | 僧团 |
| Parinibbāna | pass away | 大般涅槃 |
| Kāma | Sense-desire | 爱、欲 |
| Cattāri jhānāni | Four stages of trance | 四禅 |
| Cattāro ārupā-samādhi | Four higher stages of non-material trance | 四无色定 |
| Navānupubbavihāra Samāpattiyo | Nine stages of meditation | 九次第定 |
| Tayo samādhi | Three kinds of meditation | 三昧 |
| Sabhāva lakkhaṇa | Self nature | 自相 |
| Samañña | Common characteristics | 共相 |
| Pahīna-kilesa | Dispelling illusions | 断除迷惑 |
| Adhigama | Attaining truth | 证悟真理 |
| Bodhipakkhiya-dhamma | ways to enlightenment | 三十七道品 |
| Satipaṭṭhāna | Mindfulness | 念住 |
| Padhāna | Right efforts | 勤 |
| Iddhi-pāda | Roads to power | 神足 |
| Indriya | faculties | 根 |
| bala | Mental powers | 力 |
| Bojjhanga | Factors of Enlightenment | 觉支 |
| magga | Path | 道 |

| | | | |
|---|---|---|---|
| | Sammā diṭṭhi | Right view | 正见 |
| | Sammā sankappa | Right thought | 正思 |
| | Sammā vācā | Right speech | 正语 |
| | Sammā kammanta | Right bodily action | 正业 |
| | Sammā ājiva | Right livelihood | 正命 |
| | Sammā vāyāma | Right effort | 正精进 |
| | Sammā sati | Right mindfulness | 正念 |
| | Sammā samādhi | Right concentration | 正定 |
| 25. | Ekottarikāgama | (name of scripture) | 增一阿含 |
| | Rājacakkavattin | Wheel turning king | 转轮圣王 |
| 27. | apratiṣṭhita-nirvāṇa (S.) | active nirvana | 无住涅槃 |
| | Mettā | Great loving-kindness | 慈 |
| | Karuṇā | Compassion | 悲 |
| | Pāramitā | Perfection | 度 |
| | Cattāri Saṃgahavatthūni | Four all-embracing virtues | 四摄 |
| 28. | Bodhisatta | Bodhisattva | 菩萨 |
| 29. | Dāna | charity | 布施 |
| | Abhaya dāna | Givings that free one from fear | 无畏施 |
| | Khanti | Patience | 忍 |
| | Viriya | Effort and progress | 精进 |
| 30. | Peyyavajja | Kindly speech | 爱语 |

| | | | |
|---|---|---|---|
| | Atthacariyā | Beneficial conduct | 利行 |
| | Samānattatā | Equality | 同事 |
| 31. | vidyā (S.) | knowledge | 明（知识） |
| | Śabda-vidyā | Phonology and philology | 声明 |
| | Śilpakarma-vidyā | All technology, techniques, arithmetic etc. | 工巧明 |
| | Cikitsa-vidyā | Medical science and pharmacology | 医方明 |
| | Hetu-vidyā | Logic | 因明 |
| | Adhyātma-vidyā | Buddhist studies | 内明 |
| 32. | Suññatā | Emptiness | 空 |
| | Atta | Self | 我 |
| 35. | Mahākassapa | (person) | 摩诃迦叶 |
| | Sattapaṇṇi-guhā(P.) | (place) | |
| | Sapta-parṇa-guhā (S.) | | 七叶窟 |
| | Rājagaha | (place) | 王舍城 |
| | Tipiṭaka | Three baskets | 三藏 |
| | Ānanda | (person) | 阿难陀 |
| | Upāli | (person) | 优婆离 |
| 36. | Saṃgīti | Buddhist Council | 结集 |
| | Mañjuśrī | (a Boddhisattva) | 文殊师利（菩萨） |
| | Maitreya | (a Boddhisattva) | 弥勒(菩萨) |

| | | | |
|---|---|---|---|
| 37. | Vesālī | vaiśāli (place) | 毗舍离 |
| | Yasa Thero | Elder priest | 耶舍长老 |
| | aṭṭhakathā | commentary work | 注 |
| | Moggaliputta Tissa | (person) | 目犍连子帝须 |
| | Pāṭaliputta | Patna (city) | 波吒利弗城 |
| | Kusāna | (kingdom) | 大月氏国 |
| | Vasumitta | (person) | 世友 |
| | Mahāvibhāsā | (a commentary) | 大毗婆沙 |
| 38. | Dīpavaṃsa | A history of Sri Lanka | 岛史 |
| | Magadha | (kingdom) | 摩揭陀国 |
| | Buddhaghosa | (person) | 觉音 |
| 47. | Sutta-piṭaka | The basket of Buddha's discourses | 经藏 |
| | Dīgha-nikāya | Long Discourses | 长部 |
| | Dīghāgama | ( " ) | 长阿含 |
| | Majjhima-nikāya | Medium-length suttas | 中部 |
| | Saṃyukktāgama | The discourses organized according to content | 杂阿含 |
| | Saṃyutta-nikāya | ( " ) | 相应部 |
| | Aṅguttara-nikāya | The discourses collection in numerical order | 增支部 |
| | Ekottarikāgama | ( " ) | 增一阿含 |
| | Khuddaka-nikāya | Minor anthologies | 小部 |
| | Vinaya-piṭaka | The Basket of Disciplines | 律藏 |
| | Sutta-vibhaṅga | All of the precepts | 经分别 |

| | | |
|---|---|---|
| Khandhaka | Procedures for assemblies and rules for daily life | 犍度(律藏) |
| Parivāra | Interpretation of rules or appendix | 附随 |
| Abhidamma-piṭaka | The basket of commentary | 论藏 |
| Dhammasaṅgaṇi | Enumeration of Dhammas or Buddhist Psychological Ethics | 法聚论 |
| Vibhaṅga | The Book of Analysis | 分别论 |
| Dhātukatthā | Discourse on Elements | 界论 |
| Yamaka | Book of Pairs | 双论 |
| Paṭṭhāna | Book of causality | 发趣论 |
| Puggalapaññati | Description of Human Types | 人施设论 |
| Kathāvatthu | Points of controversy | 论事 |

# Chapter III

| | Pāli | English | 汉语 |
|---|---|---|---|
| 1. | Pañca-yāna | Five Vehicles | 五乘 |
| | yāna | vehicle | 乘 |
| | Pañca-sīla | Five Precepts | 五戒 |
| | Manussa-yāna | Human vehicle | 人乘 |
| | Dasa-kusala | Ten Meritorious Acts | 十善 |
| | hetu-phala | cause-effect | 因果 |
| | Devayāna | Heavenly vehicle | 天乘 |
| | Āriya-sacca | Noble Truths | 圣谛 |
| | Micchā-diṭṭhi | Wrong views | 邪见 |
| | Diṭṭhānusaya | Wrong views | 见惑 |
| | Atta-diṭṭhi | Ego-illusion | 我见 |
| | Sassata-diṭṭhi | Eternity-belief | 常见 |
| | Uccheda-diṭṭhi | Annihilation-belief | 断见 |
| | Micchā-sankappa | Defiled thought | 思惑 |
| | Lobha | Greed | 贪 |
| | Dosa | Hatred | 嗔 |
| | Moha | Delusion | 痴 |
| | Nibbāna | Nirvana | 涅槃 |
| | Sāvaka-yāna | Voice-hearer vehicle | 声闻乘 |
| | Buddha | Buddha | 佛 |
| | Sāvaka | Voice-hearer | 声闻 |
| | Buddha-Dhamma | Buddha's teaching | 佛法 |

| | | | |
|---|---|---|---|
| | Paṭiccasamupāda | Dependent Origination | 缘起 |
| | Pacceka-Buddha | Independently Enlightened One | 独觉佛 |
| | Pacceka-yāna | The vehicle of self-enlightenment | 独觉乘 |
| | Cha-pāramitā | The Six Virtuous Acts | 六度 |
| | Bodhisatta | Bodhisattva | 菩萨 |
| | Bodhisatta-yāna | The vehicle of Bodhisattva | 菩萨乘 |
| 2. | pabbajjā | Renunciation of the world, becoming a junior monk. | 出家 |
| | hetu-paccaya | cause and condition | 因缘 |
| | Sākyamuni | Sakyamuni (person) | 释迦牟尼 |
| | Mañjuśrī (S.) | Manjusri (a Bodhisattva) | 文殊师利 |
| | Maitreya (S.) | Maitreya (future Buddha) | 弥勒 |
| | Bhikkhu | Monk | 比丘 |
| | Vimalakīrti | Vimalakirti (person) | 维摩诘 |
| | Arahat | Arahant (enlightened person) | 阿罗汉 |
| 3. | Sotāpanna | The fruition of stream winning | 须陀洹果(初果，予流) |
| | Sakadāgāmi | The second fruition of once return | 斯陀含果(二果,一来) |

| | | | |
|---|---|---|---|
| | Anāgāmi | The third fruition of non-return | 阿那含果(三果,不还) |
| 4. | Kāmaloka | the sensuous world | 欲界 |
| | anattā | egolessness | 无我 |
| 5. | paribbājaka | religious mendicancy | 出家修道 |
| 8. | bhāvanā | meditation | 禅定 |
| | bodhipakkhiya-dhamma | requisites for enlightenment | 道品、觉支,菩提分 |
| | Cattāro satipaṭṭhānā | Four Foundations of Awareness | 四念处 |
| | Asubhābhāvanā | Contemplation of impurity | 不净观 |
| | Mettābhāvanā | Contemplation of mercy | 慈悲观 |
| | Nidānabhāvanā | Contemplation of cause and effect | 因缘观 |
| | Vibhaṇgabhāvanā | Contemplation of distinction | 界分别观 |
| | Ānāpānasati | Contemplation of breath | 数息观 |
| | Samādhi | Concentration | 定 |
| | Paññā | Wisdom | 慧 |
| 10. | tanhā | craving | 贪爱 |
| | Sangha | Monastic Order | 僧伽 |
| | Pārājika | Fundamental Rules | 重罪戒、波罗夷 |
| | bhikkhunī | Nun | 比丘尼 |

| | | |
|---|---|---|
| Upasampadā | Higher ordination | 受具戒 |
| thera | elder | 长老 |
| Mahāyāna | Great Vehicle | 大乘 |
| Vimalakīrtinirdesa (S.) | (a book) | 《维摩诘经》 |
| Upāsaka-sīla-sutta | Disciplines for Laity Sutta (a book) | 《优婆塞戒经》 |
| 11. Tiratana | The Three Gems | 三宝 |
| Uposatha | fast (a fortnightly event) | 持斋、半月说戒 |
| loka-dhammā | worldly laws | 世间法 |
| Sīṅgālaka | (a person) | 善生 |
| Siṅgālovāda Sutta | Singalovada Sutta (a book) | 善生经 |
| Dīghajāṇu (or Ujjaya) | (a person) | 跋阇迦 |
| Cattāro Dhammā | The Four Ways of Seeking Comfort and Balance | 四种安乐法 |
| Uṭṭhānasampadā | Perfection of professional training | 方便具足(职业修养的完备) |
| Ārakkhasampadā | Protection of one's own property, frugality without waste | 守护具足(节约不浪费财物) |
| Kalyāṇamittatā | Making worthy friends | 善知识具足(交结善友) |

| | | | |
|---|---|---|---|
| | Sammā-ājīva | Leading a decent life | 正命具足(正当的生活) |
| | Rāja | King | 国王 |
| | Cha-pāramitā | The Six Transcendent Virtuous Acts | 六度 |
| | Cattāri saṃgaha vatthūni | Four Embracing Dhamma | 四摄 |
| 12. | Dhammācariya | Doctrine master | 法师 |
| | Dhammasiddhi | (a person) | 达摩悉提 |
| 13. | sāmaṇera | Junior monk | 沙弥 |
| 15. | Upajjhāya | Master | 师、依止师 |
| 16. | Upasampadā | The higher ordination | 具足戒 |
| | Sāmaṇerī | Nun, female acceptor of the ten precepts | 沙弥尼 |
| 18. | Suttācariya | Scripture Master | 经师 |
| | Suttapiṭaka | Scripture Texts | 经藏 |
| | Vinayācariya | Discipline Master | 律师 |
| | Vinayapiṭaka | Discipline Texts | 律藏 |
| | Abhidhammācariya | Commentary Master | 论师 |
| | Abhidhammapiṭaka | Commentary Texts | 论藏 |
| | Tipiṭakācariya | Triple-Text Master | 三藏法师 |
| | Tipiṭaka | Triple-Text | 三藏 |

| | | | |
|---|---|---|---|
| 19. | Dhammarāja | religious leader, lit. "king of Doctrine" | 法王 |
| 20. | Sangha-rāja | King of Monastic Order | 僧王 |
| | Mahā-Nāyaka | Great leader of Sangha | 大导师 |
| | Nāyaka | Leader of Sangha | 导师 |
| 23. | Kamma | Action | 羯磨（会议办事） |
| 24. | Uposatha kamma | Recitation assembly | 布萨羯磨（诵戒的集会） |
| | Pātimokkha（P̣.） | Prātimokṣa（S.） book of precepts | 戒本、波罗提木叉 |
| | Pavārana | Satisfaction with self-criticism and other's exposure | 自恣 |
| 27. | Mahāvihāra | Great monastery | 大寺（丛林） |
| 29. | Thera | Elder（monks, 10 or more years after ordination） | 上座或长老 |
| | Maha Thera | Great Elder（senior monks, 20 or more years after ordination） | 大上座或大长老 |
| 32. | Sattvārtha-krīya-sīla（S.） | The Rule that all must serve the needs of sentient beings | 饶益有情戒 |

| | | | |
|---|---|---|---|
| 33. | Bodhisatta sīla | The precepts of Bodhisattva | 菩萨戒 |
| | Theravāda | A Buddhist sect | 上座部,小乘 |
| 34. | dāyaka | lay Buddhist donor | 施主 |
| 36. | Kasāya | monks' robe | 袈裟 |
| | Paramattha | truth | 真谛 |
| 37. | Brahmajāla Sutta | (a scripture) | 梵网经 |
| 38. | Sāriputta | (person) | 舍利弗 |
| | Moggallāna | ( " ) | 目犍连 |
| | Mahākassapa | ( " ) | 摩诃迦叶 |
| | Subhūti | ( " ) | 须菩提 |
| | Purāna | ( " ) | 富楼那 |
| | Mahākaccāna | ( " ) | 摩诃迦旃延 |
| | Anuruddha | ( " ) | 阿那律 |
| | Upāli | ( " ) | 优波离 |
| | Rāhula | ( " ) | 罗怙罗 |
| | Ānanda | ( " ) | 阿难陀 |
| | abhiññā | psychic power | 神通 |
| | Parinibbāna | Passing away | 大般涅槃 |
| 40. | Sanchi | Sanchi (place) | 山奇 |
| 41. | Nandimittāvadāna | Nandimitravadana (book) | 《法住记》 |
| | Āyasma Nandimitra | (person) | 庆友尊者 |

| | | | |
|---|---|---|---|
| | Siharatta | (present day Sri Lanka) | 狮子国（今斯里兰卡） |
| 43. | Mañjuśrī (S.) | (a Bodhisattva) | 文殊师利 |
| | Samantabhadra (S.) | ( " ) | 普贤 |
| | Avalokiteśvara (S.) | Guanyin (a Bodhisattva) | 观世音 |
| | Kṣitigarbha (S.) | (a Bodhisattva) | 地藏 |
| 44. | Bodhicitta | Awakened mind | 菩提心 |
| | Tisikkhā | Three Studies | 三学 |
| | Sīla | precepts | 戒 |
| | Samādhi | concentration | 定 |
| | Paññā | wisdom | 慧 |
| | Sammā-sambodhi | perfect enlightenment | 等觉 |
| 45. | Kathmandu | Kathmandu, Capital of Nepal | 加德满都 |
| 46. | Maitreya | Maitreya Buddhisattva, (the future Buddha) | 弥勒菩萨 |

# Chapter IV

| | Pāli | English | 汉语 |
|---|---|---|---|
| 1. | Buddha | Buddha | 佛陀 |
| 3. | Parinibbāna | passing away | 佛陀逝世 |
| | Mādhyamika | the Middle-way School | 中观学派 |
| | Mahāyāna | Great Vehicle | 大乘 |
| | Yogācāra | the Yoga School | 瑜伽学派 |
| | Tantrayāna | the Esoteric School | 密宗 |
| 4. | Khuddānukhuddaka-sikkhāpada | Lesser and minor precepts | 小小戒 |
| | Bhikkhu | monk | 僧 |
| | Saṃgīti | Buddhist Council | 结集 |
| | Dhamma | Buddha's teaching | 佛法 |
| | Puṇṇa | Pūrṇa (person) | 富楼那 |
| | Vinaya | Discipline | 戒律 |
| | Mahā-kassapa | (person) | 摩诃迦叶 |
| | Vappa | ( " ) | 跋波 |
| | Mahāthera | senior monk | 长老 |
| | Nikāya | sect | 部派 |
| 5. | Theravāda | Theravada Sect | 上座部 |
| | Mahāsaṃghika | Mahasamghika Sect | 大众部 |

| | | | |
|---|---|---|---|
| | Bārāṇasī | Baranasi(Kasi) (ethnic group) | 波利族 |
| | Yasa | Yasa (person) | 耶舍 |
| | Vesālī | Vaisali (place) | 毗舍离城 |
| | Vajji | Vajjian nationality | 跋祇族 |
| 6. | Mahāsaṃghika-vinaya | precepts of the Mahā saṃghika sect | 僧祇律 |
| | Sabbatthivāda-vinaya | precepts of the Sabbatthivāda sect | 十诵律 |
| | Thera | Senior monk | 长老 |
| 7. | bhāvanā | meditation | 禅定、修习 |
| 8. | Vajjiputtaka | (a Buddhist sect) | 跋祇子部或犊子部 |
| | Mahiṃsāsaka | ( " ) | 化地部 |
| | Vibhajjavāda | ( " ) | 分别说部 |
| | Ekavyohārika | ( " ) | 一说部 |
| | Lokottaravāda | ( " ) | 说出世部 |
| | Gokulika | ( " ) | 鸡胤部或牛王部 |
| | Cetiyavāda | ( " ) | 制多山部 |
| 9. | Abhidhamma Piṭaka | Commentary Texts | 论藏 |
| 10. | Saṅkhata Dhamma | Conditioned Phenomena | 有为法 |
| | hetu-paccaya | causes and conditions | 因缘 |

| | | | |
|---|---|---|---|
| | Asaṅkhata Dhamma | Unconditioned Phenomena | 无为法 |
| | Nibbāna | Nirvana | 涅槃 |
| | Ākāsa | Space | 虚空 |
| | Khaṇa | an instant | 一刹那 |
| | Atta | ego | 我 |
| | Nimmāna-kāya | phenomenal body | 化身 |
| | Sambhoga-kāya | noumenal body | 实身 |
| | rūpa-kāya | body | 色身 |
| | Sāvaka | Hearer Vehicle | 声闻乘 |
| | Bodhisatta | Bodhisattva (enlightened one) | 菩萨 |
| | metta-karuṇā | vow of mercy | 慈悲愿心 |
| | Pacceka-buddha | Self-enlightened one | 缘觉 |
| 11. | Asoka | King Asoka (Sorrow-free King) | 阿育王，阿输迦王，无忧王 |
| 12. | Magadha | Magadha (kingdom) | 摩揭陀国 |
| | Chandragupta | King Chandragupta | 旃陀罗笈多 |
| | Chandra | Chandra Caste | 旃陀罗种姓 |
| | Chandrasoka | (person) | 旃陀罗阿输迦 |
| | Punjab | the Punjab, (a place called "Five Rivers") | 五河 |
| | Gaṅgā | the Ganges River | 恒河 |
| | Nanda | Nanda Dynasty | 难陀王朝 |
| | Maurya | Maurya Dynasty | 孔雀王朝 |

| | | | |
|---|---|---|---|
| | Bindusāra | king Bindusāra | 宾头沙罗 |
| | Kāliṅga | Kāliṅga Kingdom | 羯陵伽国 |
| | Sadhamma | the ultimate doctrine | 正法 |
| | Mahinda | (person) | 摩晒陀 |
| | Saṃghamittā | (person) | 僧伽密陀 |
| 13. | Cīnapaṭṭa | bundle of silk | 成捆的丝 |
| | Cīnasukka | silk clothes | 丝织衣物 |
| | Cīna | China | 支那 |
| 14. | Chandragupta | Chandragupta (person) | 旃陀罗笈多 |
| | Kśatriya | king | 刹帝利(国王) |
| | Brahmin | priest | 婆罗门(僧侣) |
| | Dhammacakka | the Wheel of Doctrine | 法轮 |
| 17. | Pāṭaliputta | King Asoka's capital, present day Patna | 八纳(华氏城) |
| | Pāsāda | auditorium | 大讲堂 |
| 18. | Śuṅga (S.) | Śuṅga Dynasty | 撰伽王朝 |
| | Puṣyamitra (S.) | King Puṣyamitra | 富奢蜜多罗王 |
| | thūpa | pagoda | 塔 |
| | Vihāra | monastery | 寺 |
| | Milinda | King Milinda | 弥兰陀王 |
| | Bactria | Bactria (Kingdom) | 大夏国 |
| | Nāgasena | Nāgasena (a monk) | 那先 |
| | Nāgasena Bhikkhu Sutta | The Book of Monk Nagasena | 那先比丘经 |

| | | | |
|---|---|---|---|
| | Milinda Pañhā | (a scripture) | 弥兰陀问经 |
| | Pāli | Pali language | 巴利文 |
| | Gandhāra | Gandhara (place) | 犍陀罗 |
| 19. | Dravidians | Dravidian Nationality | 达罗维荼民族 |
| | Andhra | Andhra Kingdom | 案达罗国 |
| | Kaṇva | Kaṇva Dynasty | 康发王朝 |
| | Kuṣana | (a kingdom) | 大月支 |
| | Kṣāṇa | Kushān Dynasty | 贵霜王朝 |
| | Gupta | Gupta Dynasty | 笈多王朝 |
| | Kaniṣka | King Kaniṣka | 迦腻色迦王 |
| 20. | Pārśva (S.) | (person) | 胁比丘 |
| | Assaghosa | ( " ) | 马鸣 |
| | Kasmīra | (akingdom) | 迦湿弥罗 |
| | Vasumitta | (person) | 世友 |
| | Mahāvibhāṣā-śāstra (S.) | (a commentary) | 大毗婆沙论 |
| 21. | Nāgārjuna | (person) | 龙树 |
| 23. | sabhāva | self-nature | 自性 |
| | Hetupaccaya | causes and conditions | 因缘 |
| | Suñña | emptiness | 空 |
| | Majjhimāpaṭipadā | the Middle Path | 中道 |
| 24. | Sammuti-sacca | the Conventional Truth | 世俗谛 |

| | | | |
|---|---|---|---|
| | Paramattha-sacca | the First Truth or the Ultimate Truth | 第一义谛、圣谛、真谛 |
| | Bhava | Existence | 有、存在 |
| | Paramattha | the ultimate reality | 实相 |
| | paññatti | empirical concepts | 假名(假施设) |
| 25. | Deva | Deva (person) | 提婆 |
| | Sautrāntika | (a Buddhist Sect) | 经量部 |
| | Yogācāra | the Yoga School | 瑜伽系 |
| 26. | Candra Gupta | King Chandra Gupta | 月护王 |
| | Samudra Gupta | King Samudra Gupta | 海护王 |
| | Sāṃkhya | | 数论 |
| | Visesikā | Vaiśeṣika (school) | 胜论 |
| | Asaṅga | Asanga (person) | 无着 |
| | Vasubandhu | Vasubandhu (person) | 世亲 |
| 27. | Tusita | Tusita Heaven | 兜率天 |
| | Bodhisatta | Bodhisattva (being) | 菩萨 |
| | Maitreya | Maitreya ( " ) | 弥勒 |
| | Yogācariya | Yoga master | 瑜伽师 |
| | Jhāyin | Meditation master | 禅师 |
| | Jhāna | meditation | 禅 |
| | Ābhidhammika | Commentary master | 论师 |
| 28. | Trisvabhāva (S.) | three levels of Nature | 三种自性 |
| | Paratantra-svabhāva (S.) | the nature of being dependent in origin | 依他起性 |

| | | | |
|---|---|---|---|
| | Parikalpita-svabhāva (S.) | the nature of regarding the seeming as real | 遍计所执性 |
| | Tathatā | absolute reality | 真如,实相 |
| | Pariṇispanna-svabhāva (S.) | the absolutely true nature | 圆成实性 |
| | Trividhā niḥsvabhāvatā (S.) | three natures presenting non-existence | 三无性 |
| | lakṣaṇa niḥsvabhā vatā (S.) | the nature of non-existence in form | 相无性 |
| | Utpatti niḥsvabhāvatā (S.) | the nature of non-origination | 生无性 |
| | Paramārtha-niḥsvabhāvatā | the nature of emptiness in the highest sense | 胜义无性 |
| 29. | Vijñapti-mātratā (S.) | all dhammas are nothing but consciousness | 万法唯识 |
| 30. | indriya | sense organs | 根 |
| | Visaya | sense objects | 境 |
| | viññāṇa | consciousness | 识 |
| 31. | Viññāṇavāda | consciousness-only | 唯识 |
| | Ālaya-viññāṇa | the eighth, Alaya-consciousness | 第八阿赖耶识 |
| | Mana | the seventh, mana-consciousness | 第七末那识 |
| | Vāsanā | perfuming | 薰习、习气 |

| | | |
|---|---|---|
| Kusala | wholesome deeds | 善 |
| Akusala | unwholesome deeds | 恶 |
| Kamma | karma (acts) | 业 |
| Pariṇāma | give rise | 变起 |
| Bhājana-loka | the external world | 外界(器界) |
| Vipāka | future maturity | 异熟 |

| | | | |
|---|---|---|---|
| 32. | Ālaya-viññāṇa | Alaya-consciousness | 阿赖耶 |
| | atta-gāha (S. Ātma-grāha) | ego-grasping | 我执 |
| | Sāsava-viññāṇa | defiled consciousness | 有漏之识 |
| | Anāsavā-paññā | pure wisdom | 无漏之智 |
| 33. | Hetuvijja | Buddhist science of logic | 因明(逻辑学) |
| | Dinnāga | (person) | 陈那 |
| | Dharmakīrti | ( " ) | 法称 |
| 35. | Sīlāditya | King Siladitya | 戒日王 |
| | Amu Daria | Amu Daria River | 阿姆河 |
| | Vardhana | Varadhana Dynasty | 伐弹那王朝 |
| | Nālandā-sanghārāma | Nālandā Monastery | 那烂陀寺 |
| | Ābhidhammika | Commentary Master | 大论师 |
| | Sīlabhadra | (person) | 戒贤 |
| | Jñānaprabhā | ( " ) | 智光 |
| | Pañca-vārṣikamaha (S.) | mass meeting | 无遮大会 |
| 36. | Pāla | Pala Dynasty | 波罗王朝 |

| | | | |
|---|---|---|---|
| | Vikramasīla | a monastery | 超戒寺 |
| 37. | Mantra-dhāraṇī | a Tantric sect | 真言陀罗尼宗 |
| | Tantrayāna | Esoteric Vehicle | 密乘 |
| | Pakāsaniya-yāna | Exoteric Vehicle | 显乘 |
| | Dhāraṇī | mystical incantation | 密咒 |
| 38. | Mantra | True language | 真言 |
| | Maṇḍala | | 结坛（蔓荼罗） |
| | Mudrā | hand postures | 手印 |
| | abhiññā | psychic power | 神通 |
| 39. | Avalokiteśvara（S.） | Guanyin（Goddess of Mercy） | 观音 |
| | catu-saṃgaha-vatthūni | Four All Embracing Virtues | 四摄 |
| | cha-pāramitā | Six Transcendent Virtues | 六度 |
| | Vajra | Diamond | 金刚 |
| | Bodhipakiya-dhamma | condition leading to enlightenment | 道品 |
| | Nekkhamma-citta | renunciation | 出离心 |
| | Bodhi-citta | enlightenment | 菩提心 |
| | suññatā-ñāṇa | the awareness that all is emptiness | 空慧 |
| | Deva | deity | 天神 |

| | | | |
|---|---|---|---|
| 40. | Kumārila | (person) | 鸠摩梨罗 |
| | Śankara | (a Brahmin scholar) | 商羯罗 |
| 41. | Sena | Sena Dynasty | 斯那王朝 |
| 42. | Dhammapāla | (person) | 达摩波罗 |
| | Buddhagayā | (place) | 菩提伽耶， |
| | Bodhimaṇḍan | | 菩提道场 |
| | Mṛgadāva (S.) (Sarnāth) | Deer-garden | 鹿野苑 |
| | Kusināra | the place of Buddha's Parinibbāna | 拘尸那 |

# Chapter V

| | Pāli | English | 汉语 |
|---|---|---|---|
| 1. | Asoka | King Asoka | 阿育王 |
| | samaṇa | monk，mendicant | 沙门 |
| 2. | Dhamma | Buddhist Doctrine | 法 |
| | Kāsyapamatanga (S.) | (person) | 迦叶摩腾 |
| | Dharmaranya (S.) | (person) | 竺法兰 |
| | Sutta | Scripture | 经 |
| | Āgama | Scripture | 阿含经 |
| 4. | Vinaya | Discipline | 戒律 |
| | Dhammakāla | (person) | 昙柯迦罗 |
| | Devasara (or Tis-sara) | (person) | 铁萨罗 |
| 6. | Parthia | (kingdom) | 波斯国 |
| | Lokasema | (person) | 支娄迦谶 |
| | Saṃghavarman | ( " ) | 康僧铠 |
| | Saṃgīti | ( " ) | 康僧会 |
| | Semeg-kand | (kingdom) | 康居国 |
| | Dharmarakṣa (S.) | (person) | 竺法护 |
| | Sāvakayāna | Hearer vehicle | 声闻乘 |
| | Mahāyāna | Great vehicle | 大乘 |

| | | | |
|---|---|---|---|
| 7. | Hīnayāna | Small vehicle | 小乘 |
| | Āgama | Āgama texts | 阿含经 |
| | Dhyāna (S.) | Meditation | 禅数 |
| | Mahāprajñāpāramitā-sūtra (S.) | (a scripture) | 般若经 |
| | Sukhāvatī | Pure Land | 净土 |
| 9. | Vinaya Piṭaka | Discipline Texts | 律藏 |
| | Sākya | Shi (surname taken by Chinese monks) | 释 |
| | Kumārajīva | (person) | 鸠摩罗什 |
| 10. | Pātimokkha | disciplinary code | 戒本 |
| | Puṇyatāra | (person) | 弗若多罗 |
| | Dhammaruci | ( " ) | 昙摩流支 |
| | Kasmīra | Kashmir (place) | 克什米尔 |
| | Sarvāstivāda Vinaya | Discipline of Sarvastivāda | 萨婆多部十诵律 |
| | Vimalākṣa | (person) | 卑摩罗叉 |
| | Buddhayasas | ( " ) | 佛陀耶舍 |
| | Dhammagutta Vinaya | Discipline texts of Dharmagupta | 昙无德部四分律 |
| | Saṃghabhadra | Sanghabhadra (person) | 僧伽跋陀 |
| | Buddhaghosa | Buddhaghoṣa ( " ) | 佛音尊者 |
| | Samantapāsādikā | the Discipline Commentary | 善见律毗婆沙 |
| | Mahāsaṃghika Vinaya | Discipline texts | 摩诃僧祇律 |

| | | |
|---|---|---|
| Mahīśāsaka Vinaya | Discipline texts | 弥沙塞部五分律 |
| Buddhabhadra | (person) | 佛驮跋陀罗 |
| Kapilavatthu | Kapilavastu (kingdom) | 迦毗罗卫国 |
| Buddhajīva | (person) | 佛陀什 |
| Kamma | Karma | 羯磨 |
| Theravāda Vinaya | Theravada discipline | 上座部律 |

| | | | |
|---|---|---|---|
| 11. | Sutta Piṭaka | Scripture texts | 经藏 |
| | Abhidhamma Piṭaka | Commentary texts | 论藏 |

| | | | |
|---|---|---|---|
| 13. | Mādhyamika | Middle way | 中观 |
| | Nāgārjuna | (person) | 龙树 |
| | Mūlamadhyamaka-kārikā | (a scripture) | 中论 |
| | Śataśāstra (S.) | ( " ) | 百论 |
| | Dvādaśamukha-śāstta (S.) | ( " ) | 十二门论 |
| | Vimalakīrti-nirdeśa | ( " ) | 维摩经 |
| | Saddharmapuṇḍrīka-sūtra | ( " ) | 法华经 |
| | Cūḍaprajñāpāramitā-sūtra | ( " ) | 小品般若经 |
| | Vajracchedikāprajñā-pāramitā-sūtra | ( " ) | 金刚经 |
| | Mahāprajñāpāramitā-śāstra | ( " ) | 大智度论 |
| | Dhammatā | Dhamma-nature school | 法性宗 |
| | Satyasiddhi-śāstra | a book | 成实论 |

| | | | |
|---|---|---|---|
| 14. | Mahāyāna-Suññatāvāda | Emptiness School of great vehicle (a sect) | 大乘空宗 |
| | Āryadeva | (person) | 提婆 |
| | Buddhabhadra | ( " ) | 觉贤 |
| | Buddhāvataṃsaka-mahāvaipulya-sūtra | (a scripture) | 华严经 |
| | Dharmarakṣa | (person) | 昙无谶 |
| | Mahāparinibbāna-sutta | (a scripture) | 大般涅槃经 |
| | Guṇabhadra | (person) | 求那跋陀罗 |
| | Lankāvatāra-sutta | (a scripture) | 楞伽经 |
| | Bodhiruci | (person) | 菩提流支 |
| | Vasubandhu | ( " ) | 世亲 |
| | Yogācāra | yoga | 瑜伽 |
| | Daśabhūmika-śāstra | (a scripture) | 十地经论 |
| | Mahāyāna-saṃparigraha-śāstra | ( " ) | 摄大乘论 |
| | Mahāyāna-saṃgraha-bhāṣya | ( " ) | 释论 |
| | Abhidhammakosa-śāstra | ( " ) | 俱舍论 |
| | Paramattha | (person) | 真谛 |
| 15. | Sīlabhadra | (person) | 戒贤 |
| | Dhammapāla | ( " ) | 护法 |
| | Ālambanapārīksā | (a scripture) | 无相思尘论 |

| | | | |
|---|---|---|---|
| | Hastavālaprakaraṇa | ( " ) | 解拳论 |
| | Dinnāga | (person) | 陈那 |
| | a-gotra | without Buddha-nature | 无佛性 |
| | Parikalpita | illusory | 遍计所执 |
| | paratantra | empirical | 依他起 |
| | Cetasika | constituents of consciousness | 心所 |
| | Pravṛtti-vijñāna-śāstra | (a scripture) | 转识论 |
| | Ādānavijñāna | (consciousness) | 阿陀那 |
| | Bhāvaviveka | (person) | 清辨 |
| | Suñña | emptiness | 空 |
| | Bhava | existence | 有 |
| | Buddhapālita | (person) | 佛护 |
| | Suññatāvāda | emptiness school | 空宗 |
| | Svātantrika | Independent reasoning | 自续 |
| | Prāsaṅgika | Depending on opponent | 应成 |
| | Candrakīrti | (person) | 月称 |
| | Candragomin | ( " ) | 月官 |
| | Dharmakīrti | ( " ) | 法称 |
| | Hetuvidyā | logic | 因明 |
| 17. | Nālandā | Nalanda monastery | 那烂陀寺 |
| | śloka | line (32 syllables) | 颂(32 节为一颂) |
| | Catuhśatakavrtti | (a book) | 广百论释 |
| | Vijñapti-mātratāsiddhi-śāstra | ( " ) | 成唯识论 |

| | | | |
|---|---|---|---|
| | Bhavavāda | Existence Sect | 有宗 |
| | pañca-vārṣikamaha | assembly | 无遮大会 |
| | Śīlāditya | King Harṣa | 戒日王 |
| | Mahāyānadeva | Deity of Great Vehicle | 大乘天 |
| | Vajrasamādhi | (person) | 金刚三昧 |
| | Uposatha | fast day | 斋日 |
| 19. | Jñānagupta | (person) | 阇那崛多 |
| | Dānapāla | ( " ) | 施护 |
| | Paññā | ( " ) | 般若 |
| | Mandra | ( " ) | 曼陀罗仙 |
| | Saṅghapāla | ( " ) | 僧伽婆罗 |
| | Amoghavajra | ( " ) | 不空(金刚) |
| | Dhammatā | Dhamma Nature School | 法性宗 |
| | lakkhaṇa | Phenomena, appearance | 相 |
| | Śānta-rakṣita | (person) | 寂护 |
| | Kamalaśīla | ( " ) | 莲花戒 |
| | Padma-saṃbhava | ( " ) | 莲华生 |
| | Bhadanta | high priest | 大德 |
| | Vikramaśīlavihāra | Vikramasīla Monastery | 超戒寺 |
| | Ārya Atīśa | (person) | 阿底峡尊者 |
| | Cikitsā-vidyā | medical science | 医方明 |
| | Śabda-vidyā | linguistics | 声明 |
| 21. | Dhamma Pakati | Dhamma-nature | 法性 |
| | Dhamma-Lakkhaṇa | Phenomena | 法相 |
| | Avataṃsaka | Avataṃsaka School | 华严宗 |
| | Jhāna | Meditation School | 禅宗 |
| | Sukhāvatīvyūha | Pure Land School | 净土宗 |

| | | | |
|---|---|---|---|
| | Tantra | Esoteric School | 密宗 |
| | Mantrayāna | Mantrayana School | 真言宗 |
| 22. | Śata-śāstta | (a doctrine) | 百论 |
| | Dvādaśamukha-śāstta | (a doctrine) | 十二门论 |
| | Paramattha-sacca | the ultimate truth | 真谛 |
| | Sammuti-sacca | the conventional truth | 俗谛 |
| | Majjhima-paṭipadā | the Middle Path | 中道 |
| 23. | Paṭiccasamupāda | Dependent Origination | 缘起 |
| | Bhava | exist | 有 |
| | Rūpa | matter | 色 |
| | pañca-khandha | the five aggregates | 五阴 |
| | dvādasa-āyatanāni | the twelve Spheres (or bases) | 十二处 |
| 24. | Maitreya | (person) | 弥勒 |
| | Asaṅga | ( " ) | 无著 |
| | Vasubandhu | ( " ) | 世亲 |
| | Saṃdhinirmocana-sūtra | (a scripture) | 解深密经 |
| | Yogacāra-bhūmi-śāstra | (a scripture) | 瑜伽师地论 |
| | Vijñaptimātratā-siddhi-śāstta | ( " ) | 成唯识论 |
| | Dharma Lakaṣaṇa Vijñānavāda | Viññāṇavāda School | 法相唯识宗 |
| | āśraya-parivṛtti | convert consciousness into wisdom | 转识成智(转依) |

| | | | |
|---|---|---|---|
| 25. | pañca-dhamma | the five categories of dhammas | 五法 |
| | Nāma | name | 名 |
| | Lakkhaṇa | form or appearance | 相 |
| | vikalpa | discrimination | 分别、妄想 |
| | Sammā-ñāna | Right wisdom | 正智 |
| | Tri-svabhāvatā | Triple-nature | 三自性 |
| | Parikalpita | the illusory aspect | 遍计所执性 |
| | Paratantra | the dependent aspect | 依他起性 |
| | Parinisṣpanna | the perfected aspect | 圆成实性 |
| | Pudgala-nairātmya | the non-existence of self | 人无我 |
| | Dharma-nairātmya | the non-existence of dhamma | 法无我 |
| | Saṅkhatadhamma | conditioned dhamma | 有为法 |
| | anāsava | pure | 清净 |
| | sāsava | impure | 染 |
| | abhinivesa | grasp | 执取 |
| | grāhaka | subjective things | 主观事物 能取 |
| | grāhya | objective things | 客观事物 所取 |
| | kamma | karma | 业 |
| | kāma-loka | Sensuous world | 欲界 |
| | rūpa-loka | Fine-material world | 色界 |
| | arūpa-loka | Immaterial world | 无色界 |
| | mano | mind | 心 |
| | citta | mind | 意 |
| | anattā | egolessness | 无我 |

| | | | |
|---|---|---|---|
| | Viññāṇa-vipas-sanā | meditation on consciousness | 唯识观行 |
| 26. | Saddharmapuṇḍarīka-sūtra | Lotus Scripture | 法华经 |
| | Mahāprajñāpāramitā-śāstra | (a scripture) | 大智度论 |
| 27. | Sākyamuni-Tathāgata | (a title of Buddha) | 释迦如来 |
| | Vaipulya | (a period) | 方等 |
| | Prajñā(Paññā) | (wisdom) | 般若 |
| 29. | Tivipassanā | the Threefold Contemplation | 三观 |
| 35. | Samādhi | meditation practice | 定、三摩地 |
| 36. | Bodhidhamma | (person) | 菩提达摩 |
| | Laṅkāvatāra-sūtra | (a scripture) | 楞伽经 |
| | Vajracchedika-prajñāpāramitā-sūtra | ( " ) | 金刚般若婆罗密多经 |
| 37. | Sukhāvatīvyūha | the Pure Land School | 净土宗 |
| 40. | Amitāyus-sūtra | (a scripture) | 无量寿经 |
| | Amita Buddha | Amita Buddha | 阿弥陀佛 |
| | Amitābha | Amita Buddha | 无量光佛 |
| | asaṅkhya | a long period of time | 阿僧祇劫 |

| | | | |
|---|---|---|---|
| 42. | Tisso sikkhā | Three categories of Studies | 三学 |
| | adhisīla | discipline | 戒学、增戒学 |
| | adhicitta | contemplation | 定学、增心学 |
| | adhipaññā | wisdom | 慧学、增慧学 |
| 43. | Dhammagupta Vinaya | (a set of precepts) | 四分律 |
| | upasaṃpadā | the Full Commandments | 具足戒 |
| | Vassa | the institution of rainy season retreat | 安居法 |
| | Uposatha | the institution of fortnightly assembly | 布萨法 |
| | Brahmajāla-sīla-sutta | (a scripture) | 梵网戒经 |
| | Upāsaka-sīla-sutta | ( " ) | 优婆塞戒经 |
| | Saṃvara-sīla | the moral precepts | 摄律仪戒 |
| | Kusala-dhamma-saṃgrāhaka sīla | the precepts of the acquisition of all good | 摄善法戒 |
| | Sattvārtha-kriyā-sīla | the precepts of benefiting all sentient beings | 饶益有情戒 |
| 44. | Pārājika | the most fundamental precepts | 根本戒 |
| | Saṅghādisesa | precepts | 僧残 |
| | Bhikkhunī | precepts | 尼戒 |

| | | |
|---|---|---|
| | Pātimokkha | | |
| 45. | Subhakarasiṃh | (person) | 善无畏 |
| | Vajrabodhi | (person) | 金刚智 |
| | Amoghavajra | ( " ) | 不空 |
| | Mahāvairocana-sūtra | (a scripture) | 大日经 |
| | Vajrasikhara-sūtra | ( " ) | 金刚顶经 |
| | guruyogā | specific Buddha or master | 本尊法 |
| | abhiṣeka | pour water on the head, anoint | 灌顶 |
| 46. | guru | the specific Buddha or master | 本尊 |
| | vijjārāja | (a wise king) | 明王 |
| | mudra | hand signs | 手印 |
| | mantra | the Honored One's spell | 真言 |
| | bīja | seed | 种子 |
| | akāra-ādyanutpādah | no origination | 不生 |
| 47. | Abhidhamma-kosa (school) | the Kosa School | 俱舍宗 |
| | Abhidhamma-kosa-śāstra | (a commentary) | 俱舍论 |
| | Satyasiddhi (School) | the Satyasiddhi School | 成实宗 |
| | Satyasiddhi-śāstra | (a doctrine) | 成实论 |
| | Mahāpari-nibbāna-sutta | (a scripture) | 大般涅槃经 |
| | Mahāyāna-saṃpari-graha-śāstra | (a doctrine) | 摄大乘论 |

| | | | |
|---|---|---|---|
| | Daśabhūmika-sūtra-śāstra | ( " ) | 十地经论 |
| 48. | Dhammapakati | the Nature School | 法性宗 |
| | Dhammalakkhaṇa | the Appearance School | 法相宗 |
| 50. | Sūraṃgama-mahā-sūtra | (a scripture) | 楞严经 |
| 51. | Padmasaṃbhava | (person) | 莲华生 |
| 52. | Mahānayāka Atīśa | (person) | 阿底峡尊者 |
| 56. | Mettā-karunā | love and compassion | 慈悲 |
| | Upekkhā (or saṃnatta) | equality | 平等 |
| 57. | Sata-upamā-sutta | (a scripture) | 百喻经 |
| | Aśvaghoṣa (S.) | ( " ) | 马鸣 |
| | Buddhacarita | ( " ) | 佛所行赞 |
| 59. | Gandhāra | (place) | 犍陀罗 |
| 60. | Jātaka | (a scripture) | 本生 |
| | Avalokiteśvara | Avalokitesvara (a being) | 观音 |
| | Arahat | Arahant ( " ) | 罗汉 |
| 61. | Bhāśā | chanting and singing | 梵呗 |

| | | | |
|---|---|---|---|
| 64. | Loka-dhamma | Worldly Conditions | 世间法 |
| | Lokattara-dhamma | Supermundane Conditions | 出世间法 |
| | Dasa Kusala | Ten Good Acts | 十善 |
| 65. | hetu-phala | the law of causality | 因果律 |
| 67. | anuttara sammā-sambodhi | perfect Enlightenment | 无上正觉 |
| 68. | Dāna | charity | 布施 |
| | Khanti | Forbearance | 忍辱 |
| | Variya | Effort or energy | 精进 |
| | bhāvanā | Contemplation | 静虑 |